INTERRELIGIOUS ENCOUNTERS

INTERRELIGIOUS ENCOUNTERS

OPPORTUNITIES AND CHALLENGES

MICHAEL AMALADOSS

edited by

JONATHAN Y. TAN

ORBIS BOOKS
Maryknoll, New York 10545

Founded in 1970, Orbis Books endeavors to publish works that enlighten the mind, nourish the spirit, and challenge the conscience. The publishing arm of the Maryknoll Fathers and Brothers, Orbis seeks to explore the global dimensions of the Christian faith and mission, to invite dialogue with diverse cultures and religious traditions, and to serve the cause of reconciliation and peace. The books published reflect the views of their authors and do not represent the official position of the Maryknoll Society. To learn more about Maryknoll and Orbis Books, please visit our website at www.maryknollsociety.org.

Manufactured in the United States of America.
Manuscript editing and typesetting by Joan Weber Laflamme.

Library of Congress Cataloging-in-Publication Data

Names: Amaladoss, M. (Michael), 1936– author. | Tan, Jonathan Y., editor.
Title: Interreligious encounters : opportunities and challenges / Michael
    Amaladoss, S.J. ; edited by Jonathan Y. Tan.
Description: Maryknoll : Orbis Books, 2017. | Includes bibliographical
    references and index.
Identifiers: LCCN 2016055608 (print) | LCCN 2017008549 (ebook) | ISBN
    9781626982215 (pbk.) | ISBN 9781608336869 (e-book)
Subjects: LCSH: Asia—Religion. | Religions—Relations. | Religious
    pluralism—Asia. | Cultural pluralism—Asia.
Classification: LCC BL1035 .A43 2017 (print) | LCC BL1035 (ebook) | DDC
    201/.5—dc23
LC record available at https://lccn.loc.gov/2016055608

To P. R. John, SJ

Friend and Co-Searcher

Contents

Part II

RESPONDING TO RELIGIOUS PLURALISM

Acknowledgments

The essays in this volume were written on various occasions and presented to various groups in India and abroad. Chapter 2 was previously published as "Which Is the True Religion? Searching for Criteria," in *Co-worker for Your Joy: Festschrift in Honour of George Gispert-Sauch, S.J.*, ed. S. Painadath and Leonard Fernando (Delhi: Vidyajyoti/ISPCK, 2006), 45–60. Chapter 5 was previously published as "Religioês: Violência ou diálogo," *Perspectiva Teologica* 34 (2002): 179–96. Chapter 8 was previously published as "Ethics in a Multireligious Context," *East Asian Pastoral Review* 44 (2007): 207–20. Chapter 13 was originally published as "Hindu and Christian: Conflict or Challenge?" in *Indian and Christian: Changing Identities in Modern India,* ed. Cornelis Bennema and Paul Joshoua Bhakiaraj (Bangalore: SAIACS, 2011), 135–54. Chapter 14 was previously published as "From Syncretism to Harmony," *Chakana* 2 (2004): 4, 43–60. Chapters 1, 3, 4, 6, 7, 9, 11, 12, and 15 previously appeared as chapters 16, 15, 3, 1, 2, 11, 7, 12, and 9 of Michael Amaladoss, *Beyond Dialogue: Pilgrims to the Absolute* (Bangalore: Asia Trading Corporation, 2008). The essays were edited for this volume.

Acronyms

AAS   *Acta Apostolicae Sedis.*

AG   *Ad Gentes*, Vatican II, *Decree on the Church's Missionary Activity,* 7 December 1965.

CD   *Christus Dominus*, Vatican II, *Decree on the Bishops' Pastoral Office in the Church,* 28 October 1965.

CDF   *Congregatio pro Doctrina Fidei*, Congregation for the Doctrine of the Faith.

DEV   *Dominum et Vivificantem*, encyclical letter of Pope John Paul II, 18 May 1986.

DH   *Dignitatis Humanae*, Vatican II, *Declaration on Religious Freedom,* 7 December 1965.

DP   *Dialogue and Proclamation*, Statement of the Congregation for the Evangelization of Peoples and the Pontifical Council on Interreligious Dialogue, 19 May 1991.

DV   *Dei Verbum*, Vatican II, *Dogmatic Constitution on Divine Revelation,* 18 November 1965.

EG   *Evangelii Gaudium*, apostolic exhortation of Pope Francis, 24 November 2013.

EN   *Evangelii Nuntiandi*, apostolic exhortation of Paul VI, 8 December 1975.

FABC   Federation of Asian Bishops' Conferences.

FR   *Fides et Ratio*, encyclical letter of John Paul II, 14
            September 1998.

GS   *Gaudium et Spes*, Vatican II, *Pastoral Constitution on
            the Church in the Modern World*, 7 December 1965.

IDCR   Institute of Dialogue with Cultures and Religions,
            University of Madras, Chennai.

LF   *Lumen Fidei*, enyclical letter of Pope Francis, 29 June
            2013.

LG   *Lumen Gentium*, Vatican II, *Dogmatic Constitution
            on the Church*, 21 November 1964.

NA   *Nostra Aetate*, Vatican II, *Declaration on the Relation-
            ship of the Church to Non-Christian Religions*, 28
            October 1965.

NBCLC   National Biblical, Catechetical, and Liturgical Centre
            (Bangalore, India).

OT   *Optatam Totius*, Vatican II, *Decree on Priestly Forma-
            tion*, 28 October 1965.

RM   *Redemptoris Missio*, encyclical letter of John Paul II,
            7 December 1990.

SC   *Sacrosanctum Concilium*, Vatican II, *Constitution on
            the Sacred Liturgy*, 4 December 1963.

ST   Thomas Aquinas, *Summa Theologiae*.

TRC   Truth and Reconciliation Commission.

UR   *Unitatis Redintegratio*, Vatican II, *Decree on Ecumen-
            ism*, 21 November 1964.

VL   *Varietates Legitimae*, Congregation for Divine Wor-
            ship and the Discipline of the Sacraments' Fourth
            Instruction for the Right Application of the Conciliar
            Constitution on the Liturgy, 37–40, 29 March 1994.

Editor's Preface

Michael Amaladoss, Interreligious Theologian Par Excellence

In the postcolonial Indian Catholic Church, one unassuming theologian has transformed the face, shape, and directions of Indian theology as he walks his own theological pilgrimage into the various dimensions of India's ancient spiritual-religious and contemporary sociocultural landscapes. His name is Michael Amaladoss, SJ: theologian, missiologist, liturgist, musician, and above all, a hybridized Hindu Christian who is defined by his own nondual advaitic theological vision of unity-in-plurality.

As a child, Michael Amaladoss was exposed to Hindu social, cultural, and religious experiences, because he grew up in a Hindu village in Tamil Nadu in southern India in one of only two Catholic families. Central to this village life is a popular temple dedicated to the Goddess. As a result, he was steeped in the rituals and cycles of Hindu festivals and calendrical celebrations, all of which would later shape his own theological exploration of the boundaries of religious pluralism and interreligious engagements. Indeed, throughout this book Amaladoss emphasizes that Hinduism is not the "stranger" or "other" for him and his family. Rather, Hinduism is deeply embedded in his life and upbringing, and together with his deep Catholic faith, comprises the foundation and roots of his own faith life and theological journey.

Amaladoss brought this abiding interreligious Hindu-Christian dimension with him when he joined the Society of Jesus in 1953. As a novice, he was deeply influenced by Ignatius Hirudayam, SJ. Hirudayam not only established the Inter-Faith Research and Dialogue Center (Aikiya Alayam) in Madras but was also a trailblazer in inculturation, Hindu-Christian dialogue, and the introduction of Indian music and the arts in the Indian Catholic Church. Hirudayam introduced young Amaladoss to the karnatic (South Indian) classical music tradition and Indology, and nurtured the seeds of inculturation and interreligious dialogue that were beginning to take sprout in Amaladoss's faith imagination. Indeed, one little known fact outside India about Amaladoss is his proficiency in the classical karnatic music tradition as a result of two years of intensive study at the Tamil Nadu College of Music, Madras. Amaladoss has composed more than two hundred bhajans, or devotional songs, as well as songs with Christian themes for the South Indian classical dance, Bharata Natyam, in addition to publishing primers on karnatic music and ragas for beginning students and managing the liturgical music publication, "Isai Aruvi" (Fountain of Music).

Another turning point in his life as a Jesuit scholastic was a pilgrimage with two of his confreres, T. K. John and the late Thomas Nallail, to Hindu shrines in northern India, which brought them to Haridwar, Rishikesh, Delhi, Mathura, Brindavan, Varanasi, and Bodh Gaya. Staying in ashrams and observing Hindu rituals and practices, and engaging sannyasis in conversation, gave him and his companions new insights into Hindu faith life and, in the process, transformed their lives and perspectives.

Upon completing his philosophy and theology studies in India, Amaladoss went to France to pursue graduate theological studies in liturgy and liturgical inculturation at the Institut Catholique in Paris, studying under Pierre-Marie Gy and Jean-Yves Hameline. It was Hameline who introduced him to the social sciences, thereby shaping the interdisciplinary orientation of his subsequent theological oeuvre and informing his theological approach, which sees that the starting point of theologizing generally, and interreligious theologizing in particular, is a social analysis of the situation of people's lived experiences within the matrix of their sociocultural location and context.

Returning to India in 1973 after completing his doctorate in liturgy in Paris, Amaladoss found a lively post–Vatican II Indian Church that was gingerly dipping its toes into indigenization and inculturation. He was the first Indian editor of *Clergy Monthly*—subsequently renamed *Vidyajyoti Journal of Theological Reflection*—which he juggled with another appointment as a theology professor at St. Paul's Seminary in Tiruchirapalli. He also found time to participate actively in the pioneering work of the National Biblical, Catechetical, and Liturgical Centre (NBCLC) in Bangalore, where he was involved in research seminars and planning groups that worked on the Indian Rite of the Mass, the inspiration of non-Christian scriptures, and so forth. As time went on, he joined Vidyajyoti in Delhi and would become its dean, as well as the vice-provincial for formation, before being appointed assistant to the General of the Society of Jesus in Rome, where he also became a member of the executive board of the Documentation and Research Centre and the president of the International Association of Mission Studies.

Nonetheless, Amaladoss's heart and interests lie in the development of Indian theology generally, and interreligious[1] and liberationist[2] theologizing within Indian theology in particular. This has led him to exploring and writing on religious pluralism and interreligious dialogue for the Federation of Asian Bishops' Conferences (FABC), where his contributions made their way to the final statements of the FABC's early plenary assemblies. One could also see clearly his insights and influence in the FABC Theological Advisory Commission's *Theses on Interreligious Dialogue*.[3] Indeed, this was an especially productive and creative period for him, with numerous essays and book chapters, as well as ground-breaking monographs on the challenges of caste,[4] inculturation,[5] and dialogue,[6] seeing Jesus through Asian eyes,[7] harmony as a theological response to the challenges of pluralism,[8] and the challenges of globalization.[9]

In order to understand and appreciate Amaladoss's theological approach, one should be aware of its deep advaitic roots. While he does not hew closely to a specific school of advaita, he is interested in

---

[1] Michael Amaladoss, *Making All Things New: Dialogue, Pluralism, and Evangelization in Asia* (Maryknoll, NY: Orbis Books, 1990).

[2] Michael Amaladoss, *Life in Freedom: Liberation Theologies from Asia* (Maryknoll, NY: Orbis Books, 1997).

[3] Federation of Asian Bishops' Conference Theological Advisory Commission, *Theses on Interreligious Dialogue: An Essay in Pastoral Theological Reflection*, FABC Papers, no. 48 (Hong Kong: Federation of Asian Bishops' Conferences, 1987).

[4] Michael Amaladoss, *A Call to Community: The Caste System and Christian Responsibility* (Anand, Gujarat: Gujarat Sahitya Prakash, 1994).

[5] See Michael Amaladoss, *Becoming Indian: The Process of Inculturation* (Bangalore: Dharmaram Publications, 1992); and idem, *Beyond Inculturation: Can the Many Be One?* (Delhi: ISPCK, 1998).

[6] See Michael Amaladoss, *Walking Together: The Practice of Inter-Religious Dialogue*, Series XI—Jesuit Theological Forum Reflections (Anand, Gujarat: Gujarat Sahitya Prakash, 1992); and idem, *Beyond Dialogue: Pilgrims to the Absolute* (Bangalore: Asian Trading Corporation, 2008).

[7] Michael Amaladoss, *The Asian Jesus* (Maryknoll, NY: Orbis Books, 2006).

[8] Michael Amaladoss, *Making Harmony: Living in a Pluralist World* (Chennai: IDCR, 2003).

[9] Michael Amaladoss, ed., *Globalization and Its Victims as Seen by the Victims* (Delhi: ISPCK, 1999).

and inspired by advaita's *Grundnorm*—seeing reality around oneself through the eyes of unity-in-duality or unity-in-multiplicity, eschewing dialectical oppositions and binary dichotomies. He acknowledges that advaitic mutuality and unity pose a challenge to the fundamental Greek ontology that has shaped the contours of Christian theologizing, which is premised upon dichotomy and duality. Amaladoss would make the case for reformulating the basic doctrines of Christianity, which have been articulated based upon a Greek philosophical framework, within a contemporary Indian context using Indian hermeneutical tools and approaches. This is seen beginning with his doctoral thesis and his very first monograph[10] and culminating with his impassioned discussion in Chapter 13 of this book, entitled "Hindu and Christian: Conflict or Challenge?"

Within the ongoing debates on the theology of religions and the use of the convenient but highly simplistic and reductionistic framework of exclusivist-inclusivist-pluralist perspectives to classify an approach to religious diversity and pluralism, Amaladoss has consistently eschewed being pigeonholed into any one of these categories, as is clear throughout this entire book. If one could discern a position, Amaladoss's own advaitic approach to Christian theologizing would place him somewhere in the theological continuum between pluralism (on the issue of Christianity vis-à-vis other religions) and inclusivism (on the narrow issue of salvific efficacy of Jesus, the Christ). In this book Amaladoss outlines and unpacks his own position on this issue in Chapter 9 ("God of All Names and Interreligious Dialogue") and Chapter 12 ("Double Religious Identity: Possible? Necessary? A Reflection from an Indian Experience").

Unfortunately, this highly nuanced position is not often appreciated by his detractors, which has resulted in the investigations of his writings by Vatican's Congregation for the Doctrine of the Faith. Amaladoss's complete and unabridged response to the CDF is reproduced in this book as Chapter 15 ("Interreligious Dialogue Fifty Years after Vatican II"). In addition, the reader's attention is also directed to the Epilogue, "Pope Francis and Dialogue," where Amaladoss updates his discussion to take into account the new developments that have been ushered into the church by Pope Francis.

This volume collects Amaladoss's important (albeit hitherto inaccessible) papers and writings exploring and responding to the challenges

---

[10] See Michael Amaladoss, *Do Sacraments Change? Variable and Invariable Elements in Sacramental Rites* (Bangalore: Theological Publications in India, 1979).

of religious pluralism and the diversity of theological positions and responses to interreligious engagements. His writings speak of crossing borders, encountering and relating to others, sharing worship, reading the scriptures of other religions, finding new criteria to judge the truth of religions, seeking harmony through diversity and pluralism, and achieving liberation through dialogue and collaboration. To be clear, there is no discussion of dialogue or religious pluralism in the abstract, but rather of living life to the full in a multireligious world. Amaladoss's goal here is giving readers flashes of lived experience that call for reflection and question accepted certitudes and attitudes rather than producing an abstract theological treatise. In today's transnational and hyper-connected world, shaped by massive migrations and other challenges of globalization, it is hoped that this book will afford readers new insights and perspectives on age-old issues, as peoples of various faiths and religions rub shoulders in new ways and in new social locations and cultural contexts.

—JONATHAN Y. TAN

Introduction

A Call to Continuing Dialogue

Occasionally we hear calls for a third Vatican council. The calls may be too early. We have not fully absorbed and implemented the Second Vatican Council yet. Fifty years after the beginnings of the council it is time to assess the progress we have made and to look forward. Though the council produced sixteen documents, I think that its major new thrusts were in three areas: the universal church as a communion of local churches; the church as primarily the people of God, at whose service there are ministers; and a church in dialogue with the world, with other religions, and with other churches.

A Communion of Churches

The Second Vatican Council's very first document on the liturgy laid the groundwork for a vision of the universal church as a communion of local churches. It spoke of the need to inculturate the liturgy and gave this responsibility to local bishops' conferences (SC 37–50). The use of local languages and music visibilize the variety of local churches. National and regional conferences of bishops meet regularly. The Synod of Bishops is also celebrated regularly (CD 36–38). Though how autonomous the local churches really are remains a question, the framework is there (LG 13). In India, for instance, while the official liturgy has been a touchy point, some movement is visible in the area of popular religiosity, spirituality, and theology. The Christians are also in dialogue with secular society, as Dalit, tribal, feminist, and ecological theologies bear witness. That the church organization is strongly centralized is also undeniable. But in a postcolonial era the people cannot be totally dominated. People in positions of leadership are probably more sensitive to centralization than others. An occasional challenge is thrown our way, as when John Paul II wrote in *Fides et*

Ratio: "An immense spiritual impulse compels the Indian mind to an acquiring of that experience which would, with a spirit freed from the distractions of time and space, attain to the absolute good. This is the time, above all for Indian Christians, to unlock these treasures from their inheritance" (72). When the Hindutva brigade calls Christianity a foreign religion, we cannot really jump up and say that we are fully Indian, self-financing, self-propagating, and self-governing. We still have a long way to go to become an Indian Church, not merely the church in India. It is our task; it will not be anyone else's gift.

The Church as the People of God

The second major thrust of the council is the self-understanding of the church as the people of God (LG 9–17). The First Vatican Council focused on the authority of the pope. The Second Vatican Council balanced this with episcopal collegiality. The various bishops' conferences and the synod of bishops offer a framework for the exercise of collegiality. But the structure and the forces of centralization in the church today seem strong, reducing episcopal collegiality to a mere consultative role. The Latin Church is nowhere near the synodal system of the Asian churches. John Paul II asked theologians to explore the nature and function of the papal office in the church. Though there have been some studies and statements like the one on authority in the church by an Anglican–Roman Catholic Commission, there has not been much movement. It is true that the Syro-Malabar and Syro-Malankara churches in India have succeeded in acquiring some autonomy, which the Latin Church does not have.

The development that has been largely ignored in practice is the realization of the church as the people of God. The council, before talking about its hierarchical structure, presents the church as the *people of God*. The church is the people of the new covenant with the law of God written in their hearts (cf. Jer 31:31–34). St. Peter calls it "a chosen race, a royal priesthood, a holy nation. . . . Once you were not a people, but now you are God's people" (1 Pet 2:9–10). The people are priests participating in the priesthood of Christ, offering not only Christ's sacrifice as his body, but themselves. The presbyters have only a ministerial or service role. The people of God also share in Christ's prophetic office. The council says: "The whole body of the faithful . . . cannot err in matters of belief. This characteristic is shown in the supernatural appreciation of the faith *(sensus fidei)* of the whole people, when 'from the bishops to the last faithful' they manifest a universal consent in matters of faith and morals" (LG 12). There is a fine balance here between the "sense of the faithful" and the official teaching of the pope and the bishops. The Holy Spirit also gives special gifts to the people, not for their own benefit, but for the service of the people (cf. 1 Cor 12:7–11). Unfortunately, the church remains largely and strongly clergy dominated. Rather than being a consensual, not majoritarian, democracy, the church is seen as essentially hierarchical and autocratic, with the leaders enjoying absolute authority.

A Church in Dialogue

While these two thrusts can be seen as internal to the church, the third makes the church look outside itself. At the Second Vatican Council the church entered into dialogue with the world. In *Gaudium et Spes (Pastoral Constitution on the Church in the Modern World)* it does not take a merely negative view of the modern world, with its secularization and even atheism, but seeks to dialogue with it, focusing particularly on the family, culture, socioeconomic development, political life, and peace. As a matter of fact, the document is addressed not only to Catholics but to the whole of humanity. It has a section on dialogue between the church and the world (GS 40–44). In true dialogical fashion it is not only ready to offer but also to receive from the world (GS 44). In *Dignitatis Humanae (Declaration on Religious Liberty)* it dialogues with political structures demanding freedom not only for itself, but for all religions. We can say that it indirectly dialogues with the religions, too, acknowledging them as legitimate holders of rights. The desire for dialogue is more explicit in *Nostra Aetate (Declaration on the Relationship of the Church to the Non-Christian Religions)*, which deals with the church's relationship to other religions, focusing particularly on Islam and Judaism. It opens up finally to other ecclesial communities in *Unitatis Redintegratio (Decree on Ecumenism)*. A certain theological background to such dialogue, especially with reference to other religions, is provided in the constitution on the church, *Lumen Gentium (Dogmatic Constitution on the Church)*, *Dei Verbum (Dogmatic Constitution on Divine Revelation)*, and *Ad Gentes (Decree on the Church's Missionary Activity)*. I think that this is an important development, one that is going to determine increasingly the identity and action of the church in the world in the twenty-first century. So I will focus on it in the rest of this chapter. I start with the dogmatic statements, move on to the pastoral directives, and then reflect on the theological vision and implications for mission. At the end I show how this links to the other two thrusts that I mentioned in the beginning: the universal church as a communion of local churches and the church as the people of God.

The Mission of God

I think that what we have in the council documents are two inter-related ways of God's presence and action in the world. But their relationship can be interpreted in different ways. While the council speaks of both ways, it is not always clear about the relationship between them. Perhaps our Indian experience and reflection may give some insight into this.

The *Decree on the Church's Missionary Activity (Ad Gentes)* speaks on what is called popularly today the mission of God or *missio Dei*:

> The Church on earth is by its very nature missionary since, according to the plan of the Father, it has its origin in the mission of the Son and the Holy Spirit. This plan flows from "fountain-like love," the love of God the Father. . . . God in his great and merciful kindness freely creates us and moreover, graciously calls us to share in his life and glory. He generously pours out, and never ceases to pour out, his divine goodness, so that he who is creator of all things might at last become "all in all" (1 Cor 15:28). (AG 2)

This presence and action of the Word and the Spirit, starting with creation, are obviously found everywhere and always. But God's mission acquires a new form with Jesus Christ:

> However, in order to establish a relationship of peace and communion with himself, and in order to bring about brotherly union among men . . . God decided to enter into the history of mankind in a new and definitive manner, by sending his own Son in human flesh . . . so that he might make men sharers in the divine nature. (AG 3)

> To do this, Christ sent the Holy Spirit from the Father to exercise inwardly his saving influence, and to promote the spread of the Church. Without doubt, the Holy Spirit was at work in the world before Christ was glorified. On the day of Pentecost, however,

he came down on the disciples that he might remain with them forever (cf. Jn 14:16). (AG 4)

The question we can ask is whether the mission of the Word and the Spirit from creation ends when the Word became flesh and the Spirit was given to the church or continue, not in a parallel, but in a deeper, related way. In *Gaudium et Spes* we read:

> The Christian . . . as one who has been made a partner in the paschal mystery, and as one who has been configured to the death of Christ . . . will go forward, strengthened by hope, to the resurrection. All this holds true not for Christians only but also for all men of good will in whose hearts grace is active invisibly. For since Christ died for all, and since all men are in fact called to one and the same destiny, which is divine, we must hold that the Holy Spirit offers to all the possibility of being made partners, in a way known to God, in the paschal mystery. (GS 22)

It seems clear that, while it is possible for all humans to have a share in the paschal mystery, for some it comes through the church, while for others it is accessible through other ways known to God. The fundamental unity behind the pluralism of religions is affirmed in *Nostra Aetate*:

> All men form but one community. This is so because all stem from the one stock which God created to people the entire earth (cf. Acts 17:26), and also because all share a common destiny, namely God. His providence, evident goodness, and saving designs extend to all men (cf. Wis 8:1; Acts 14:17; Rom 2:6–7; 1 Tim 2:4). (NA 1)

The question, then, is this: what is the relationship between these different ways through which God seems to be reaching out to humanity? Let us look at some more texts before we take up the question again. Since we know well and agree about God's saving action in Jesus Christ and the church, let us focus on the mission of God. *Dei Verbum* asserts:

> God, who creates and conserves all things by his Word, (cf. Jn 1:3) provides men with constant evidence of himself in created realities (cf. Rom 1:19–20). And furthermore, wishing to open up

the way to heavenly salvation, he manifested himself to our first parents from the very beginning. After the fall, he buoyed them up with the hope of salvation by promising redemption (cf. Gen 3:15); and he has never ceased to take care of the human race. For he wishes to give eternal life to all those who seek salvation by patience in well-doing (cf. Rom 2:6–7). (DV 3)

This describes the *missio Dei* or mission of God. It then goes on to talk about Abraham, Moses, and Jesus Christ. *Lumen Gentium* makes a similar affirmation:

Those who, through no fault of their own, do not know the Gospel of Christ or his Church, but who nevertheless seek God with a sincere heart, and, through the dictates of their conscience—those too may achieve eternal salvation. (LG 16)

Gaudium et Spes says:

It is by the gift of the Holy Spirit that man, through faith, comes to contemplate and savour the mystery of God's design. Deep within his conscience man discovers a law which he has not laid upon himself but which he must obey. His voice, even calling him to love and to do what is good and to avoid evil, tells him inwardly at the right moment: do this, shun that. For man has in his heart a law inscribed by God. His dignity lies in observing this law, and by it he will be judged. (GS 15–16)

Conscience is evoked here as the place where God makes God's presence and will felt.

Conscience is given a collective dimension in *Dignitatis Humanae:*

It is through his conscience that man sees and recognizes the demands of the divine law. He is bound to follow this conscience faithfully in all his activity so that he may come to God who is his last end. Therefore he must not be forced to act contrary to his conscience. Nor must he be prevented from acting according to his conscience, especially in religious matters. The reason is because the practice of religion of its very nature consists primarily of those voluntary and free internal acts by which a man directs himself to God. . . . His own social nature requires that man give external expression to these internal acts of religion,

that he communicate with others on religious matters, and profess his religion in community. (DH 3)

Here we see not merely one's individual conscience, but one's collective and religious conscience given freedom and protection. God
reaches out to humans not merely as individuals but also in their
socio-religious structures (cf. AG 3). This is, of course, balanced with
statements such as this one from *Ad Gentes:*

The Lord Jesus . . . founded his Church as the sacrament of
salvation; and just as he had been sent by the Father (cf. Jn
20:21), so he sent the apostles into the whole world. . . . Hence
the Church has an obligation to proclaim the faith and salvation
which comes from Christ. (AG 5)

The Church's Mission at the Service of God's Mission

Looking at all these texts it seems clear that in many of its documents the council holds on to the vision that God, the Word, and
the Spirit are present and active everywhere and always. That this
happens not only in human hearts, but also in their religions, seems
to be indicated, though this would be developed further by Asian
theologians. This presence and action of God is salvific. But all
salvation is a participation in the paschal mystery of Christ, either
known and acknowledged or unknown. At the same time, Jesus
Christ, God's incarnate Word has proclaimed and is realizing God's
kingdom in history and has commissioned the church to proclaim
it to all peoples and to make disciples (Mt 28:18–20). We know
as a historical fact that the majority of humanity so far has not
been members of the church; they have salvation available to them
through ways known to God alone.

  How do we come to terms with this complex experience of the mission of God through the Word and the Spirit always and everywhere
and the mission of the same God in and through Jesus Christ and the
church? There seems to be two paradigms in the council itself. One
is the paradigm of preparation-fulfillment. We move from God's covenant in nature and go on to Abraham, Moses, and Jesus. Jesus is the
fulfillment of all that has gone before. Once Jesus is there, the others
are no longer relevant except as promises pointing to the fulfillment
that has already been reached (AG 3). The previous manifestations

of God are at the service of God's self-manifestation in Jesus and the church, preparing for it and leading to it. Dialogue with them is a way of preparing them for their fulfillment in the church. God's mission is at the service of Christ's and the church's mission. This is the paradigm that is generally accepted in the church today (RM 28–29). The problem is that most humans in the past, in the present, and probably also in the future do not seem to follow this path. They never reach such fulfillment in the church in this life. They are beyond the reach of the church.

The second paradigm is not so unilinear; it is pluralistic without being relativistic. God is manifesting God's self to people in various ways in history. All such manifestations, since they are divine, are salvific. One of these manifestations is the incarnate one in Jesus Christ, continued in the church. This particular manifestation may be more perfect, but it does not abolish or do away with other manifestations. Rather, it is at their service, reaching out to them and bringing all God's manifestations to a communion. This is an eschatological goal. In the meantime the church is helping them toward this goal through dialogue. The mission of the church is at the service of God's mission, which is broader and more inclusive. God's mission, unlike the church, is actually reaching out to everyone at any given time, in ways known to God.

This second paradigm is the common one in Asian theology today. One way to understand this is to contrast the church and the kingdom of God. The kingdom of God is the goal of God's mission. The church is not the kingdom but only a pilgrim movign toward it. As *Lumen Gentium* says:

> The Church, endowed with the gifts of her founder and faithfully observing his precepts of charity, humility and self-denial, received the mission of proclaiming and establishing among all people the kingdom of Christ and of God, and she is, on earth, the seed and the beginning of that kingdom. While she slowly grows to maturity, the Church longs for the completed kingdom and, with all her strength, hopes and desires to be united in glory with her king. (LG 5)

The whole chapter 7 of *Lumen Gentium* speaks of the church as a pilgrim that will "receive its perfection only in the glory of heaven" (LG 48). Therefore, it is not proper to set up the church as the fulfillment of other religions. The church, like the other religions, is also a pilgrim on its way. Its own fullness is in the future. It cannot be presented as the fullness of other religions.

All religions, including the church, are not merely God's initiative, but also human response and therefore may be tinged by limitations and even sin. It is in mutual dialogue that these can be challenged and corrected. The church is not exempt from this situation.

A theological consultation, Evangelization in Asia, organized by the Office for Evangelization of the FABC, writes:

> The Kingdom of God is therefore universally present and at work. Wherever men and women open themselves to the transcendent Divine Mystery which impinges upon them, and go out of themselves in love and service of fellow humans, there the Reign of God is at work. . . . "Where God is accepted, where the Gospel values are lived, where the human being is respected . . . there is the Kingdom." In all such cases people respond to God's offer of grace through Christ in the Spirit and enter into the kingdom through an act of faith. . . .
>
> This goes to show that the Reign of God is a universal reality, extending far beyond the boundaries of the Church. It is the reality of salvation in Jesus Christ, in which Christians and others share together; it is the fundamental "mystery of unity" which unites us more deeply than differences in religious allegiance are able to keep us apart.[1]

The Indian bishops in their response to the *Lineamenta* before the Asian Synod write:

> As God's Spirit called the Churches of the East to conversion and mission witness (see Rev 2–3), we too hear this same Spirit bidding us to be truly catholic, open and collaborating with the Word who is actively present in the great religious traditions of Asia today. Confident trust and discernment, not anxiety and over-caution, must regulate our relations with these many brothers and sisters. For together with them we form one community, stemming from the one stock which God created to people the entire earth. We share with them a common destiny and providence. Walking together we are called to travel the same paschal pilgrimage with Christ to the one Father of us all (see Lk 24:13ff., NA 1, and GS 22).[2]

---

[1] Franz-Josef Eilers, ed., *For All the Peoples of Asia, Vol. 2: Federation of Asian Bishops' Conferences Documents from 1992 to 1996* (Manila: Claretian, 1997), 200.

[2] See Peter C. Phan, ed., *The Asian Synod: Texts and Commentaries* (Maryknoll, NY: Orbis Books, 2002), 21.

They continue:

> In the light of the universal salvific will and design of God, so
> emphatically affirmed in the New Testament witness, the Indian
> Christological approach seeks to avoid negative and exclusivistic
> expressions. Christ is the sacrament, the definitive symbol of
> God's salvation for all humanity. This is what the salvific unique-
> ness and universality of Christ means in the Indian context. That,
> however, does not mean there cannot be other symbols, valid
> in their own ways, which the Christian sees as related to the
> definitive symbol, Jesus Christ. The implication of all this is that
> for hundreds of millions of our fellow human beings, salvation
> is seen as being channeled to them not in spite of but through
> and in their various sociocultural and religious traditions. We
> cannot, then, deny a priori a salvific role for these non-Christian
> religions.[3]

It is my contention that the council has laid the basis for such a
vision by making it clear that the mission of God continues in the
world and by not identifying it with the mission of the Church. The
council is also telling us, both directly and indirectly, that the way of
mission (for the church) is dialogue with God's mission manifested
in various ways in history. This is done in *Gaudium et Spes, Nostra
Aetate, Dignitatis Humanae,* and *Unitatis Redintegratio.* How does
this link to the two thrusts that I mentioned in the beginning?

First of all, since God is speaking to a particular people in a particular time, place, and culture, it is bound to be *inculturated.* The
Christian community can dialogue with God's mission in that culture
only if it is also inculturated. That means that it must become an authentic local church, more local than it happens to be. As a matter of
fact, the Asian bishops at their first FABC assembly said that it is by
dialoging with culture that the church becomes a local church. If it is
not local, it will be neither credible nor relevant. The church therefore
has to become local in order to engage in mission credibly, leading
to transformation from within. In an era of globalization, the local
churches have to dialogue with one another so that they can offer a
collective challenge to the world. In the course of such dialogue the
local churches also may challenge each other prophetically.

Second, dialogue with God's mission will have to be primarily the
dialogue of life. The focus should be on the collaboration of believers

---

[3] Ibid., 22.

in transforming life and society. *Gaudium et Spes*, after speaking about dialogue in general, goes on to spell out concrete areas for dialogue: the family, cultures, social and economic life, the political community, and the peaceful coexistence of nations. For dialogue at these levels we need, not so much the clerics, who have a special function within the church, but the people who live in the (secular) world. We have to declericalize and secularize the church at this level. We have to encourage the people of God to commit themselves to transform the world in collaboration with all people of good will. Addressing other religious leaders in Chennai in February 1986, Pope John Paul II said:

> By dialogue we let God be present in our midst; for as we open ourselves in dialogue to one another, we also open ourselves to God. . . . As followers of different religions we should join together in promoting and defending common ideals in the spheres of religious liberty, human brotherhood, education, culture, social welfare and civic order.[4]

Challenges

If the Second Vatican Council has shown us that dialogue is the way of mission, what have we done in the last fifty years? A true answer would be: nothing much, except occasional symbolic gestures. Mistrust, conflicts, and violence among and between religions have increased. Ecumenical movements are nearly dead. The secular world has moved further away from the church, necessitating a special synod on new evangelization. It would not be fair to lay all the blame at the doors of the church. Consumerism, individualism, secularization, fundamentalism and communalism, monopoly capitalism, unfair trade practices, militarism and the arms race—all these and more are responsible for injustice, violence, and war in the world. But the church cannot escape responsibility for failing to be prophetic. I shall limit myself to three comments in this context.

First, in spite of the inspiration of *Gaudium et Spes*, the church sees itself as the depository of a spiritual message. Some charitable activity is acceptable, but the church is not really in the world in order to transform it from within, following the way of the incarna-

---

[4] Pope John Paul II, *Origins* 15 (1986): 598. For similar sentiments, see John Paul II's address to leaders of other religions in New Delhi after the publication of *Ecclesia in Asia* entitled "The Interreligious Meeting," *Vidyajyoti Journal of Theological Reflection* 63 (1999): 884–86.

tion. Liberation theologies in the Third World, especially in Latin America, have been more or less successfully suppressed, accused of promoting a this-worldly kingdom in the Marxist manner. The church is satisfied with proclaiming general spiritual and moral principles in its social encyclicals. Its focus seems to be on otherworldly salvation. It prefers not to dirty its hands on the ground. In this sense there is a proclamation of a message of justice but no active involvement. For example, in the area of peacemaking, the church prays for peace but does not animate any active movement for peace. That is left to others. There is no dialogue with the world. The church seems to limit itself to offering a spiritual message that others are expected to listen to. Placing itself on a pedestal, it may not invite listeners. The leaders in post-Christian Euro-America seem to be anticlerical. The Islamic world is not interested. Those in India and China would be suspicious in a postcolonial context.

Second, the church has a superiority complex that is very detrimental to dialogue. It is true that Jesus Christ as the incarnate divine Word is the fullness of Truth. But the church does not possess Christ. It does not fully understand him either. It is only a pilgrim church, going ever deeper into the mystery that it has received. So it cannot think of itself as the fullness to which all the others have to come. I think that the church is misled by the Old Testament–New Testament paradigm. The events narrated in the New Testament are seen as accomplishing the prophecies of the Old Testament. But it cannot project this paradigm onto the mystery of the mission of God in the universe. The other religions and churches may witness to aspects of the divine mystery which the church itself has not experienced. Anyway, the church is called to be at the service of God's mission, not to dominate it. If the church is aware of its limitations as a pilgrim church, it will certainly be open to dialogue, to give and to receive. Otherwise, it can think only of a monologue, and the others will not be interested. Though the Second Vatican Council talks much about the mission of God in the universe, I do not think that the church has really interiorized this mystery and opened itself to dialogue with other manifestations of the One Truth of Jesus Christ. Its political status and organizational strength in the world today, for historical reasons, also allow it to dominate any formal or informal conversation with other cultures, religions, and ideologies. So there is no real mutuality in dialogue, and the other partners are not interested to be only subaltern vis-à-vis the church. As a matter of fact, with rising religious fundamentalism, each religion thinks of itself as the only true religion. When they meet, at the religious level, there can be a clash of absolutes rather than dialogue.

Third, the church seems to instrumentalize dialogue as a preparation for and a first step toward proclamation. Mission is seen primarily as the proclamation of the kingdom of God as revealed and realized by Jesus Christ. Dialogue is then perceived as only a step toward proclamation. Sometimes it is even seen as a threat to proclamation. It is not seen as meaningful in itself. The religious others then see in it a hidden agenda and are not interested. St. Irenaeus speaks of Christ and the Spirit as the two arms with which the Father holds up the universe. Perhaps we can see proclamation and dialogue as the two arms of mission, equal in dignity.

Conclusion

I would like to suggest that the Second Vatican Council has pioneered a new era of dialogue in the church and in the world. Pope Saint John XXIII called it a pastoral council. Dialogue with the world is the pastoral thrust that the council gave to the church. This dialogue operates at all levels, secular and sacred, socioeconomic, political, cultural, and religious. This is clearly seen in *The Church in the Modern World*, supported by other pastoral and dogmatic documents, as I have tried to show above. After fifty years we have not yet fully understood dialogue and engaged in it, apart from some sporadic attempts at official and unofficial levels. While we are aware of the mission of the church, we have to become aware increasingly of the mission of God. These two have also to dialogue with each other. If we become conscious of the mission of God in the universe, which is to build up a better human community of freedom, fellowship, and justice—though it is never-ending process, then it will also challenge us to go beyond dialogue to collaboration to gather all things together so that God will be all in all (cf. Eph 1:3–10; Col 1:15–20; 1 Cor 15:28).

PART I

RETHINKING RELIGIOUS PLURALISM

OPPORTUNITIES AND CHALLENGES

Chapter 1

The One and the Many

The world we face is characterized by multiplicity and diversity. There are many sorts of people, animals, trees, and flowers. All these living things are born or come to be and then disappear through death or destruction. This is true also of the material world. Even a child in the school knows that what we see in the world around us can be reduced to basic chemical elements and their compounds. But these elements are different. How can we understand this reality? At the risk of simplification we can say that the Jains with their *anekantavada* simply affirm that reality is made up of many things and we have to accept them as given. The Buddhists, however, claim that though things and persons are many in the world, they are all mutually dependent. They form a sort of network that keeps constantly changing. If we take human persons, they are born of male and female parents whose genes they inherit. Each one's body is made up atoms and molecules of various kinds. These are constantly in movement. Even an atom is made up of particles.

Today, scientists discuss whether the basic reality in matter is a particle or a wave. In any case everything is in motion. As a baby grows it is nourished by food which it transforms into energy. It learns its language and culture from the community in which it grows. It inherits a symbolic world, to the development of which it can also contribute creatively. People construct not only symbolic worlds but also real machines and instruments that can control nature and use its laws for manufacturing goods. People die, and new ones are born. The world continues in mutual dependence and in constant change and movement. While trying to transcend this changing reality, the Buddha refuses to speculate on questions like what, why, and how. Hinduism, however, proposes an *advaitic vision* of Reality. I highlight its originality here.

3

The Questions

The *Kena Upanishad* asks: "Who sends the mind to wander afar? Who first drives life to start on its journey? Who impels us to utter these words? Who is the Spirit behind the eye and the ear?"[1] People seek to understand. To understand means to know the causes and the destiny of things. The answer of the *Kena Upanishad* is: "It is the ear of the ear, the eye of the eye, and the Word of words, the mind of mind, and the life of life. . . . What cannot be spoken with words, but that whereby words are spoken: Know that alone to be *Brahman*, the Spirit." This thought process suggests that the multiplicity that we experience is not ultimate. The basic reality is Brahman. Brahman then can be said to be source and cause of everything. The One is the cause of the many. Much of the thinking of the Upanishads and of later Indian philosopher-theologians is an effort to understand and spell out the reality of and the relationship between the One and the many.

Such questions were not peculiar to India. In Greece, Aristotle posited a *Prime Mover*. He saw the universe as a giant machine. God is the one who constructs the machine and then sets it going. The dynamism of the movement is communicated by the One who sets the whole thing into motion. Like an automatic watch the machine can go on forever under the force of its own movement. The Bible thinks that there was nothing in the beginning, only God. God then creates the world out of nothing: "In the beginning when God created the heavens and the earth, the earth was a formless void and darkness covered the face of the deep" (Gen 1:1–2).

We can say that among the thinkers, both in the East and the West, there was a consensus that the many we experience is caused by the One. The problem, of course, is that the One is posited, but not directly experienced, as we experience the many. Second, there were many attempts to relate the many to the One. Some thought that the One and the many were radically different. Others thought that reality is one and the many are dependent and secondary so as to be almost nonexistent. A third group suggested that the many were related to the One as the body to the Spirit in the humans. These three positions correspond roughly to the opinions of the three well-known Indian philosopher-theologians, Madhava, Sankara, and Ramanuja. The position of Madhava was more or less similar to what the philosophers in the West held. To understand this position we focus on the Western

---

[1] The translations from the Upanishads throughout this chapter are taken from Juan Mascaró, *The Upanishads* (Hammondsworth: Penguin, 1965).

philosophers. *The thoughts of Sankara and Ramanuja were typically Indian. I would like to show that they are more satisfying than the Western view. They are a creative contribution to world thought.* This can be seen clearly if we follow the development of thought in the East and in the West. Let me start with the West.

From Creationism to Atheism

We saw above that, according to Aristotle, God was the *Prime Mover* of the universe. The *Prime Mover,* of course, is not known directly by our senses. It is a logical conclusion from the effect (the universe) to a cause (God). We see a manifold and changing universe, marvelously organized and we posit a supremely intelligent organizer. We cannot think of a complex machine assembling itself by itself. There must be a designer and an assembler.

In the course of philosophical history this vision encountered two sorts of difficulties. Science began progressing in the Middle Ages. Science was based on observation by the senses and experimentation. While science was also busy with causes and effects, it refused to posit non-observable causes. So it tried to explain phenomena without reference to non-observable causes. For example, there is rain. Rain is caused by clouds. Clouds are caused by water evaporating from the seas and rivers. There is no need to make God responsible for the rain. In this sense the phenomenon, according to science, was immanent to the universe, not needing a transcendent cause. The origin of the living beings and of their various species, including humans, can be explained by the theory of evolution. Scientists in the Middle Ages did believe in God. But God was no longer necessary to explain the universe. In later centuries some denied God, who was no longer necessary to explain the universe. It was not that they had explained all the mysteries in the universe. But there was a hope that with the advancement of science any mystery can eventually be explained. A non-necessary God slowly disappeared from the horizon. This is the process of secularization. The Sacred or God is denied. Only the *saeculum* or the world—the secular—remains.

The second sort of difficulty arose from the theory of knowledge. René Descartes proved his own existence, not by any experience of his body by his senses, for example, but by the awareness of his reflecting mind. He said: "I think, therefore I am." Knowledge is related to thought. Any link between the senses and thought is denied. But the thinking mind does not see, feel, touch, hear, or experience anything outside itself. So Immanuel Kant later concluded that we cannot know any reality outside our own thinking mind. He did not deny such reality. But it cannot be known. What we know are our own thoughts and the shape that our thought gives to reality. Even the thinking self is not thinkable, except through its thoughts. Here again it is only one more step to say that what we cannot reach by our thoughts, independent of themselves, does not perhaps exist. So we are left with our thoughts, which have no reality outside of themselves to relate to. But thoughts suppose a thinking self. The only reality that I actually know is my thinking self. This One is affirmed absolutely, while the many are only its manifestations. This was Idealism.

Some said that if thoughts are all that we have, then only thoughts are real and they are what we think they are. We have no means of going beyond our thoughts. Since we—humans—are many, our thoughts are many. So there is pluralism of thoughts. This is what is called postmodern pluralism. Modernity believed in material reality that science studied and worked on. Even if it is still there, it takes as many forms as our mind gives to it. And one wonders: what actually is the "real" behind all these many forms? The many remain, either as mere thoughts or as scientific objects. The One has disappeared. It is not only unknown and unknowable, but does not—need not—exist. It is a sort of *anekantavada*, which affirms multiplicity, not of objects, but of thoughts.

There are still Realists in the West—those who believe that God (One) created the world (many). But they are not the dominant philosophical voice. I am not going into all the intricacies of phenomenological, idealistic, and hermeneutical thinking in the West. There is no space, and it is not necessary for our purpose. For some, the One is there. But we cannot think it, because it thinks us. For the others, we think only of the many. Perhaps there is no One behind the many. In any case the relation between the One and the many is no longer a live question.

The One in the Many

Let us now go back to the history of Indian thought. In India we do not have mere philosophers, but rather philosopher-theologians. Reflection starts with the Upanishads. The Vedantic thinkers start with the Upanishadic affirmations as given. We have had materialists like the Charvakas, or phenomenologists like the Jains, or agnostics like the Buddhists. But the Hindu mainstream based itself on the

Upanishads and interpreted them. Let us therefore go to the Upanishads and see what they say about the One and the many. After that we can explore what the commentators say.

I quoted above the questions of the *Kena Upanishad* and its brief answer. Let us look at the story that it tells us to explain its answer. For reasons of space I am only summarizing it.

> Once upon a time, Brahman, the Spirit Supreme, won a victory for the gods. All the gods think that the victory is theirs and feel proud. Brahman wants to teach them a lesson and appears to them. They do not recognize him. So Agni goes on their behalf to find out. He boasts of his power, but is unable to burn a straw placed before him by Brahman. Similarly, Vayu and Indra are also humiliated. Then Uma appears and tells them: "He is Brahman, the Spirit Supreme. Rejoice in him, since through him you attained the glory of victory." The gods indeed fought. But they did not realize that Brahman was fighting in them, so to speak, and was ultimately responsible for the victory. So they have to glory not so much in themselves, but in Brahman.

This story affirms a relationship between the One (Brahman) and the many (the gods) that is significant for the whole of Indian thinking. This relationship is explained in various ways in the different Upanishads. The frequent use of the image of light in this context is significant and interesting.

The *Isa Upanishad* says: "Behold the universe in the glory of God: and all that lives and moves on earth. . . . The Spirit filled all with his radiance. . . . He is the supreme seer and thinker, immanent and transcendent."

In the *Katha Upanishad* the god of death, Yama, tells Nachiketas: "Concealed in the heart of all beings is the Atman, the Spirit, the Self; smaller than the smallest atom, greater than the vast spaces. . . . When the wise realize the omnipresent Spirit, who rests invisible in the visible and permanent in the impermanent, then they go beyond sorrow."

The *Mundaka Upanishad* says: "In the supreme golden chamber is Brahman indivisible and pure. He is the radiant light of all lights, and this knows he who knows Brahman. There the sun shines not, nor the moon, nor the stars; lightnings shine not there and much less earthly fire. From his light all these give light; and his radiance illumines all creation."

The *Svetasvatara Upanishad* personalizes Brahman. It says:

This is the God whose light illumines all creation, the Creator of all from the beginning. He was, he is, and forever he shall be. He is in all and he sees all. Glory to that God who is in the fire, who is in the waters, who is in plants and in trees, who is in all things in this vast creation. Unto that Spirit be glory and glory. . . . All this universe is in the glory of God, of Siva the god of love. The heads and faces of men are his own and he is in the hearts of all. . . . God is in truth the whole universe: what was, what is, and what beyond shall ever be.

Then we come to the *Chandogya Upanishad,* in which Svetaketu's education is being completed by his Father. The conversation goes thus:

> Bring me a fruit from this banyan tree.
> Here it is, father.
> Break it.
> It is broken, Sir.
> What do you see in it?
> Very small seeds, Sir.
> Break one of them, my son.
> It is broken, Sir.
> What do you see in it?
> Nothing at all, Sir . . .
> My son, from the very essence in the seed which you cannot see comes in truth this vast banyan tree. Believe me, my son, an invisible and subtle essence is the Spirit of the whole universe. That is Reality. That is Atman. THOU ART THAT (*Tatvamasi*).

The father goes on to give two more examples—salt in water and a man blindfolded. But the teaching is the same.

The *Bhagavad Gita* confirms this teaching. Lord Krishna tells Arjuna:

> He who sees me everywhere, and sees all in me,
> I am not lost to him, and he is not lost to me.
> He who standing in oneness,
> Worships me abiding in all beings,
> Exists in me, whatever happens. (6:30–31)[2]

---

[2] The translations from the *Bhagavad Gita* are taken from Antonio de Nicolas, *The Bhagavad Gita* (York Beach: Nicolas-Hays, 1990).

. . . .

Whatever reality has glory, majesty and power,
Understand that to be sprung from a spark of my
    light. (10:41)

. . . .

That radiance in the sun which illumines the entire
    world,
The radiance in the moon and in fire:
Know that radiance as mine. (15:12)

The Commentators

As I said earlier, philosophical-theological reflection in India is not
a rational investigation of the world but an attempt to understand
the scriptural revelation, especially the Upanishads and the *Gita*. But
finally the truth of revelation is experienced in spiritual practice. The
commentators on these texts are many. Well-known among them are
Sankara, Ramanuja, and Madhava. Madhava is a dualist whose reflections correspond more or less to that of the Realists of the Western
tradition. Sankara teaches advaita (nonduality), while Ramanuja
exposes visistadvaita (qualified nonduality). What is common among
them is nonduality, which is interesting as a point of comparison with
Western thought. Let us see, briefly, what Sankara and Ramanuja
teach. Then, I point out the special significance of nonduality in the
understanding of the world and of us today.

Sankara

Sankara is popularly considered a monist. He is said to have affirmed
that ultimate reality is One. Everything else is *maya* (illusion) or unreal. Some of Sankara's own students may have misunderstood him in
this way. German idealist philosophers thought that they had an ally in
Sankara and acclaimed him as a monist in modern times. But serious
students of Sankara point out that he remained a nondualist and did
not become a monist. The starting point is, of course, our experience
of multiplicity. Our question is: what is real? As we experience the
world with its many relativities and limitations we discover that the
Real is "not this, not this" *(neti, neti)*. Our enquiry leads us through
the different levels or sheaths *(kosas)* of reality.

As we reach the heart of the Real we are enlightened. We realize
that the Real we have been seeking is not an object. It is the Subject,

the Subject of our own selves. Once we have reached this center we look back on all the sheaths that we have crossed but from a new point of view, from within. We realize that our previous perceptions have been wrong, due to our ignorance of the Real. We understand that the Real is the only Absolute. It is at the heart of everything and illumines everything. It is One without a second. It does not depend on any other light. But it lights up everything else. The relationship is not mutual. It is like the sun and the moon. The moon reflects the light of the sun. The sun is the source of light and is not dependent on the moon. If we keep looking only at the moon, we think that it is our light. But once we have discovered the sun, then we realize that the sun is the real and only light and the source of all light in the solar system. We see this not from the outside but from within—from the sun, so to speak. Everything else shares the light of the sun. The sun is the only source.

There are not two sources, but rather one—nonduality. To be liberated is to realize experientially that "I am the sun." I identify myself with the center of my being and not with any peripheral sheaths. "Thou are That." "You are the Sun." Then I look back on the world with new eyes, in a new perspective. The world is not nothing. But it is not the Ultimate. My "ego" is not nothing. But, it is not the Ultimate. Once this is realized, the Ultimate lives and works in "me" and in the "world." At the *vyavaharika* (phenomenal) level I may still feel the multiplicity and difference. But, at the *paramartika* (ultimate) level all duality disappears. This experience is not monistic, but nondual.[3]

Ramanuja

Ramanuja reads the scriptures in the light of the bhakti tradition of the Alvars of South India. For him, Brahman is personified as Lord Vishnu, who manifests himself in various ways in the history of the world. Rama and Krishna are two such manifestations *(avatars)*. At the same time he cannot ignore the unity of Brahman so strongly affirmed in the Upanishads and particularly in the *Gita*.

Guided probably by the embodiment of Vishnu in Rama and Krishna, Ramanuja sees the world as the body of God. He rejects what he sees as the monism of Sankara. He affirms a certain duality of relationship between the Lord and the devotee. But this duality is not that of two separate things. The One and the many relate to each

---

[3] To understand this interpretation of Sankara, see Sara Grant, *Sankaracarya's Concept of Relation* (Delhi: Motilal Banarsidas, 1998).

other as spirit and body. The Spirit is the ultimate reality. But the body is dependent on it. It has no reality on its own. It cannot act on its own either. The Spirit is the real actor in the composite. Ramanuja calls this qualified nonduality. The point is that it is nonduality, however qualified it may be.[4]

Conclusion: Advaitic Unity

Idealistic monism makes the world unreal. Mere pluralism lacks purpose and is meaningless. When the One and the many are seen from a dualistic perspective, either the One dominates the many, rendering them subservient, or the many declare their independence and deny the One, affirming pluralism. When the autonomy of the secondary causes is stressed one-sidedly, they tend to cut themselves loose from the Primary Cause. The vision of the advaita, the One-in-the-many, integrates and unifies Reality. The many are dependent on the One, but the dependence is not subservient loss of selfhood, but the experiential rediscovery of one's roots. Rootedness is the source of true freedom, because it is not subservience caused by ignorance and alienation. We experience our rootedness in the One by total self-surrender—*prapatti*. This is the true use of freedom that leads to self-realization.

Jesus gave a glimpse of an advaitic perspective, when he said: "The Father and I are one" (John 10:30). He wished to lead everyone to this awareness. He said that a branch produces fruit only so long as it is part of the tree nourished by its sap. Cut off from the plant it withers. (John 15:1–6) However, this perspective was not favored very much in the West. In the Middle Ages, Meister Ekhart, who revived this vision, was almost condemned as a heretic. Ignoring this perspective has led the West to the final state of ignorance and alienation which is the denial of the One Real. I have explained this above.

I think that the basic difference between the West and India is that the West starts with a mechanistic model of objects that are created and manipulated by an Agent. When the objects discover that they are "subjects," they revolt and affirm their difference, losing their roots in the process. Indian thought, on the contrary, starts with a personal model. It privileges relationship and encounter rather than difference. The selves are not alienated as objects but integrated in the Self. When selves relate to the Self an experience of communion transcending

---

[4] Cf. Swami Tapasyananda, *Bhakti Schools of Vedanta* (Chennai: Ramakrishna Math, 1990).

difference is possible. It is not a phenomenon of the Self dominating objects that are "other" than itself. It is the experience of becoming aware of the hidden aspects of oneself. It is an interior experience of unity. It is two-becoming-one without ceasing to be two. It is an experience of nonduality. The Upanishads give an image that is even more telling than Ramanuja's spirit-body complex. The *Brihadaranyaka Upanishad* says: "As a man in the arms of the woman beloved feels only peace all around, even so the Soul in the embrace of Atman, the Spirit of vision, feels only peace all around. All desires are attained, since the Spirit that is all has been attained, no desires are there, and there is no sorrow."

Chapter 2

The One Spirit and Many Gods

The Spirit is a source of pluralism in the Christian tradition. The recognition of the presence and action of the Spirit in other religions may lead us to see the many Gods of different religious traditions as manifestations in history and culture of the One Absolute beyond name and form. This is the substance of the argument that I shall try to lay out in the following pages.

In the Bible, the Spirit appears as the divine creative force. Hovering over the primal void she presides over the emergence of the cosmos. She inspires the prophets and kings to become mediators of divine power in the course of history. She overshadows Mary when the Word becomes human in her womb, descends on Jesus at his baptism, and initiates his public ministry. Jesus acknowledges the power of the Spirit in him as he proceeds to proclaim and realize the good news among the poor. He promises the gift of the Spirit to his disciples to help carry on the work of the reign of God. The Spirit is indeed the wisdom and the power of God that animates the realization of God's plan in the world. She is the power within the cosmos and humans, inspiring and creating.

Speaking in Many Voices

The Spirit appears as a source of pluralism on the day of Pentecost. Mary and the disciples of Jesus—about one hundred and twenty of them—were gathered in the upper room. The Spirit comes upon them in the form of a strong wind and tongues of fire resting on each of them. "All of them were filled with the Holy Spirit and began to speak in other languages, as the Spirit gave them ability" (Acts 2:4). The gathering crowd is bewildered. There were people from all parts of the Mediterranean wondering: "How is it that we hear, each of us, in our own native language?" (Acts 2:7)

13

Here we see two kinds of pluralism. First of all, the disciples speak in tongues. The same message is communicated in different languages to different groups of people. It is often suggested that this is the contrary of what happened at the tower of Babel. When people were getting together to assert their power independent of God, the diversity of languages broke up their unity and provoked their dispersion. Now people speaking different languages are coming together as one community responding to the same message. The diversity of languages is not suppressed. People do not miraculously understand the message proclaimed in one language, say Aramaic. Rather, people hear the same message, each in their language. The diversity of languages is affirmed. But it does not become a factor for division. The Spirit is conveying the same message through the different languages. The message is exposing God's deeds of power that starts a new age in which the young shall see visions and the old shall dream dreams. The gift of the Spirit is promised to all who are ready to repent. The repentance is shown in their breaking of bread together and celebrating community. (cf. Acts 2) Here we see the many becoming one without losing their differences rooted in their languages. This is the miracle of the tongues.

There is also a second kind of pluralism here that is rarely noted. There were one hundred and twenty disciples in that upper room when the Spirit came upon them. The power of the Spirit must have been manifested in these one hundred and twenty people—the mother and brothers of Jesus and other women and men followers—in different ways. The narrative in Acts focuses on Peter and the other apostles. It ignores the various prophetic charisms of the many others, especially the women, present in that group.

Many Charisms in One Community

Paul, in his letter to the Corinthians, attends to this variety of charisms forced by the tensions in that community. He writes:

> Now there are varieties of gifts, but the same Spirit; and there are varieties of services, but the same Lord; and there are varieties of activities, but it is the same God who activates all of them in everyone. To each is given the manifestation of the Spirit for the common good. (1 Cor 12:4–7)

He then goes on to list some of the charisms and concludes: "All these are activated by one and the same Spirit, who allots to each one individually just as the Spirit chooses" (1 Cor 12:11). This is followed by an affirmation of equality and community: "In the one Spirit we were all baptized into one body—Jews or Greeks, slaves or free—and we were all made to drink of one Spirit" (1 Cor 12:13).

Paul's point here is that every charism is the gift of the Spirit for the service of the community. They are different but equal. So they should not be the cause of conflict, considering some as superior to the others. In our context here we emphasize this focus on the fact of the plurality of charisms, equal in difference and oriented to the service of one community. Paul's use of the image of the body in this context could become problematic, if it is interpreted in a hierarchical sense opposing the body to the head.

Beyond Institutional Borders

The Spirit is also the inspirer and agent of another kind of pluralism. The apostles saw their experience of the life, death, and resurrection of Jesus in the context of the Jewish tradition. They did not immediately perceive its relevance for the others. It is the Spirit that leads them to understand that the good news of Jesus is for all humans, not only the Jews. The Acts of the Apostles narrates for us the story of how the Spirit delicately leads Peter to the house of Cornelius (Acts 10). The invitation comes from Cornelius. Peter is prepared by the vision that warns him not to call unclean anything created by God. As Peter is telling the story of Jesus in the house of Cornelius, the Spirit takes the initiative of giving herself to the "pagan" household. Peter and his companions "were astonished that the gift of the Holy Spirit had been poured out even on the Gentiles, for they heard them speaking in tongues and extolling God" (Acts 10:45–46). Peter has no choice but to celebrate the gift of the Spirit symbolically by baptizing them. He explains the event to the others back in Jerusalem: "If then God gave them the same gift that he gave us when we believed in the Lord Jesus Christ, who was I that I could hinder God?" (Acts 11:17). Here we see the Spirit manifesting another kind of pluralism: the eschatological gift of the Spirit is not merely for the Jews, but for all peoples in the world.

The Spirit of Freedom

The pluralism of the Spirit is rooted in its freedom. She is not bound by our structures and dividing walls. We need to be reborn in the

Spirit to become members of the reign of God. But the Spirit is free to blow where she wills. Jesus affirmed this to Nicodemus: "The spirit blows where it chooses, and you hear the sound of it, but you do not know where it comes from or where it goes. So it is with everyone who is born of the Spirit" (John 3:8). We tend to limit the Spirit to a particular community, culture, or religion. We may even claim power over her. But she is free. Paul affirms this freedom of the Spirit in his letter to the Romans:

> All who are led by the Spirit of God are children of God. For you did not receive a spirit of slavery to fall back into fear, but you have received a spirit of adoption. When we cry "Abba! Father!" it is that very Spirit bearing witness with our spirit that we are children of God, and if children, then heirs, heirs of God and joint heirs with Christ." (Rom 8:14–17)

This freedom is not something given but is to be acquired and experienced. It is a process. Creation itself participates in this process and becomes free (Rom 8:22). The Spirit also helps us in our weakness and prays in us. "And God, who searches the heart, knows what is the mind of the Spirit, because the Spirit intercedes for the saints according to the will of God" (Rom 8:25). Freedom in the Spirit is opposed, on the one hand, to the obligations and institutional structures of the Law and, on the other, to the "flesh," as the principle of human weakness (Rom 7). "You are not in the flesh; you are in the Spirit, since the Spirit of God dwells in you" (Rom 8:9).

The Spirit, therefore, is the principle of freedom and creativity, pluralism and community. She is the presence and action of God in humans and in the cosmos. She blows where she chooses. It is in this experiential faith context that we have to explore the implications of the presence of the Spirit in other religions and cultures.

The Spirit in Other Religions

The Second Vatican Council makes a very broad statement about the presence and action of the Spirit in humans. In *Gaudium et Spes*, after describing the action of the Spirit in the Christians, it affirms:

> All this holds true not for Christians only but also for all men of good will in whose hearts grace is active invisibly. For since Christ died for all, and since all men are in fact called to one and

the same destiny, which is divine, we must hold that the Holy Spirit offers to all the possibility of being made partners, in a way known to God, in the paschal mystery. (GS 22)

✗ Religious inclusivism !

While affirming the centrality of the paschal mystery in the event of salvation, the church suggests that a participation in this mystery is possible for all, in ways unknown to us, but known to God, through the Holy Spirit. Theologians like Karl Rahner would suggest that the various religions may actually be the locations where such a divine-human encounter takes place, given the social-symbolic nature of humans.[1] This is confirmed by John Paul II in his encyclical *Redemptoris Missio:*

> The Spirit manifests himself in a special way in the Church and in her members. Nevertheless, his presence and activity are universal, limited neither by space nor time (DEV 53). . . . The Spirit's presence and activity affect not only individuals but also society and history, peoples, cultures and religions. . . . Thus the Spirit, who "blows where he wills" (cf. Jn 3:8), who "was already at work in the world before Christ was glorified" (AG 4), and who "has filled the world . . . holds all things together (and) knows what is said" (Wis 1:7), leads us to broaden our vision in order to ponder his activity in every time and place (DEV 53). . . . The Church's relationship with other religions is dictated by a twofold respect: "Respect for man in his quest for answers to the deepest questions of his life, and respect for the action of the Spirit in man." (RM 28–29)

Is Spirit a gender fluid term?
Is Church a feminine term?

The Other Religions and the Church

How do we understand the presence and action of the Spirit in human hearts and other cultures and religions? We can see two approaches that seem to be in tension. One approach tends to link the work of the Spirit not only to the paschal mystery of Christ but also to the church. Pope John Paul II says:

> Whatever the Spirit brings about in human hearts and in the history of peoples, in cultures and religions serves as a preparation

---

[1] See Karl Rahner, *Theological Investigations,* vol. V (London: Darton, Longman and Todd, 1969), 128.

for the Gospel and can only be understood in reference to Christ, the Word who took flesh by the power of the Spirit "so that as perfectly human he would save all human beings and sum up all things." The universal activity of the Spirit is not to be separated from the particular activity within the Body of Christ, which is the Church. Indeed, it is always the Spirit who is at work. Both when he gives life to the Church and impels her to proclaim Christ, and when he implants and develops his gifts in all individuals and peoples, guiding the Church to discover these gifts, to foster them and receive them through dialogue. (RM 29)

There is, of course, no problem with such an interaction between the church and various other religions. But the question is whether the other religions need to have a historical link with the church (and Jesus). It seems that they need not. For John Paul II also says:

Since salvation is offered to all, it must be made concretely available to all. But it is clear that today, as in the past, many people do not have an opportunity to come to know or accept the Gospel revelation or to enter the Church. The social and cultural conditions in which they live do not permit this, and frequently they have been brought up in other religious traditions. For such people salvation in Christ is accessible by virtue of a grace which, while having a mysterious relationship to the Church, *does not make them formally part of the Church* but enlightens them in a way which is accommodated to their spiritual and material situation. (RM 10)

Here a mysterious relationship with the church is affirmed that obviously is not historical. So we have a pluralism of religions animated by the Spirit. The document *Dialogue and Proclamation* is more clear and forthright:

Concretely it will be in the sincere practice of what is good in their own religious traditions and by following the dictates of their conscience that the members of other religions respond positively to God's invitation and receive salvation in Jesus Christ, even while they do not recognize or acknowledge him as their Savior. (DP 29)

The Spirit of God, therefore, is present and active in other religions. This activity is related, in ways unknown to us, but known only to

God, to the paschal mystery. But it is not related to Jesus as known and experienced in faith by us, nor to the church as a visible, historical institution. This means that various religions facilitate salvific divine-human encounter in various ways. We can see this as a manifestation of the pluralism characteristic of the Spirit of God. The Spirit is at the source of the pluralism of religions. This is made possible by the freedom of the Spirit who blows where she wills and the freedom of the humans who respond to her in various cultural and historical ways. The unity of humanity in the salvific plan of God at the mystery level is manifested and realized in multiple ways at the level of history, cultures, and religions. Since it is difficult to speak of this pluralism with reference to the historical Jesus, it is attributed to the Spirit. But let us remember that where the Spirit is, the Father and the Word are also.

Religions and the Spirit of God

It is in this context that we can attempt to gain a little more clarity about how actually the Spirit of God is operative in the various religions and cultures. The document *Dialogue and Proclamation* speaks of the "sincere practice of what is good in their own religious traditions." What does this mean? The reflections of Indian theologians over two related issues are worth recalling here. They have had two seminars, one The Inspiration of Non-biblical Scriptures[2] and the other Sharing Worship.[3] The first concluded that the other religious scriptures can be considered inspired and so used in Christian liturgy. If the Spirit of God is present in other religions, she must have spoken through their scriptures, though the message was primarily addressed to their followers. The second said that we can participate in the worship of other religions since all religions worship, through various symbols, the one God. An act of faith in what is happening will obviously be required. Both these conclusions depend on the acceptance of other religions as facilitating salvific divine-human encounter through

---

[2] See also my further discussion in Chapter 4 in this book, entitled "The Scriptures of Other Religions: Are They Inspired?" For additional perspectives, see D. S. Amalorpavadass, ed., *Research Seminar on Inspiration in Non-Biblical Scriptures* (Bangalore: NBCLC, 1974); and George Gispert-Sauch, "Vatican II and the Use of Indian Scriptures," in *Theological Explorations,* ed. Jacob Kavunkal, 35–48 (Delhi: ISPCK, 2008).

[3] See Paul Puthanangady, ed., *Sharing Worship: Communicatio in Sacris* (Bangalore: NBCLC, 1988).

their proper scriptures, symbols, rituals, and institutions. The Spirit of God, active in them, enables such divine-human encounter.

From such a perspective we can say that the Gods of other religions are various manifestations of the one God. They are not mere idols but real mediations. They are not merely different "names" of one and the same Reality. They are actualizations in a people's history and culture. They represent interventions of God in their history. The people narrate such interventions and relive them in sacred times and places and through appropriate images. These give the Absolute a name and a form. Their worship is directed not to these images, but rather through them to the Absolute that they represent and mediate. So when we are looking at the many religions in the world and their Gods, we are not really encountering many Gods but many historical, cultural, and religious manifestations of the one God.

One God in Many Manifestations

Once this principle of pluralism in unity at the level of God and God's manifestations is accepted, we can envisage the possibility that there can be many manifestations of God within the same religious tradition. Among the many religions known to us, Hinduism makes provision for such a possibility. The advaitic (nondual) tradition speaks of the Absolute-without-qualities *(Nirguna Brahman)* and of the Absolute-with-qualities *(Saguna Brahman)*. The *Saguna Brahman* is the manifestation of the *Nirguna Brahman* and can be many. At the level of manifestations, pluralism is possible for personal, histori-cal, and geographical reasons. Sankara, the *advaitic* theologian, has beautiful devotional songs to Siva, Vishnu, and Devi (the Goddess). Saiva Siddhanta is another nondual school. In its tradition Siva has many manifestations in different places under different circumstances to different people. The many manifestations are expressed in vari-ous images installed in various places. They have their local histories and commemorations. But they are many forms or manifestations of one Siva. In the tradition of Vishnu, the Absolute takes many *avatars* or manifestations to restore righteousness in the cosmos on different historical occasions. It is traditional to speak of ten *avatars*, with the tenth one still to come. These *avatars* are worshiped as divine manifestations. But there is no doubt in the devotee's mind that they are manifestations of one God—Vishnu. In an atmosphere of such a variety of Gods and Goddesses in India, at a popular level one tends to relate them to one another as members of one large divine family.

But the wise sages would insist that they are manifestations of the one Absolute. The actual way that the relationship between the many and the one is understood depends on various philosophical worldviews and presuppositions. The basic image is that of one-in-the-many. From such a perspective the Hindus find it easy to integrate the Gods of other religions into their system.

There is a surprising Christian parallel, even if it is only hypothetical, to this vision. Asking whether many incarnations are possible, St. Thomas Aquinas answers:

> The power of a divine person is infinite, not limitable in regard to anything created. . . . We must hold that beside the human nature actually assumed, a divine person could take up another numerically distinct. (ST 3, 3, 7)

We believe today only in one incarnation of the Word of God in Jesus. Since the whole cosmos participates in the paschal mystery, there is no need for other incarnations. But in principle other incarnations are possible. If, on the model of Jesus, each incarnation is seen as a divine-human person, then we will have many human incarnations of one divine Person. We would not certainly consider them as many Gods, but as different incarnations of one God. The unity of God will not be affected by God's many incarnations.

Conclusion

We see in the Bible the Spirit of God as the principle of freedom and pluralism not limited by human, historical structures. Though the New Testament speaks only of the pluralism of tongues and charisms, the church today evokes the presence and action of the Spirit to understand the pluralism of religions. But to accept religious pluralism is to acknowledge the diversity of divine manifestations in the religions, considered Gods by them. Since God is one, these can only be different manifestations of the one Absolute.

Chapter 3

Which Is the True Religion?

In the ensuing decades after the Second Vatican Council, one can say that among Asian Christian theologians there has been a growing positive appreciation of other religions. John Paul II has recognized that the Spirit of God is present and active in other cultures and religions (RM 28–29). This recognition has been prepared and supported both by a priori and a posteriori arguments. The council had said that God makes it possible for everyone to have a share in Jesus Christ's paschal mystery through the Spirit, but in ways known to God alone (GS 22). Karl Rahner suggested that God will have to reach out to humans in a human way, respecting their bodily and social nature and responding to their own search for God. The religions with their symbols and rituals seem to be obvious candidates for this role. This is an a priori argument. Rahner says:

> In view of the social nature of man and the previously even more radical social solidarity of men, however, it is quite unthinkable that man, being what he is, could actually achieve this relationship to God—which he must have and which if he is to be saved, is and must be made possible for him by God—in an absolutely private interior reality and this outside of the actual religious bodies which offer themselves to him in the environment in which he lives. . . . If man can always have a positive, saving relationship to God, and if he always had to have it, then he has always had it within *that* religion which in practice was at his disposal by being a factor in his sphere of existence.[1]

---

[1] Karl Rahner, *Theological Investigations,* vol. V (London: Darton, Longman and Todd, 1969), 128.

The bishops in Asia also suggest a positive view of other religions. But they base their assessment on the fruits of holiness that they experience in the members of other religions. Theirs is an a posteriori argument:

> In Asia especially this (evangelization) involves a dialogue with the great religious traditions of our peoples. In this dialogue we accept them as significant and positive elements in the economy of God's design of salvation. In them we recognize and respect profound spiritual and ethical meanings and values. Over many centuries they have been the treasury of the religious experience of our ancestors, from which our contemporaries do not cease to draw light and strength. They have been (and continue to be) the authentic expression of the noblest longings of their hearts, and the home of their contemplation and prayer. They have helped to give shape to the histories and cultures of our nations. How then can we not give them reverence and honor? *And how can we not acknowledge that God has drawn our peoples to Himself through them?*[2]

Such a positive view of other religions supposes the acknowledgment that God is reaching out to people through their own religions. This leads us to take the phenomenon of religious pluralism seriously and positively. But when we do so, we are always warned of the dangers of relativism.

The Dangers of Relativism

The problem is that here again there are two broad ways of looking at the pluralism of religions. One way is a priori. This is the approach of people like John Hick.[3] They look at the phenomenon of many religions. Considering them from a Kantian perspective they suggest that these religious phenomena are human attempts to express the Real—the *Noumenon*—which is actually beyond the reach of any or all of them. Being mere human efforts they are conditioned by all human limitations. They are subjective. There is no objective quality

---

[2] Gaudencio Rosales and C. Arevalo, eds., *For All the Peoples of Asia: Federation of Asian Bishops' Conferences Documents from 1970–1991* (Manila: Claretian, 1992), 14.

[3] See, for example, John Hick, *A Christian Theology of Religions: A Rainbow of Faiths* (London: SCM Press, 1995).

about them. All religions are the same or at least in the same boat. This is obviously a relativistic point of view. It denies the possibility of knowing or getting in touch with any objective reality. Such a view is also limited to the level of knowledge and truth. The Truth or the Real cannot be known. What we have are the relative truths of our own making, if we can call them truths at all. This is obviously relativism. It does not take any religion seriously. This is not the way that the religions look at themselves. This is the way someone, who claims to have an outsider's (superior?) perspective looks (down?) at them. From this point of view it is easy to say that all religions are the same. They are all equally relative.

It is understandable that Pope Benedict XVI condemns such relativism, because it denies the possibility of knowing the truth or the Real. He warned the cardinals at the mass for electing the new pope (April 18, 2005): "We are moving towards a dictatorship of relativism which does not recognize anything as certain and which has as its highest goal one's own ego and one's own desires." While sharing the pope's concern for relativism, it may not be necessary to attribute such moral depravity to all relativists, since relativism can simply be a consequence of a particular theory of knowledge based on Kantian philosophical principles.

Other philosophers oppose "critical realism" to the Kantian theory of knowledge. They suggest that reality can be known. We are not prisoners of our own minds. Through our body and our senses we—our minds—can reach out to reality. But this does not mean that we can know reality exactly as it is. Our knowledge is conditioned by our own limitations, our intellectual capacity, our emotions, our desires and prejudices, our cultural perspectives, our language—all of which structures our universe. We can, therefore, know the real. But our knowledge is relative, because it is conditioned. We constantly attempt to reach at the content of our knowledge through interpretation. That is why this approach to knowledge is called critical realism. To accept that our knowledge is relative in this sense is acceptable. We do not say that truth is relative. But we say that our knowledge of it is relative to our capacity and to the conditions of knowing. We are not completely cut off from the truth as the real relativists are. We can know the truth. But we never know it in all its fullness. We do not know it exactly as it is. We can always know more of it. We may not be able to express all that we know about it. We can call this a posteriori relativism.[4]

---

[4] See Michael Amaladoss, *Making Harmony: Living in a Pluralist World* (Chennai: IDCR, 2003), 91–116.

Corresponding to these two kinds of relativism—a priori and a posteriori—we can think of two kinds of pluralism. The first kind of pluralism is subjective and phenomenal. We do not reach the Real at all. We only have our own images of it that we have evolved. The second kind of pluralism is objective. All of us know the Real. But our many ways of knowing are conditioned in various ways. So we may know different aspects of the same reality in different ways. They may overlap. Our knowledge is true, though limited in various ways and therefore different. A dialogue with others may even lead to a better or deeper grasp of the truth. Pluralism in this sense is not merely objective but positive and beneficial.

The Pluralism of Religions

We cannot simply apply these two theories of pluralism to understand the pluralism of religions. The reality of religions is more complicated. Before going into this, perhaps we can say that we are not interested in the relativistic, a priori, agnostic pluralistic theory of John Hick in our attempt to understand the pluralism of religions. Actually we *reject* it. So we need not bother about it any further.

What complicates the issue of pluralism in relation to the religions is the fact that most religions do not present themselves merely as valid human efforts to know Reality or God. They claim to be God's self-revelations and human responses to them. God's self-revelation is enshrined in the scriptures: the Bible, the Qur'an, the Vedas, and so on. Theories of revelation differ. Vedic revelation is eternal, heard by the seers. The Qur'an is literally dictated to Muhammad by an angel of God. The Bible is a record of God's actions in human history. It also reports the discourses of Jesus. God's own word about God obviously has an absolute character. God's demand in terms of cultic and moral behavior cannot be ignored. Religion is nothing but a symbolization and systematization of God's call and the human response to it. God's intervention gives the religions an absolute character.

Such an absolute character, however, may be qualified in two ways. First of all, though God speaks, God does so in a particular human language to a particular human community at particular times of its history. God's self-revelation is put in writing by humans and transmitted to succeeding generations. All these activities are conditioned by limitations of humans—their cultures, languages, and historical circumstances. Therefore, these texts need to be interpreted when read in other contexts. So we get into a hermeneutical circle, the ultimate guarantee being the faith-commitment of a community that recognizes its identity in the texts of scripture. We cannot demonstrate the truth of the scriptures of any religion rationally to a nonbeliever. Interpretations, of course, can be pluralistic, but within the community. Islam, for example, has four main schools of interpretation of the Qur'an.

The second qualification comes from the experience of religious pluralism itself. There is no problem as long as we hold that ours is the only true self-revelation of God. But if we have a positive appreciation of other religions, we cannot a priori refuse the possibility that God may have spoken to the members of other religions. It is the same God who speaks. But God does not have to say the same things to every group. An infinite God may manifest different aspects of Godself to different groups of people. God's self-revelation itself may be conditioned by the history and culture of the people to whom God is speaking. Otherwise, God may not be understood. The response of the people is also conditioned by their history, culture, and the depth of their commitment. If we add to this the freedom of God who reveals and the freedom of the people who respond, then pluralism seems inevitable.

A third element that may complicate the situation further is that people's intellectual limitations, emotional attitudes, and moral deviations like egoism and desire may condition or even block their understanding of God's self-revelation and/or falsify it and misinterpret it in various ways. Did not Jesus complain about his hearers: "They look but do not see and hear but do not listen or understand" (Matt 13:13). What we call religion, as a sociocultural and historic institution, embodies all these. That is why every religion is and has to be self-critical and has prophets who keep challenging its misrepresentations and abuses periodically. Such criticisms of religion are significant for the believers only when they come from within.

Pluralism as a Problem

All that we have been saying so far looks at religious pluralism in a general way. This does not answer the questions of concrete individuals or groups when they are faced with the experience of religious pluralism. We may accept in general the possibility that there can be many ways of divine-human encounter. Yet, in a concrete situation we may not be able to see a particular religion as a way of divine-human encounter. We may consider it as misguided or false. We must also contrast the attitude of a "neutral" observer and a believer. Someone who is a phenomenologist or a historian may look at various religions, compare and contrast them and mark convergences and divergences, avoiding every kind of value judgment. Believers, on the other hand, believe their own religion to be true and consider all other religions they know as false or at least imperfect and inadequate, even though in theory they are open to the idea of a possibility of many religions, as I have outlined above.

When we discuss the pluralism of religions in the classroom or the conference hall, for example, someone will usually raise a question whether religious pluralism means that all religions are the same or that all religions are true or that all religions are equal. Others will say that in practice religions seem to be contradictory to one another—Islamic monotheism and the Christian Trinity, for example. These are comparative statements that are best avoided. A truly religious person can only talk in terms of his or her own faith. I believe in the truth of my religion. But I am open to the possibility that God may also have spoken to others in different ways. I am not, however, facing many ways from which I have to choose one. I am not in a supermarket of religions where there are a number of religions on offer and I can choose one of them for whatever reason. If God has spoken to me and called me in a particular way, that way is obviously mandatory for me. I have no choice in the matter, even when I accept that God could have called others in various other ways.

Believers also usually think that their own religion is the ultimate one so that, even when they are open to the possibility that God has spoken to others, the other religions are considered as somehow "ordained" to their own. They may think that this "ordination" is transcendental or eschatological, since it is not experienced historically, where the reality is one of pluralism. For instance, Christians believe that Jesus Christ is the universal and only savior and that everyone who is saved is related to the church in some (unknown to us) way. Krishna, the *avatar* of Vishnu, says in the *Bhagavad Gita* that though people may worship different gods, all their worship comes to him, he being the only true God. But even these people have to face the fact that historically there is a pluralism of religions and people live, die, and are saved in them—however the ultimate technology of salvation is understood by particular believers. They have to make space for the other religions within their own perspective. It is the God in whom they believe and who has called them in this way, who is also reaching out to others through other religions.[5]

Making space for other religions within our own faith perspective does not involve that we accept a priori all other religions as good and holy. In the public, political sphere we may observe a spirit of tolerance or noninterference. We respect the right of the others to practice any religion of their choice. We do not seek to judge them as religions. But such noninterference may have its limits. On the one hand, we may protest against a particular religion if we see that it violates what we consider the fundamental rights of human beings. In India, for instance, we may have reservations about how Muslims treat women and how Hindus treat the Dalits, while the Hindus may not understand why the Christians (Catholics) oppose divorce and contraception. On the other hand, when we have to live and work together with members of other religions, we are not satisfied with abstract and general affirmations of their legitimacy. We would like to evaluate them concretely. We would like to say what is good and bad in them and so be critical, while collaborative. It is here that the question arises: what are the criteria for such a judgment? We are seeking to go beyond a political policy of noninterference to a socio-religious policy of dialogue and collaboration for the good of all. We may even suspect that without the second the first—the policy of noninterference—may not succeed. So we have to explore the criteria by which we can "judge" religions, including our own.

Truth as a Criterion

Religions based on revelation set great store by what God has revealed to them about Godself, humans, and the world. They consider this information true. They codify this truth in a creed. They would suggest that truth could be a criterion for judging among religions. For instance, Christians feel that they have the fullness of truth. Jesus Christ said: "I am the truth." In Jesus Christ we possess the truth. Therefore we must be able to evaluate and judge any religion with this truth as the criterion. Whatever is contrary to what we believe cannot be true, because we have the truth. The reality, however, is not that simple. Jesus is indeed the truth—the fullness of truth. He is the

---

[5] For an effort in this direction with regard to different religions, see ibid., 117–44.

Word of God itself. But how much do *we* know this truth? Jesus's own manifestation was kenotic. St. Paul tells us: "Though he was in the form of God . . . he emptied himself, taking the form of a slave" (Phil 2:6–7). Jesus tells his apostles on the last day of his life: "I have much more to tell you, but you cannot bear it now. But when he comes, the Spirit of truth, he will guide you to all truth" (John 16:12–13). The idea of the development of dogma through which we go deeper into truth and have a better grasp of it over time is well recognized in the church. The need for the gospel to encounter various cultures in the world and take form in them is also a widely accepted principle today. It is therefore difficult to claim that we have the fullness of truth in an effective manner, so that we can judge everyone else using our knowledge of truth as a criterion.

On the other hand, while we may not know the full truth in a conscious and effective way, what we say about God—in our creed, for example—is true. Anything that contradicts this cannot be true. The problem is whether we tend to assume contradictions too easily and quickly. For example, Muslims would assume that the Christian doctrine of the Trinity contradicts Islamic monotheism. But Christians would say that the Trinity is not tritheism but is monotheistic. So they seek to explain the apparent contradiction. Similarly, is the advaita of Hinduism contrary to the "I—Thou" perspective of Christianity? We can point to many mystics like Meister Eckhart who seem to have had an advaitic (nondual) experience of God. If we go behind symbols and myths to basic meanings many seeming contradictions may disappear. Besides this we have to take cultural pluralism seriously. Theologians have shown how even dogmatic pluralism is possible.

If God has spoken differently to different people, we may envisage a certain pluralism of truths as pointing to various aspects of the infinite truth that is God. Apophatic theology shows that God is beyond what we can know or say about God. The fact of limited affirmations about the truth of God makes place for other limited affirmations about God. In such a case we may say that while an affirmation that is really contradictory to my affirmation may not be true, an affirmation that is merely contrary to mine can be true. It is said that in Asian thought one is more open to the perspective of *both-and* than to the perspective of *either-or.* We may have to speak more of complementarity and convergence than merely non-contradiction.

Given the complex nature of truth and its knowledge and affirmation, I wonder whether "truth" can be the only criterion to judge other religions. Swami Abhishiktananda, for example, wrote the book *Saccidananda* to show how the advaitic experience of Ramana Maharishi finds its fulfillment in the Christian Trinity.[6] Toward the end of his life, however, he was less sanguine about this, looking on advaitic experience as being beyond both the Hindu and the Christian *nama rupa* (name and form). He did not deny the Trinity. But he thought that we can go beyond it into the depths of God where only oneness is experienced.[7]

It may not, therefore, be acceptable today to use the truth as we experience and express it as the only criterion to judge other religions. The fact that our perception, experience, and expression of truth are mediated by a culture and a language besides our limitations as humans makes it problematic as a sole criterion of judgment. We are not masters of truth but its servants. Given our own limited perspectives we may not be able to interpret adequately the truth of other religions. There has also been a growing emphasis on experience rather than knowledge in religious matters. Mystics may be more reliable guides than theologians. The primary purpose of religion is not to reveal the truth about God, humanity, and the universe. Religion is meant to help us to live meaningfully. The Word of God became human in Jesus Christ, not to communicate to us a creed or a list of truths, but to liberate us from all our oppressions and to share God's life with us. Religion is not a body of truths, much less a philosophy. It is an encounter, an experience of life and freedom. When Jesus said "I am the way, the truth and the life" (John 14:6), he was not revealing to the disciples a body of truths; rather, he was presenting himself as the true mediation of encountering God, the Father. That is why he continues: "No one comes to the Father except through me. If you know me, then you will also know my Father" (John 14:6–7).

The insistence on truth and on faith as belief in a series of affirmations as central to religion may be peculiar to Christianity. With it goes the importance given to theology. When the theology of liberation emphasized praxis as a criterion for authenticity, it was seen as something new. Islam tends to stress praxis: prayer, fasting, almsgiving, pilgrimage—besides confession faith in Allah. Hinduism and Buddhism insist rather on experience reached through concentration. It is not that scripture and theology are not important to them, but they are secondary.

---

[6] Swami Abhishiktananda, *Saccidananda* (Delhi: ISPCK, 1970).

[7] Swami Abhishiktananda, *Ascent to the Depth of the Heart* (Delhi: ISPCK, 1998).

From Their Fruits (Matt 12:33)

We have seen above how the Asian bishops used the fruits of holiness of the members of other religions to conclude that God is present and active in them. This is certainly a good criterion. When someone in the crowd told Jesus that his mother and his brothers were waiting outside for him, he replies: "Whoever does the will of my heavenly Father is my brother, and sister, and mother" (Matt 12:50). In the same way he declares that the truly blessed are "those who hear the word of God and keep it" (Luke 11:28). This insistence on praxis is confirmed when Jesus evokes the scene of the final judgment. The criterion for approval is feeding the hungry, clothing the naked, welcoming the stranger, caring for the sick, and visiting those in prison (Matt 25:31–45). Such insistence on praxis goes well with what we have said about the other religions in the previous paragraph.

However, good behavior by itself can again only be a partial criterion of true religion. While all religions insist on moral behavior, their prime insistence seems to be on ritual or other meditative experiences. In Hinduism and Buddhism moral observance is only the preparation for real *sadhana* (religious practice), which is meditation. Christianity too tends to stress sacramental practice. In modern times we also have the experience of people who may be morally good though they may not believe in any religion. The basic moral law of doing good and avoiding evil may be in the heart (conscience) of every human being independently of what religion the person belongs to. Moral behavior can become a significant criterion to judge religion only when it is linked to some sort of religious commitment of which it is seen as a consequence. In practice, too, moral behavior is an excellent criterion to judge individuals, but not necessarily religious groups. It may be rather hard today to find a Christian community that acts like the first community that is reported in the Acts of the Apostles. "All who believed were together and had all things in common; they would sell their property and possessions and divide them among all according to each one's need" (Acts 2:44–45). Some communities of religious try to live this ideal. Buddhism has its community of monks *(Sangha)*. Hindus have their *sannyasis*.

Religious groups tend to get politicized. Every religious group has indulged in violence at some time or another in the name of its religion, even if it is only for perceived self-protection. Some people in every religious group tend to become fundamentalist. Therefore, behavior of its adherents is an ambiguous pointer to the quality of a religion, though good behavior can always be a good recommendation.

Perhaps the criterion of behavior shows us that there are good and bad elements in every religion. Behavior may be one way of discerning the principles that inspire it. Jesus tells us the story of the good Samaritan. While he goes out of his way to help the wounded person who could have been a Jew, the Jewish priest and Levite pass the man by. We appreciate the goodness of the Samaritan. But we would hardly use it as a criterion to say that the Samaritan religion is better than Judaism. We do not use the example of Mahatma Gandhi to prove that Hinduism is a good religion. Gandhi drew his inspiration from many religions and had his own brand of Hinduism that had little to do with official, institutional Hinduism.

Vision and Values

Religion is for life. A good criterion for judging religion may be the kind of ideal that it proposes and the hope that it offers to make life worth living. Christianity, for example, is the symbol and servant of the kingdom of God. Jesus proclaimed the kingdom of God as a community of freedom, fellowship, and justice. It is marked by love and reconciliation, sharing and service. It seeks to do away with social divisions and marginalization. This kingdom remains on the horizon both as a vision and a challenge.[8] Jesus establishes the church as a symbol and servant of this kingdom. Its purpose is precisely to promote the communities of the kingdom in the world, not itself. The kingdom is a vision of hope toward which the church is constantly moving. It is a gift of God but also a task for the church. The kingdom is also the criterion to judge the authenticity of the church. The church is true only insofar as it promotes the kingdom and seeks to be its visibilization. The church is not its own justification. It is judged in terms of how effective it is in living and promoting the values of the kingdom, not in terms of its creed, its sacramental system, or its institutional structure. These values are not identified with the church. It can promote them even where it cannot promote itself (RM 20). It can collaborate with other religions and ideologies and with all people of good will in promoting the values of the kingdom. The kingdom seems a secular reality, even though the church feels intimately connected to it.[9]

---

[8] George Soares-Prabhu, "The Kingdom of God: Jesus' Vision of a New Society," in *The Indian Church: The Struggle for a New Society*, ed. D. S. Amalorpavadass (Bangalore: NBCLC, 1981), 579–608.

[9] By *secular* I refer to something that is not anti-God or antireligious but common to all religions.

I wonder whether the vision of the kingdom and its values can be a criterion to judge not only Christianity, but also other religions. It is a nonreligious criterion, of the kind proposed by Jesus in his story of the judgment of the nations. So no religion need feel that it is being judged in terms of another religion.

A rapid look at the other world religions and ideologies seems to suggest that the vision of community that Christianity calls the kingdom is also found in them. The Muslims speak of the *Umma* as a world community of justice and peace.[10] Buddhism looks forward to the ideal of inter-being, which is the fruit of the denial of egoism and desire that are divisive. It extends to the whole cosmos, which discovers itself interdependent and interconnected.[11] Hinduism is working toward an advaitic (nondual) community of life where all reality becomes one.[12] All of these visions have one common enemy, namely egoism in its many manifestations.

Such a common vision has the advantage of being a continuing challenge to all religions. The authenticity of a religion consists in how actively it is pursuing this vision and its values. Its structures may be inadequate. Its successes may be limited. But it is open to be influenced and challenged by its vision. That is what is giving it the dynamism that keeps it alive. Such a vision finds expression in a text like Jesus's Sermon on the Mount. It attracted people like Gandhi. It is a Christian vision. But there is nothing sectarian about it. It could be a Hindu, Buddhist, or Muslim vision too.

There is a difference between the criterion of vision and values and the one of moral behavior. It is the difference between vision and praxis. A religion may offer excellent ideals. But the people who claim to be the followers of that religion may not follow those values at all. This does not mean that the religion is bad. It means that while the good behavior of people can be a recommendation for a religion, their bad behavior need not lead to an adverse judgment of the religion itself. The religious institution may not adequately embody the values that the religion proposes. Its followers may not practice what they preach—as the saying goes.

By focusing on vision and values we also give less importance to the organizational and ritual structures that each religion develops to

---

[10] Cf. Asghar Ali Engineer, *Islam and Liberation Theology* (Delhi: Sterling Publishers, 1990).

[11] See Thich Nhat Hanh, *Inter-being* (Berkeley: Parallax Press, 1987); and Bhikku Buddhadasa, *Dhammic Socialism* (Bangkok: Thai Interreligious Commission for Development, 1986).

[12] Swami Agnivesh, "Vedic Socialism," *Seminar* 339 (1987): 18–22.

carry on its project in the world. These structures are under the constant judgment of the vision and values. For example, it is the vision and values of the kingdom of God that help us to be critical of the unjust social structures of slavery and discrimination against women that even Paul seems to support.

Conclusion

As a Christian I would like Christianity to be judged by the vision and values of the kingdom of God as preached, lived, and inaugurated by Jesus and by the saints who have tried to translate this vision in their lives than by the praxis and institutional aspects of the church.[13] It is true that one cannot adequately separate the vision from the institution. A vision cannot be translated into practice without some sort of institutional mediation. But the institutions always remain imperfect *avatars* of a perfect ideal that animates our hope.

In India, for instance, Hinduism is often condemned because it justifies the caste system. The unequal and discriminatory caste system is an evil. We do not know how it came into the Hindu social order. There is no doubt that it is justified by its ritual praxis in terms of purity and pollution. But I do not think that it belongs to its vision of an ideal society. Many saints in the bhakti tradition have been against the caste system playing any role in divine-human interaction. The love of God transcends caste. A sannyasi also renounces caste because it is seen as belonging to this phenomenal world. One way to fight the caste system in India is precisely to show that it is not part of the deeper vision of the ideal Hindu society. It belongs to the practical ordering of society promoted by the Dharmasastras and can be abolished in the light of our contemporary awareness of the dignity of every human being and of participatory democracy as the necessary social framework.

Contemporary Islam would benefit by a distinction between what Muhammad and the Qur'an intended and the Arabic sociocultural customs and practices in which this vision has been expressed. Its vision of a socioeconomic and political order subject to God and concerned for justice and for the poor is inspiring.[14] With regard to

---

[13] Michael Amaladoss, *Vision and Values for a New Society: Responding to India's Social Challenges* (Bangalore: NBCLC, 2004), 3.

[14] Ali Shariati, *What Is to Be Done? The Enlightened Thinkers and an Islamic Renaissance* (Houston: IRIS, 1986).

other religions, Muhammad had an attitude of tolerance that does not seem to have filtered down to most contemporary Muslims.

Religions, therefore, must be judged by the vision and values that they propose and by the saints who seek to live them and not so much by their theological, ritual, and institutional manifestations. If we explore these criteria we would be amazed at the kind of convergence that we find among the various religions of the world. Christians believe that Jesus Christ is related in a unique and special way to the project of realizing this vision. However, Christians also believe that God is realizing this universal vision everywhere, through the Word and the Spirit, in ways known to God alone (GS 22). Some of these ways could be other cultures and religions in which the Spirit of God is present and active (RM 28).

Chapter 4

Are the Scriptures
of Other Religions Inspired?

Every religion has its foundational myths, normally stories of origins and ends and of divine self-manifestations.[1] These are narrated, sometimes even reenacted, during important rituals of the community. In the more developed religions these narratives are written down. These are the scriptures. These are the foundational documents in which the community recognizes the sources of its faith.

Insofar as these narratives are considered by the community as divine self-manifestations, they are said to be revealed. They are also recognized as having human authors. But these are guided by God in a special way. They are inspired. This inspiration guarantees their authenticity and veracity and therefore their authority in the community. They have to be interpreted to become relevant in varying circumstances of space and time. But they remain unalterable foundations of the religious tradition to which one has to return constantly.

Some Questions

How do we, Christians, look at the scriptures of other religions? Do they have any value for us? Can we draw inspiration from them? Does

---

[1] I am not subscribing to theories like "all religions are the same" or "all religions are equal." Each religion will have to make space for other religions within its own perspective. So the term *religion* in this chapter is used analogically. Similarly, the terms *revelation* and *inspiration* are used analogically. I do not consider the other scriptures as equally revealed and inspired *for me* as the Bible. The value I give to them will depend on the value I give to the other religions within themselves and in relation to me in dialogue. If I believe that the Spirit is present and active in other religions, this will be true also of their scriptures in a proportionate manner. This has to be discerned and not affirmed a priori.

37

God speak to us through them? I am reflecting on these questions as a Christian, in the context of my own faith in God's self-manifestation in Jesus and in the divine plan for the world. Each religion has its own view of the origin and nature of its scriptures. For Muslims, the Qur'an is the revelation of God's word to Muhammad. Hinduism believes that the Vedas are eternal sounds present in the atmosphere and heard by sages who wrote them down. I am not going to discuss such special origins. I am simply taking the scriptures as privileged documents of a religious community in which they "hear" the word of God.

Why should we be concerned by the other religions and their scriptures? How should we look at them? A simple reason could be that in the course of my life I encounter believers of other religions and their scriptures. Some of them make an impression on me and I wish to know what attitude I should adopt toward them. This attitude can be dictated by good neighborliness; that is, I have a desire to know more about others or I feel that I should respect them. These reasons are good as far as they go. But our attitude can be dictated also by our vision of faith. Is there a Christian way of looking at these scriptures? I think that there is.

Christians and Other Scriptures

Here is my general thesis: *Scriptures are foundational documents of a religious community. They share the same value that we give to that religious community. If we believe that the Spirit of God is present and active in the other religions (cf. RM 28), then the presence and action of God can also be recognized in their scriptures and rituals.*

Religions, their scriptures, and rituals are also the fruits of human creativity. So they will be marked by the creative elements, but also by the limitations of human agents. Yet it is in and through these limited creations that we discover the divine self-manifestation. This is obviously a hermeneutical process. This view supposes that we believe that God is the common origin and goal of all peoples and their religions. These have a specific place and role in the plan of God. They are also interrelated. How we understand this interrelationship depends on how we see the plan of God. At the moment there are two ways of looking at it, through a unilinear framework or a pluralistic one.

A Unilinear Framework

The relation we experience between the Old Testament and the New Testament is projected on to the other scriptures. The paradigm is one that goes from preparation or promise to fulfillment. The other religions and their scriptures are seen as pre-Judaic. They have the "seeds of the word" as compared with the Bible which is the word of God. A seminar of Indian theologians held at Bangalore in 1974—The Inspiration of Non-Biblical Scriptures—evoked a vision of history with three covenants of God with humans: the cosmic or natural in creation, the Judaic through Abraham and Moses, and the new covenant in Jesus Christ. Just as the New Testament reads and interprets the Old, it can also read and interpret in its own light the scriptures of other religions. We can see the mystery of Christ adumbrated in the other religions. Christianity has the fullness of the light of Truth, whereas the other religions have some "rays" of it piercing through the clouds of darkness. These partial truths will have to be recognized and saved by Christianity. The people who hold those partial truths are invited to discover the fullness in Jesus Christ by becoming Christian.

While this paradigm of promise-fulfillment may hold good when it is applied to the history of one particular people—namely, the Jews, even though the Jews who have not become Christians may not see it that way—one wonders whether this can be projected onto other peoples, their histories, and their cultures. Any real experience of other religions like Hinduism, Buddhism, and Islam sees them as very different from the Judeo-Christian framework.

A Pluralistic Framework

Some theologians today suggest that we must respect and accept the real pluralism among religions. This is the consequence of the respect we owe to the freedom of the Spirit active in human hearts and religions and to the freedom of these people who respond to the Spirit in their own way (cf. RM 28). But this pluralism does not mean that all the religions are the same or say the same thing in different words. It is a pluralism that is coordinated in mysterious ways by the one God who is at the source of everything and who has only one plan for the universe. We know its goal. We even confess the place of Christ in it. But we have no blueprint to guide us. We do not know how it is actually being achieved. We are called to discover it and collaborate with it in history.

We, not being God, cannot understand a priori their interrelationship. But we can discover this a posteriori through dialogue. We are also called to be at the service of God's plan, which is manifested to us as a gathering of all things together or universal reconciliation so that finally God will be all in all (1 Cor 15:28).

When we think of religions as being ways of salvation, we tend to think of them as objects in the abstract. Religions are not objective entities that we can compare and contrast. The world is not a supermarket of religions from which we can choose according to our preferences and specifications. Religions are only mediations of an encounter between God and a group of humans. This encounter finds expression in symbols: images, rituals, narratives, and so on. These have no value apart from the encounter that gives them birth. They cannot be treated or judged as objects. If God has called a person or a group in a particular way, that way is unique to them. They are not simply choosing one way among many others displayed before them. A certain way that is God's will for one person may not be God's will for another. God may call people to change ways for whatever reason. But changing ways is not purely a human choice. To say that different people reach God in different ways so that all these different ways lead to God does not mean that all of them are equally good ways for everyone.

To say that God has manifested Godself in the various scriptures does not mean that they are objective statements that can be freely interpreted by everyone and compared and contrasted. They are documents of faith that have a special significance in the relational context in which they have been produced. They do not have the same significance outside this context.

Such a specificity of religions and their scriptures does not mean that they are monads that are not accessible to others. But it does mean that they can be properly and adequately accessed only in the context of a dialogical relationship with the community to which they belong. They should not be read and interpreted outside that context. This is a common principle of hermeneutics. It is not for us to interpret others' scriptures for them.

Our Response to Other Scriptures

In this context, how do I respond to the other scriptures? All the scriptures, like all the religions, do not have an equal value for me. God has called me in a particular way in which I too have responded to God. This is special for me. My respect and appreciation for another religion and its scriptures are only consequences of my respect for the other believers and their religious experiences. Such a contact goes beyond the approach of the study of comparative religions or the reading of scriptures as literature, even devotional literature, and drawing inspiration from them at that level. We find in the market a number of books of collections of texts from various scriptures that try to show how all of them speak well of peace, love, service, and so on. Eventually such quotations can also come from non-scriptural sources.

I can think of three levels of such contacts with the others and their scriptures. At a first level we are in dialogue with the other believers. It starts as dialogue of life and dialogue of collaboration in the defense of common human and spiritual values. But this experience of life and action may lead us to share also our religious experiences and even to pray together. In such a dialogical context the identity of each one is respected. Each group reads and interprets its scriptures, and we admire them particularly for the way that they inspire the other believers. We may appreciate and learn from their example. A certain comparison may not be out of place here. But it is not an "objective" comparison. It is always in the living context of the others and of our relationship with them.

At a second level such dialogue with the other may lead me to have some authentic understanding and appreciation of the other scriptures. I may see in it aspects of God-experience that is different from mine and which challenges me in some way. It may provoke me to correct and go beyond my personal, historical, and cultural limitations. It may even point to depths of my own scriptures that I have not so far understood. It may make me read my scriptures with new eyes. I remain rooted in my religious experience. Yet I am enriched by my dialogue with the other. But my use of the scriptures of the other depends on a previous listening to the other. Today such listening may be through the mediation of books or discourses in the media. But then I go beyond this listening to reinterpret the text of the other in the context of my own experience and my scriptures. This is based on the conviction of faith that God is speaking to me through the other. God is not calling me to become the other. But the other has a prophetic message for me that enables me to grow deeper in my own tradition.

At a third level some people may feel called to experience God through two traditions. These people try to read the scriptures from within the tradition. Today we come across people who claim to be Hindu-Christians or Buddhist-Christians. This can happen in two ways. An Indian, born and brought up as a Christian, may discover his roots in Hinduism, seeing it, not as a foreign religion, but as the tradition of his or her ancestors. The person may seek to integrate it in some way. But integration may not be easy and one may tend, not to syncretize, but to alternate between two experiences, mutually enriching.

We may also have a similar movement from the opposite direction. A Hindu may hear the call of Christ without feeling obliged to leave his or her own tradition. The two experiences are seen neither as the same nor as complementary but as different. We also seem to have examples of people who come from the European Christian tradition to encounter the Hindu or the Buddhist tradition. They feel loyal to both without easily integrating one with the other; they live in tension, which can be painful but creative. These people may rise beyond the social and ritual aspects of a religion. Perhaps we need not worry about such rare cases. But it is good to keep them in mind to realize the actual width of the spectrum of interreligious encounters.

Some Difficulties

We can now look at some of the difficulties that are usually raised. If we define concepts like revelation and inspiration narrowly, as they are understood in Christian, not to say Scholastic, theology, obviously we cannot apply them to other religions. That is why we have tried to focus on conditions of possibility of divine-human encounter in general, without limiting our gaze to its particular form in biblical-Christian history.

Revelation and inspiration are often spoken of with reference to truths. One then speaks of more or less truth(s). When there are many truths, one tries to reduce them to a unity either in terms of a hierarchy or in terms of complementarity. I have tried to avoid this by talking about relationships. These may be more or less intimate. But as long as there is a relationship, the degree of intimacy is not immediately relevant. Relationships can be different without being hierarchized or compared. The difference can be due not merely to human, historical, and cultural conditioning, but also to God's will. A certain unity or convergence, however, is assured because one pole of all the relationships is the same, namely, God. Because of God, the unity need not necessarily be fully historical. It can be transcendent.

When one speaks of interpretation and discernment, there is always a question on criteria. When we speak in terms of difference, one relationship cannot set itself as the criterion for all the others. Criteria must be looked for in terms of non-contradiction, analogy, or convergence because it is the same God. One can also speak of the fruits of the Spirit of which St. Paul speaks: "love, joy, peace, patience, kindness, generosity, faithfulness, gentleness, and self-control" (Gal 5:22–23).

Phenomena like revelation and inspiration need not be limited to developed religions and written scriptures. They are present also in cosmic religions with their orally transmitted mythical narratives. As a matter of fact, all the scriptures have an oral origin.

Conclusion

Such a broadening of the notion of inspiration and revelation makes interreligious dialogue a spiritual challenge. We could say that God is an active, if invisible, partner of such dialogue. The participants should listen, not only to each other, but also to God. Interreligious dialogue is no longer an option but is a necessary means of collaborating in God's mission to reconcile all things at the end of time. It is an eschatological responsibility that has to be fulfilled in history. Revelation and inspiration are not once-for-all events. They are a dimension of history. That is why we have to be alive to the signs of the times constantly. No one need claim to be an exclusive spokesperson for God. God is an ever-present mystery in history.

Chapter 5

Violence or Dialogue between Religions?

In today's world, dialogue between religions has acquired a new dimension and a new urgency. Believers in different religions are not just living together; in many places they are fighting each other in the name of religion. Religions inspire and legitimate violence. Hence, a dialogue between religions seems urgent for the survival and peace of humans on this earth. We have, therefore, to look at dialogue between religions not only in a missionary and religious, but also in a sociopolitical context. Both contexts are related in life and in ideology.

Violence in the Name of Religion

Violence between people professing different religions has a long history. Every religion has its martyrs. The Crusades and the European wars of religions are part of world history. If we look only at the second part of the twentieth century, interreligious violence in the world was widespread. Hindu-Muslim violence in India; Buddhist-Hindu violence in Sri Lanka; Christian-Muslim violence in the Philippines, Indonesia, and the former Yugoslavia; inter-Christian violence in Ireland; Jewish-Muslim violence in the Middle East; Buddhist-Christian violence in Myanmar—the list can go on. There has been antireligious violence in the former and present Communist countries. Even the United States and Japan have not escaped violence by fundamentalist sects. Religious minorities and converts to new religious movements have had a difficult time in most countries.

But the link between religion(s) and violence seems to have caught the imagination and attention of people everywhere after the terrorist attack on the twin towers of the World Trade Center in New York on

45

September 11, 2001. People thought that the predictions of Samuel Huntington regarding the "clash of civilizations" have been proved true.[1] Huntington identified civilizations with religions and suggested that the next major conflict would be between Christianity and Islam. Disclaimers to the contrary, popular imagination, both of Christians and Muslims, probably sees the ongoing conflict in West Asia or the Middle East as one between the two religious communities.

A few years earlier, on the occasion of the Second World Parliament of Religions in 1993, in Chicago, the participants proclaimed that there can be no peace in the world without peace between religions.[2] This project had been symbolically dramatized by leaders of all religions coming together in Assisi to pray for peace in October 1986 and January 2002. This is the context in which we are raising this question: why are believers fighting among themselves, and how can we avoid such conflict?

Interreligious violence rarely has only religious reasons. There are always socioeconomic and political causes behind religious conflicts. Religion justifies them and adds its own reasons. So we shall adopt a broad approach in our effort to understand religious violence.

Defending One's Identity

One of the roots of religious violence is the quest for social identity. Our identities are socially constructed. Individuals become aware of their identity by interacting with significant others starting with their mothers, fathers, siblings, the wider family, and neighbors. At the same time they also build up a social identity by interiorizing symbolic structures of communication and relationship through language and ritual. The lifecycle and seasonal rituals particularly contribute to the building up of the group. Initiation rites may play a key role at a crucial moment of personal development. These are constituents of culture. The individual belongs to a group that distinguishes itself in contrast to other groups: "we" against "them." Psychologists suggest that when there are two groups, each sees the other not merely as different, but as competitive and inimical and inferior to itself. This is based on the feeling of the in-group against the out-group. There is no attempt to know the other, giving rise to ignorance and prejudice.

---

[1] Samuel P. Huntington, *The Clash of Civilizations and the Remaking of World Order* (London: Touchstone Books, 1996).

[2] Cf. Hans Küng and Karl-Josef Kuschel, eds., *A Global Ethic* (London: SCM Press, 1993).

These feelings may be dormant at normal times but get aggravated in moments of tension.[3]

Religion is the deepest element of individual and group identity. As providing answers to ultimate questions, religion touches the deeper elements of human identity and behavior like searching for meaning, goal setting, and decision making. Even people who are not practicing their religion are rooted in a tradition. Or they may substitute for religion some ideology that provides them with an ultimate frame of reference.

Religion is also an important element of group identity. Every individual is socialized in the context of a social group, as we have seen. The family plays a primary role in this. The religious community comes closely behind the family, so we can call it a wider family. Religion provides the rituals like lifecycle rituals and festivals that are means of social integration in the community. Sudhir Kakar, a psychoanalyst, explains:

> The inner space occupied by what is commonly called the 'self'— which I have been using synonymously with 'identity'—not only contains mental representations of one's bodily life and of primary relationships within the family but also holds mental representations of one's groups and its culture, that is, the group's configuration of beliefs about man, nature, and social relations (including the view of the Other).[4]

When people belonging to different religions live together and socialize in school, in the street, in the marketplace, and in the place of work, the reasons for such socialization are always limited. The primary socialization seems to remain the family and the religious group. The other groups are really "other" and different. Psychologists suggest that this sense of identity develops and becomes fixed in early childhood, by the age of three or four. Because it is often unconscious, it is also strong. Kakar suggests:

> At some point in early life, like the child's 'I am!' which heralds the birth of individuality, there is also a complementary 'We are!' which announces the birth of a sense of community. 'I am' differentiates me from other individuals. 'We are' makes me aware of the other dominant group (or groups) sharing the physical and

---

[3] Sudhir Kakar, *The Colours of Violence* (Delhi: Viking, 1995).
[4] Ibid., 242.

cognitive space of my community. . . . (The mere perception of two different groups is sufficient to trigger a positive evaluation of one's own group and a negative stereotyping of the other.)[5]

All of us belong to different social groups in different social contexts and for different purposes. Normally we are able to live without conflict. The tolerance may be no more than a negative attitude of "live and let live." But such tolerance is possible. Conflicts come when the relationships among different groups enter into a competitive mode.

Such divisive group feelings are further strengthened by religion, which is a powerful cementing force. A group may feel that it has been specially chosen by God and has a special revelation. Or it may claim a special experience of the Ultimate. Others then may be seen as questioning and threatening this special relationship, especially if they claim a different experience of the Divine.[6]

In a conflictual situation people tend to project their own drawbacks and evils onto the other. In a religious context such a projection may become the demonization of the "other," identifying oneself with the Divine.[7] Kakar explains this process of projection:

Because of early difficulties in integrating contradictory representations of the self and the parents—the 'good' loving child and the 'bad' raging one; the good, care taking parent and the hateful, frustrating one—the child tries to disown the bad representations through projection. First projected to inanimate objects and animals and later to people and other groups—the latter often available to the child as a preselection by the group—the disavowed bad representations *need* such 'reservoirs'. . . . These reservoirs—Muslims for Hindus, Arabs for Jews, Tibetans for the Chinese, and vice versa—are also convenient repositories for subsequent rages and hateful feelings for which no clear-cut addressee is available. Since most of the 'bad' representations arise from a social disapproval of the child's 'animality', as expressed in its aggressivity, dirtiness, and unruly sexuality, it is

---

[5] Ibid., 242–43.

[6] See Veena Das, ed., *Mirrors of Violence* (Delhi: Oxford University Press, 1990); Gerald James Larson, *India's Agony over Religion* (Albany: State University of New York Press, 1995).

[7] Mark Juergensmeyer, *Terror in the Mind of God: The Global Rise of Religious Violence* (Berkeley and Los Angeles: University of California Press, 2000).

preeminently this animality which a civilized, moral self must disavow and place in the reservoir group.[8]

Religious Communalism

Conflicts between groups arise when they are forced to share the same geographical, economic, and political space. Such togetherness involves a question of power: who controls the situation, who dominates? Such need to dominate seems to be a basic need for humans as political animals. Political control, however, becomes crucial when there is a competition for limited resources in the economic sphere. In such a situation individuals find group support indispensable. The religious group, of course, will be the strongest because it believes it has God on its side. A religious group may be even more closely knit than a class group.

Religion, then, becomes communalistic.[9] Communalism is the political use of religious group identity. People who belong to the same religion are made to think that they share the same economic and political interests. The actual struggle may start with the economic and political sphere, justified by religion. But it easily spills over into the religious sphere, and religious symbols are attacked. In these cases religions are involved in economic and political conflicts. There may be some truly religious people in every group who may see such abuse of religion and regret or stand against it. Every religion will have its prophets who condemn its abuse and instead try to use it for promoting peace.

Religious Fundamentalism

Sometimes religion itself can become a cause of division and conflict. Every religion has its fundamentalist groups.[10] Fundamentalists defend what they think are the fundamentals of their religion when they feel that these are under attack. For example, many of the modern reformers in Islam were equally opposed to the secularist atheism promoted

---

[8] Kakar, *The Colours of Violence*, 243–44.

[9] S. Arockiasamy, ed., *Responding to Communalism* (Anand, Gujarat: Gujarat Sahitya Prakash, 1991).

[10] Lionel Caplan, *Studies in Religious Fundamentalism* (London: Macmillan, 1987); John Locke, *The Call to a Renewed Church in Asia and the Challenge of Religious Fundamentalism*, FABC Papers no. 92m (Hong Kong: FABC, 2000).

by the consumer culture of the West, represented by the United States, and to the Marxist atheism of the Communist powers.[11] Some of them promoted a literal interpretation of the Qur'an. Unfortunately, this fundamentalist struggle became communalistic because these two cultural-religious currents were supported by the political and military dominance of the Western powers led by the United States and the Communist bloc led by the former Soviet Union. So it became not only a religious but also a political and military struggle. Guerilla warfare and terrorist attacks are the "weapons of the weak." Violence is then justified as self-defense.

Exclusivism in religion can be considered a mild form of fundamentalism.[12] Exclusivists think that their religion is the only way to salvation. Consequently, they are also universalistic or global. They believe that they are responsible for the salvation of all. This feeling of responsibility urges them to "save" others—through force, if necessary. The force could be political, social, economic, and today also the media. In the past Islam and Christianity have not hesitated to use even military force for the purpose—of course, as they would claim, for the ultimate good of the people.

Religious Violence

Our analysis so far may make us think that social groups are responsible for violence for economic and political causes. The power of religion is often co-opted to legitimize such conflict. Even religious fundamentalism does not seem to become violent unless it is also mixed up with political factors and, perhaps, not-so-hidden economic interests. We might be tempted to think that religions in themselves are promoters of personal/inner and social peace. Unfortunately, religions are very ambiguous in this matter.[13]

All religions start as a quest for a solution to the problem of evil as unmerited suffering. Suffering is seen as punishment for sin. The evil of sin can be attributed only to humans, not to God. But sin seems so enormous that most religions feel the need for an evil power, like Satan, who tempts and provokes humans. Satan may eventually be

---

[11] John L. Esposito, ed., *Voices of Resurgent Islam* (New York: Oxford University Press, 1983).

[12] Gavin D'Costa, *The Meeting of the Religions and the Trinity* (Maryknoll, NY: Orbis Books, 2000).

[13] R. Scott Appleby, *The Ambivalence of the Sacred* (Lanham, MD: Rowman and Littlefield, 2000).

conquered by God. But in the meantime we have an ongoing conflict between good and evil that takes historical, human, and social form. The struggle is directed against those—people and structures—that are seen as the agents of Satan in this world. Violence against these "agents" is not only accepted but even encouraged. This is how a "just war" slips into a "holy war"—a *jihad,* a crusade.

The scriptures of all religions are full of such wars. The Old Testament is full of the wars of God's people against their enemies. They are often humanly unjustified, divine election and favor being seemingly the only justification. The New Testament speaks of the struggle between Jesus and Satan, though eventually it is Jesus who is killed. Jesus's death is interpreted as a punishment for the sins of humanity. Hinduism has its epic wars between the good and evil forces in the Ramayana and the Mahabharata. In the Qur'an, Muhammad is at the head of an army, even if the last battle for Mecca passes off nonviolently. Only in Buddhism is the struggle between good and evil seen as a moral, interior one. Even then the Buddha chooses the middle path between rigorous asceticism and indulgence. But the Buddhists are as violent as others, justifying it in terms of the conflict between good and evil spirits. Thus all religions tend to the demonization of the enemy and justify or even encourage violence. Supporters of just wars are very much alive today. Therefore, one cannot say religions do not support or justify violence. Unfortunately, they do. I am not saying that religions are inherently violent. But they do justify violence under certain circumstances.

Sacrificial Violence

There is still another religious principle that also seems to justify violence. All religions speak of sacrifice. In the history of religions we have a spectrum that extends from human sacrifice to "spiritual" sacrifice. Sacrifices are spoken of in the context of sin, guilt, and propitiation. Strictly speaking, sacrifice is the offering of oneself, of one's own life. But this is done symbolically by offering other lives, often animals. Life is symbolized by blood. So sacrifice involves killing and violence. Jainism in India, Buddhism, and some forms of Hinduism have done away with bloody sacrifices. But they have done so by focusing on self-realization through meditation for ultimate liberation. They no longer speak about a God whom one has to propitiate or satisfy by offering sacrifices. We Christians have not abandoned a sacrificial language in understanding the redemption wrought by

Jesus. The offering of oneself as a sign of love and service has deep meaning. But we must free this self-offering from any sense of reparation or satisfaction involving suffering as punishment. We must also distinguish self-offering from suffering. Suffering may be incidental. One can even take on suffering as a way of showing love in particular circumstances. But it is not an essential element of love or offering. One can regret it even while accepting it.

Religions for Peace

While religions can, in various ways, provoke violence, they also can inspire peace. All religions speak of peace: Shalom! Salam! Shanti! Just as religions, in the process of being rooted in a particular place, tend to acculturate themselves and justify existing socioeconomic and political structures, religions, or at least some of its serious practitioners, challenge injustice and violence in the name of the Ultimate. Economical and political structures will always be guided by profit and power. The quest for justice and peace can come only from religion(s). Even those who justify violence always propose peace as their goal. How can the religions promote peace in practice? I think that each religion has to answer this question for itself.

But religions can hardly promote peace if they are not at peace among themselves. Hence we have to ask, first of all, how religions can promote peace among themselves. What can we do, not only to avoid communalistic conflagrations, but also to reduce communal tensions? I shall make a tentative attempt to answer this question.

Communal Conflicts

Any community with a diversity of members and interests will not be entirely without conflict. Conflicts indicate there are tensions in the community, and they may be due to valid instances of discrimination, injustice, and misunderstanding related to unequal or inadequate distribution or availability of resources, illegitimate divisions of power, or disputes about status in society. The community, then, is enabled to intervene in such problematic situations, resolve conflicts, and restore justice. What is important is not to pretend to avoid all conflicts but to solve them in creative ways without allowing the eruption of violence. Writing on conflict resolution E. Franklin Dukes asserts:

In a democratic society conflict is the basis for social change. If there is to be just relationship, if change is to occur, latent conflicts must be made visible to all parties. It is through confrontation and advocacy that needs gain currency and legitimacy; in many situations it is this confrontation alone that forces the recognition of interdependence that makes negotiation possible.[14]

The need to become peacemakers seems particularly present when conflicts erupt into destructive violence. Our response to such conflicts, however, can be explored both in short-term and long-term perspectives. In the short term, soon after a conflict which has led to violence and destruction, we need to collaborate with multireligious peace-and-reconciliation committees. We have to, first of all, help and reassure the victims and defend them, if necessary. We have to procure aid for them and help in their rehabilitation. Second, we have to condemn the violence and use all possible legal means to find out its perpetrators and help to bring them to justice. This might involve putting pressure on the government, not only to inquire into the incidents impartially, but also to take appropriate action to restore justice by punishing the culprits and by compensating the victims, as far as possible. We obviously cannot bring people back to life. But we can rebuild houses, offer help to restart small businesses that may have been destroyed, and so forth.

Any peace or reconciliation has to be based on justice and fairness, not on appeasement of the powerful and violent. This might be a long, drawn-out process that involves collaborating with the inquiry, putting pressure on the government through all legal means to act on the inquiry, and to initiate public interest litigation processes if the government is not responsive. Such actions will reassure the victims by making them feel that they are not alone. Even when this is happening, the process can be subverted in so many ways. Hence, there is the need for the peace committees to be vigilant and to follow up developments. Multireligious peace committees must resist every attempt to politicize or again communalize the issues. This is the reason that we should take seriously the suggestions of practitioners of conflict resolution that third-party mediation is always helpful.[15] We could

---

[14] E. Franklin Dukes, *Resolving Public Conflict: Transforming Community and Governance* (Manchester: Manchester University Press, 1996), 164.

[15] See Ronald J. Fisher, *Interactive Conflict Resolution* (Syracuse, NY: Syracuse University Press, 1997).

qualify the idea of the third party as actually a multireligious group, where there are third-party elements, but also credible representative of the religious groups in conflict. We do have some nongovernmental organizations that engage in this kind of activity. Interreligious groups are sometimes formed on an ad hoc basis to do some immediate relief work. But we do not have stable multireligious committees, preferably based in the affected areas themselves, to follow up the process of promoting reconciliation through justice. I suggest that this is a concrete way of promoting interreligious dialogue in life and action.

South Africa has given a concrete example in recent years. The authorities there, when it became a democracy after decades of apartheid, established a Truth and Reconciliation Commission (TRC).[16] Interreligious conflicts are often provoked by economic and political factors. The properties of some are destroyed, and others benefit. People are murdered. The political order too has been violated. In such a situation, we cannot speak about resolving conflicts without restoring justice. Justice does not mean revenge: an eye for an eye, a life for a life. It is not victor's justice, like the trials of Nuremberg after the Second World War. We cannot turn back the clock of history. We cannot bring dead people back to life. That is why the TRC spoke of *restorative* justice as opposed to *retributive* justice. Reparation can be made to people who have lost their property, either by people who have deprived them of it, or, if they can be identified, by the community or state. Restorative justice aims, not to go back to the old order, but to build a new community. This supposes forgiveness and reconciliation. These have to be based on truth. The truth of what actually happened must be established. One can transcend it; one need not forget it. The process of forgiveness starts from the victims, they must be ready to forgive, if not forget.

In order to forgive, the truth of what the victims have suffered must be recognized. Forgiveness supposes and demands repentance on the part of those who have done wrong. Forgiveness cannot be given if it is not asked for and accepted. People in power giving themselves or their predecessors a blanket amnesty is not reconciliation. Putting the blame on the system is not forgiveness. People who were responsible— at least the leaders—must come forward to accept responsibility and express regret. Only this kind of interaction between the oppressors and the victims can lead to the healing of memories. Memories need not be abolished, but they can be healed. The stories of avowals of

---

[16] Raymond G. Helmick and Rodney L. Peterson, *Forgiveness and Reconciliation* (Philadelphia: Templeton Foundation Press, 2001).

violence done and of pain and suffering undergone before the TRC have been cathartic to everyone. It is not difficult to imagine recognized leaders of one community asking forgiveness symbolically from another community.

What happens in many cases is that, when there is violence, order is restored by the police or army. In majority-minority conflicts the civil authorities and police, coming from the dominant communities, may play an ambiguous role between restoring order and supporting the majority. Enquiry committees are appointed. Because of the mob character of the violence, the real culprits who inspired and instigated the struggle are never brought to book. Real justice is not done to the innocent victims. Memories are not healed but simply suppressed. They just wait for another occasion to flare up, making the next conflict more violent than the first. Normal forms of dialogue are not really possible on such occasions.

In the long term we must create a growing atmosphere of mutual understanding, acceptance, and even collaboration among the believers of different religions. How can we go about this? In a world in which religions seem to be becoming sources of conflict rather than promoters of peace, we have to be clear about our vision of a multireligious community living together in harmony. If we look around the world, we can see various ways in which people have sought to solve this problem.[17] Then the people must be enabled to live as members of such communities. Let me explore this in a little more detail.

A Vision of Community

Before we speak about the role of religions in community, it is good to look at the idea of people living together in community and its implications. Today we have nation states everywhere, covering a certain geographical space, created by various kinds of historical circumstances. They all have within their national territories different kinds of ethnic, cultural, or religious groups. Conflicts among these are common today, even if they are not violent everywhere. How do people construct community in such situations?

The political theory that developed in Europe during the Enlightenment sees the state as a collection of individuals, who have their

---

[17] Peter H. Merkl and Ninian Smart, eds., *Religion and Politics in the Modern World* (New York: New York University Press, 1985); Gustavo Benavides and M. W. Daly, eds., *Religion and Political Power* (Albany: State University of New York Press, 1989).

inalienable rights, but who, in pursuit of their own self-interest, come together to set up structures of common living, spelled out in a contract. One insists on the dignity and rights of every individual. In such a situation conflicts are seen in terms of the legitimation of power, the defense of one's rights, and the search for one's interests. While we do not deny the relevance of these factors, social contract of individuals seems inadequate as the foundation of community. It ignores natural communities like families, kin groups, and so forth. The basis of community is relatedness. Every human being has the experience of being in relationship with others for his or her origin, life, culture, and celebration. To live in community is to develop such sustainable relationships. Dukes explains:

> While it (relatedness) need not exclude such dispositions as friendship, love, or altruism, it is much more than those dispositions alone. For relatedness does not depend on the good feelings one might have for others. Relatedness also found in such qualities as a sense of responsibility for one's actions; a sense of obligation to those who are dependent; and loyalty to those who have extended themselves for others. It is found in a respect for the traditions of one's own and others' cultures; recognition of one's shared humanity; and understanding of, and even empathy for, the meaning others impart to their beliefs, values and needs.[18]

Once we go beyond individualism as the basic element of society, we discover that a nation is actually a community of communities, because a nation is not a conglomeration of individuals but is made up a variety of ethnic, cultural, and religious groups. This reality has been explored, particularly with reference to cultures, as multicultur-alism.[19] People in a national community do not relate to one another only as individuals, but also as members of particular groups, each with its own identity. Each group attempts to protect its identity and deserves recognition and respect. Of course, the groups should not be allowed to stifle the freedom of individuals in the name of preserving and defending group identity. But the groups have a right to be recognized, acknowledged, and respected. It is from this point of view, for example, that Gerald J. Larson speaks of respecting "community-ship"

---

[18] Dukes, *Resolving Public Conflict,* 169.

[19] See, for example, Amy Gutmann, ed., *Multiculturalism* (Princeton, NJ: Princeton University Press, 1994); Cynthia Willett, ed., *Theorizing Multiculturalism* (Oxford: Blackwell Publishers, 1998).

side by side with "citizenship" in the Indian context. If "community-ship" is not respected, then communalism will be the result.[20]

It is in the context of a nation that is a community of communities that we see the inadequacy of a democratic system that depends on the rule of majority, because in such a system a majority community can always dominate minority communities democratically. The fathers of the Indian Constitution tried to forestall this possibility by defining and protecting the rights of minorities. The attempt by some in the majority community to claim for it the right to dominance in national affairs by virtue of its numerical majority shows up the shortcomings of the present liberal democratic system focused on the individual. This is why people who are reflecting on multiculturalism and conflict resolution are talking of strong or deep democracy. *Strong democracy* complements liberal democracy by developing institutions and structures where everyone can actively participate in discussion and contribute to the evolution of policy and decision making that affects everyone. Not only individuals, but also communities are respected. Such participative democracy is distinguished from representative democracy, where a few representatives, often more concerned for their own self-interest than for the interests of the people, decide the fate of a whole people.[21] Others speak of *deep democracy.* Judith M. Green, exploring different aspects of deep democracy, writes:

> Someone who has developed a culturally pluralistic perspective has already decentered the claims of his or her own cultural tra-dition to unique and absolute authority in favour of a perhaps inchoate belief that other voices and traditions have their own, respect-worthy insights, values, and claims to at least limited authority. Such a belief supports and is supported by an impulse toward democracy as a way of life.[22]

One who is open to pluralism does not seek to dominate or impose, but rather to converse, to dialogue, and to search for consensus. In India the role of the Rajya Sabha is to be a body of wise people, who have the good of the whole country at heart and who, in this way, counterbalance the elected representatives of the Lok Sabha. Unfor-tunately, the Rajya Sabha has been politicized too.

---

[20] Larson, *India's Agony over Religion,* 285–87.

[21] Benjamin Barber, *Strong Democracy: Participatory Politics for a New Age* (Berkeley and Los Angeles: University of California Press, 1984).

[22] Judith M. Green, "Educational Multiculturalism," in Willett, *Theorizing Multiculturalism,* 429.

The Indian democratic system has inherited its formal democratic structure from the West. It has an impersonal, universally binding legal system which is enforced by the state. But it is superimposed on a multiplicity of religious and caste groups. A person's primary loyalty is to the group. Such loyalty to one's group also conditions the behavior of politicians and bureaucrats. This subverts the system from within.[23] But the alternative does not seem to be the abolition of intermediary groups between the individual and the state. This does not seem possible in a multicultural, multireligious community. The challenge, then, is to build up a community that respects, integrates, and transcends cultural and religious pluralism.

Religions and Community

What are the implications of such a vision for the presence of many religions in a community? Some would say that the state should be totally neutral in everything that has to do with religion. But this does not mean that religions must be reduced to the private sphere of the individual, as many secularists would maintain. No true believer would accept that religious faith should not have any influence on his or her public conduct. One could therefore distinguish between the state and its institutions of governance, which must be neutral toward all religions, and the public life of the community, which has its own institutions. At the level of public life there must be a free interplay of diversity of religions, as well as of cultures and ethnic identities. In a democratic state the formal structures of governance will be guided and helped indirectly by the convergent consensus of the community. Different religious groups can find inspiration and motivation in their own religious resources for the defense of common human and spiritual values that govern public life, controlled at its own level by the state.

The present situation in India, however, is quite confusing, and no common point of view has emerged. On the one hand, we have the secularists, who do not want to have anything to do with religion either at the level of the state or at the level of public life. Here secularism becomes a quasi-religious ideology, which limits religion to the private sphere, with the supposition, of course, that religion is really something irrational, and, while it could be tolerated in the private

---

[23] Satish Saberwal, *India: The Roots of Crisis* (Delhi: Oxford University Press, 1986); idem, *Wages of Segmentation* (New Delhi: Orient Longman, 1995).

sphere, it should have no influence on public life. But such secularists in India are few, and there is a consensus among scholars that India is not secularized in that sense but remains a "religious" country. At the other extreme, we have the Hindutva ideologists who would like to make India a Hindu state, which, of course, would be tolerant of other religious minorities. They see democracy as dominance by the majority.[24] This view is obviously detrimental to the kind of community that we have envisaged above. In between we have people like Mahatma Gandhi, who wanted a secular state that will be respectful of other religions. However, he saw Hinduism itself as a kind of inclusive religion that made place for minorities; so one could say that his vision of India was a type of Hindu secular state based on the principles of *sanatana dharma* as he understood it.[25] The Muslim community led by Jinnah did not accept his vision. Others would suggest a secular state with a public order that would be nourished by all the religions, in the manner suggested above.

I think that all these four currents of opinion were represented in the Constituent Assembly, with the result that we have in the Constitution a compromise document. The state is said to be secular—not against, but neutral to all religions. But at the same time, not only the people but also the state itself are committed to protect the minorities and defend their rights. The state also claims the right to interfere even in religious matters when they concern the public good and the defense of fundamental rights. For instance, it reformed the Hindu code, and it claims the right also to legislate for the other personal religious codes, though this is done with the consensus of the religious groups concerned. In any case the state is also committed by the Constitution to move toward a common civil code. It looks as if the Constitution makers wanted to respect religious pluralism, protect the minorities, and at the same time reform the religions with regard to practices that were seen as contrary to fundamental human rights.

In the light of what we have seen in the previous section, I think that we should move toward a *state* that would remain secular as neutral toward all religions, with a common civil and criminal code and a *public life* that is multireligious, in which all religious groups are respected and accepted. There must be a dialectical and symbiotic relationship between the state and the public (community) so that the institutions of the state are constantly nourished by the developing

---

[24] Peter van der Veer, *Religious Nationalism: Hindus and Muslims in India* (Berkeley and Los Angeles: University of California Press, 1994).

[25] G. Aloysius, *Nationalism without a Nation in India* (Delhi: Oxford University Press, 1998), 70–213.

consensus in the community. This mutual influence could be institutionalized in some way. The state can and should keep public order
and ensure justice. But it is the community that can promote peace and
reconciliation. It is here that dialogue will have an indispensable role
to play. In his Introduction to the study *Citizens and Politics* (1991),
David Matthews spells out why dialogue is so important:

> Why is public dialogue so pivotal? The public dialogue is the
> natural home for democratic politics. That is the 'home' people
> feel forced out of and want back. People depend on the dialogue
> to provide opportunities for the public to hold counsel with
> itself and give public definition to the public's interest. . . . The
> only way to get at the base of the problem is through greater
> public definition of its own interests. That means the public has
> to be invested in deliberations over the difficult choices that are
> involved in delineating the public's interests. That definition is
> necessary to give direction to government. And public direction
> makes for public legitimacy.[26]

If we do not appreciate this distinction between the state and the
public, we tend to expect the state to do everything, which it is not
capable of. There is a need today to build up an active and engaged
public. Dialogue is the only way of doing this. Unfortunately, the
state's control of much of the nation's media, with the exception of
the press, makes such free discussion all but impossible.

The goal of interreligious dialogue is precisely to build up a public
that is multireligious. It should not, of course, ignore the other dimensions of dialogue, while it is aware of its own specific identity. Interreligious dialogue will be only one element in a wider dialogue that is
also intercultural, interethnic, and, in India, inter-caste. Multireligious
groups will have a special role, not only in shaping the consensus of
the community through discussion, but also in conflict resolution
when religious communities come into conflict, for whatever reason.

Conditions for Dialogue

We do not have to concentrate too much on the interreligious and
inter-caste conflicts all around us to realize that dialogue is not easy.
From a purely communicative point of view, Jürgen Habermas has

---

[26] Quoted in Dukes, *Resolving Public Conflicts*, 158.

described what he sees as an "ideal speech situation" to provide un-distorted communication. The ideal speech situation is one in which communicative action is not disturbed by power differences and co-ercion so that the interlocutors can arrive at a "rational consensus." Some of the conditions are that the statement must be true, that its author has the required legitimacy to make it, and that it is a true reflection of the intentions of the speaker.[27]

But dialogue goes beyond communicative action, because what we are looking for is not merely a rational consensus but the emergence of a community. It has, besides the rational, also emotional and personal aspects. One of the obstacles to dialogue is what social psychologists have called stereotyping. We tend to categorize others in terms of the group they belong to. The group itself is characterized as an out-group which is opposed to the in-group to which I myself belong and which gives me my social identity. The relationship between the groups is often conditioned by economic (material benefits) and political (power relations) circumstances. Such stereotyping can block communication. Stereotyping can have negative consequences when one interiorizes, for psychological, economic, and political reasons, one's own status as an underdog. When the stereotype is in place, concrete data about an individual are either ignored or seen as an exception. Stereotypes can be countered only by bringing them to consciousness and examining them in the light of the available data and by promoting alternate voluntary groupings.[28]

Dialogue can also be blocked because we do not seek to meet the need of the others for recognition, respect, and acceptance as a group and for a social space in which they can live and develop their iden-tity. On the contrary, we may tolerate them without acceptance and respect or we may try to be inclusive in a relationship of domination-subordination. The others then seek to affirm their identity in an adversarial or a revolutionary mode, giving rise to conflict. This is what happens when a group asserts its "right" to go through areas where the others tend to dominate, make noise near their holy places, and so on. It is often an aggressive demand for recognition that is not voluntarily given. Often, such refusal of mutual recognition is not conscious but symbolic. It means that there are no rituals of normal interaction between the communities.

---

[27] Jürgen Habermas, *The Theory of Communicative Action*, vols. 1 and 2 (Boston: Beacon Press, 1984, 1987).

[28] Ann E. Cudd, "Psychological Explanations of Oppression," in Willet, *Theorizing Multiculturalism*, 187–215.

When I meet a friend, a number of symbolic gestures of recognition and acceptance, without anything being said, make me feel immediately at home. Such rituals may not be available with the adversarial other. Or relationships are limited to commercial or similar transactions that never reach the level of personal depth. Any deeper interaction may even be avoided, because one is not sure what the response would be. In any case, there is no spontaneity in relationships. One cannot take anything for granted. Modern individualism in urban and semi-urban situations may aggravate such distance between communities, further increased when people tend also to live in separate geographical areas. In such a situation, first of all, there must be a basic will to recognize, respect, and accept the other as different. Second, common public rituals must be created and voluntary associative groups encouraged so that such acceptance can be mutually communicated in an experiential way. Projects for common action to promote justice and community will also be helpful.[29]

Creative Praxis

It is now time to apply what we have seen above about dialogue in the context of community building to the dialogue between people who believe in different religions. Religion, being the deepest element in culture and affecting the deeper recesses of a person with regard to his or her search for meaning in life, plays a key role in personal and social identity formation, in setting clear boundaries for in-groups and out-groups, and in the creation of stereotypes. Is it at all possible to aim at building a multireligious community through dialogue? Should one rather limit one's ambitions to living together in mutual tolerance and noninterference? Is it not enough to control fundamentalist groups from causing too much damage to community?

All religions do believe in human and cosmic harmony as the goal of history. Christians envisage the kingdom as the reconciliation of all things according to the plan of God revealed in Jesus Christ. Muslims believe in the *Umma* as a universal community. What can be more unifying than the cosmic manifestation of Krishna to Arjuna in the *Bhagavad Gita*? Buddhists believe that the whole universe is interrelated. The ideal of Confucianism is universal harmony. But looking at the present and at our country I think that, while community and

---

[29] For more on some of the ideas in this paragraph, see Jonathan H. Turner, *A Theory of Social Interaction* (Stanford, CA: Stanford University Press, 1988).

harmony remain at the horizon, what the immediate future needs is *interreligious dialogue as conflict resolution*, not only in the short term, but also in the long term. How can we go about this?[30] I shall restrict my suggestions here to the possible activities that may help in the long term.

1. *Conscientization.* Conscientization focuses on personal transformation through surfacing and changing incorrect attitudes, through coming to terms with pluralism at many levels as not only factual but legitimate, and through cultivating the capacity for analysis that unmasks the abuse of religion by economic and political forces. Our attitudes to others are conditioned by our own prejudices and stereotypes, often fed by biased information. The only way of changing this is to surface these unconscious attitudes and confront them with experiential reality. Where there are longstanding tensions that seem to indicate that such prejudices are reasonable, we have to create new experiences of community through dialogue and common action for justice. Change of attitudes takes place not through preaching or abstract argument, but by actually encountering others, preferably in multireligious groups, and talking about it. Such personal contacts in groups help not only rational discourse, but also a certain emotional involvement.

In such a dialogical situation one also learns to understand, respect, and accept the reasonableness of the other. This means that one starts to accept the possibility of pluralism. In turn, this experience of pluralism as legitimate needs to be integrated through reflection, both personally and in group. To be open to pluralism is to accept, at least implicitly, that one's own perspectives are conditioned by culture and history. Such an acceptance of pluralism normally starts with the acceptance of the right of the other to be different. It then goes on to recognize the possibility that in being different the other is not irrational or wrongheaded but may have some justification in a tradition and experience that one has not shared. Such an experience of pluralism can be further developed and deepened at the philosophical and theological levels. But

---

[30] I would like to draw the reader's attention to suggestions made by others that I have found significant. See John Desrochers, *Towards a New India* (Bangalore: Centre for Social Action, 1995), 109–37; Gabriele Dietrich, "Can the Women's Movement Be a Force against Communalism?" in *Women's Movement in India* (Bangalore: Breakthrough Publications, 1988), 187–201; Virendra Varma, "Communalism: Remedial Suggestions" and S. Usman, "Communalism: A Solution through Co-operation," in Ravindra Kumar, *Problem of Communalism in India* (New Delhi: Mittal Publications, 1990); Larson, *India's Agony over Religion*; Arokiasamy, *Responding to Communalism.*

where experience is lacking, such superstructures will be empty. To-day all major religious traditions, if we exclude the fundamentalist groups in each of them, are open to pluralism.

Another area of conscientization is developing the capacity to analyze society. In our context the analysis will focus on the role of religion in society and its distinction from the economical and political dimensions. People should become aware of the abuse made of religion by economic and political forces. The idea is not to deny the existence of economic and political injustices but to realize that we should struggle against them at their proper level. Such conscientization can be done at all levels, from peasant to city dwellers, through formal and non-formal education groups and through the media. It is advisable that such conscientization programs be organized and conducted by multireligious groups. Groups of people who are accustomed to meet in conscientization sessions are less likely to be pulled into a mass frenzy during communal and other conflicts.

2. *Creating a Multireligious Public Space.* In every community, besides the official organs of the state, there are many voluntary organizations of a cultural and social nature that give shape to the public space. The danger is that these voluntary organizations are also guided by prevalent group prejudices and stereotypes. They do not often have a multireligious character, except at the level of the elites. Even at this level the multireligious factor may be interpreted in varying ways according to the prevailing ideology. We have seen above that one of the elements that facilitates the formation of stereotypes is membership in a group, as distinguished from or even opposed to other groups. These groups often tend to be natural groups based on factors like religion, ethnicity, caste, and so on. Therefore, one way of promoting a mul-tireligious community is to facilitate the formation of multireligious voluntary groups based on a variety of cultural and social interests like music and the arts, literature and drama, sports, peace, ecology, feminism, as well as other social causes like the abolition of dowry and child labor. As people start belonging to many groups, strong and divisive group identities start breaking down. This is why one should question groups organized along religious lines for anything besides strictly religious causes. Multiple group belongingness also helps to define identity in positive terms of what brings the group together and not in terms of what sets it apart from others. One also learns not to define one's own identity in any narrow way.

In order to play such a transformative role, the groups must not only be task oriented, but find time or create occasions for symbolic celebrations of different religious and other social and national festivals and for "wasting" time together in relaxation. Such occasions allow informal, "purposeless" interactions and conversations that have a deeper influence on the persons. These groups can be started in schools and colleges and later continued in various ways. It is unfortunate that our schools and colleges seem to become centers for manufacturing of degrees and titles rather than places for community building. In this way an essential purpose of educational institutions as places for socialization is lost.

3. *Collaboration in Action.* The most effective way of building multireligious community is probably for multireligious groups to act together to promote equality and justice in the nonreligious sphere or economics, politics, and society. Commentators point out that one of the reasons why a particular group becomes fundamentalist and aggressive is its sense of deprivation and discrimination with regard to economic development and employment. This is not a religious issue. Multireligious groups can act to collaborate with governmental and nongovernmental agencies to promote the equal development of all without discrimination.

At the political level, multireligious groups can work for the neutrality of political institutions, especially of the state and of the police. When there are communal riots, the arms of the government like the civil administration and the police are often accused of being partial to the majority community. The state must keep law and order. But it must be—and must be seen as—impartial and neutral. Only active public opinion, public protests, and public-interest litigations can help to keep the state in check. Such movements must be multireligious. The media can play a great role in this. Some of our national newspapers in English are doing a good job. One is less sure of the vernacular press. The private channels of television can also play an important role. What is needed is appropriate commentary that helps to awaken and conscientize the people rather than to provoke a mad collective frenzy.

Multireligious groups that seek to collaborate in action for economic and political justice must be, as far as possible, local, based in determinate geographical area, and their attention could start with improving local facilities to promote an ecologically sound common life. But these groups must be able to join together in wide regional and national coalitions and networks for common causes. Such involvement breaks down narrow identifications. The coming together of more than two hundred groups to move the courts to demand action on the Srikrishna report on the Mumbai riots is a welcome move. Similar coalitions must increase and multiply. Such common action is the only way to defeat the basic principle of communalism that people who share the same religious beliefs also share common economic and political interests.

4. *Deepening the Relationship.* One of the tools that Gandhi used for promoting interreligious harmony was interreligious prayer meetings. At such meetings passages from different scriptures were read and devotional songs from different religious traditions were sung, concluded by an exhortation to promote interreligious peace and harmony. The aim of these meetings was to show that all religions were for peace. If we all believe in one God and we have mutual respect for and acceptance of one another, then praying together for our country and community will be a welcome religious practice. Moreover, India's national anthem—*Jana Gana Mana*—is a prayer. Such meetings to promote mutual fellowship in a multireligious context can be helpful to create an atmosphere of mutual understanding and respect, even if there are no imminent conflicts. One could also suggest the celebration of festivals, which could become occasions for sharing one's joy with one's neighbors of other religions. This happens even today in villages. In reality, at the popular level there are instances of greater involvement in the celebration of festivals and pilgrimages. However, it is unfortunate that such traditional practices are being given up in some places under pressure from fundamentalist groups.

At more elite levels common sharing of scriptures, common prayer, and common reflection in a multireligious context on questions that arise from contemporary life can lead to a deepening of understanding both of one's own religion and of the religion of the other. Such groups can also comment and enlighten the public on books and artistic productions that are fundamentalist in tone or inspiration, seeking to promote division rather than harmony. The very fact of growing in religious depth together will also enable them to be critical and challenging of the shortcomings in each other's religious tradition in a constructive way.

Elites groups can also engage in research that will help to remove obstacles and facilitate the process of conversation. I shall indicate just three areas. Each religious tradition needs to be interpreted in keeping with new situations. Though most religions have known other religious traditions in the course of history, religious pluralism is being taken seriously only recently. Even today only some Christians accept the legitimacy of other religions and are ready to meet them on an equal footing. Islamic scholars who make place for other religions are very few indeed. Hinduism is traditionally tolerant, but its tolerance tends to be inclusive and limited to offshoots of its own tradition. Its own advaitic perspective on reality is seen as underlying and unifying all other religions. In such a situation scholars have to delve deep into the tradition, engage in reinterpretation, and make space in each tradition for the pluralism of religions that would justify dialogue between them.

Another area in which research is necessary is political theory. Although there are a variety of solutions offered by the different political structures across the world to the problem of religious pluralism, an adequate democratic structure is still to emerge. I think that the Indian and the Indonesian Constitutions are the most creative in this area. But even these need to be revised in the light of experiences and difficulties.

A third area of research will be personal and social psychology. How do people evolve their personal and social identity? How do they live an experience of multiple belongingness? How do they overcome prejudices and stereotypes? How do they prevent mass behavior in which violent and blind emotion seems to take over from reason as the guide of action? These questions do not have ready and clear answers.

Conclusion

I have limited my reflections in this chapter to the phenomenon of religious pluralism. But real life is much more complicated, with cultural, ethnic, and social (caste) pluralisms, not to speak of class differentiations in the economic and political sphere. In India we see a resurgence of subaltern caste and tribal groups affirming their separate identity and demanding recognition and respect. In countries like Canada and the United States there is a lively discussion around the phenomenon of multiculturalism. Religion is involved in some of these tensions as it has tended to legitimate discriminative practices in the past, as in the caste system, for example. But whatever may be the differences and tensions, we are called to build up humanity as one community in harmony and peace, in which all the various pluralisms will be respected and accepted, but in which all are invited to participate in a convergent movement toward community through conversation and collaboration. We do not have ready-made models for such community. That keeps the field open for all our imaginative and creative energies.

Jesus said that the Sabbath is for humans, not humans for the Sabbath. Similarly, we can say that the religions are for the people and their life in the world; people do not live for their religions. The basic commandment is to love one another and to love God in the other, not to fight about which symbol of God is true. On the last day Jesus will not ask about which God people worshiped, but whether they served the poor and the needy (Matt 25). God is not exclusive; people and their religions are. Once we are assured that God's saving love in Christ and the Spirit is reaching out to all people in ways unknown to us (GS 22), we can witness to the self-emptying love of Jesus without anxiety and aggressivity. The way of Jesus is kenotic service, not domination (Phil 2:6–12). We can leave to God how God will bring together all things so that God will be all in all (cf. 1 Cor 15:28). We can respect God's freedom and the freedom of all people. To acknowledge and accept the freedom of the other is to be ready for dialogue. Then violence in the name of religion will be no more.

Chapter 6

Responding to Fundamentalism

In many contemporary societies around the world, people are living in fear. Violence is in the air. People are protecting themselves in various ways. The search for security is leading to new forms of discrimination. Everyone speaks of fundamentalism. In the popular media in most parts of the world it is associated with Islam. It is seen as the source of violence. Violence provokes or justifies violence, and it becomes a spiral. At the moment no one seems to know what to do about fundamentalism. I would like to make an effort to understand it and then reflect on what we could do about it beyond condemning it and protecting ourselves from it.

Fundamentalism is often associated with religion.[1] As a matter of fact, it is a very complex phenomenon. Looking at it, even cursorily, I see it as the interplay of four elements mutually influencing and strengthening each other. One or another of these elements may be dominant in a given situation. Fundamentalism therefore can take different forms in different places.

1. Fundamentalism begins by being religious. Threatened by modern scientific discoveries or by liberal cultural and political ideologies, some believers hang on to what they consider the fundamentals of their religion. They may organize themselves to defend their belief. They may be perceived as conservative or revivalist.

2. A particular group of people, gathered together in the name of religion, ethnicity, caste, language, on other criterion may think that the members share the same economic and political interests that they seek to pursue and defend together. This is more commonly called communalism (at least in South Asia). This may happen when there

---

[1] This seems to be the thesis of Martin E. Marty and R. Scott Appleby, *Fundamentalisms Observed*, vol. 1 of *The Fundamentalism Project* (Chicago: University of Chicago Press, 1991).

are wide economic and social disparities in society and a group feels unjustly exploited and/or discriminated against.

3. A communal group may imagine itself as a nation, discovering its historical roots. A very powerful force that can weld such a group together is religion. History also manifests itself to it as historical memory of joys, but especially of sufferings. Such a group may fight for autonomy or independence or seek domination over other groups. The ideology of nationalism strengthens group identity.

4. Finally, a group with a strong identity looks on other groups, not only as different, but as inimical to its interests. In a religious setting others can be demonized when one group thinks that God is "on its side." This can lead to defensive or aggressive violence, particularly when the group experiences itself as the victim of deprivation, injustice, and oppression. Indiscriminate violence against the innocent is called terrorism. It can be fanatical. One or another of these four elements may be predominant at a given moment, in a given place. A good analysis of the situation and any effort to suggest a remedy must focus on all these elements. Rather than explain these elements in the abstract, we can see them emerge as we tell stories of different situations across the world. For convenience, I take different religious groups.[2] I start with Christianity, which gave birth to the term *fundamentalism*.

Christian Fundamentalism

The term *fundamentalism* had its origin in Christian circles in the southern United States of America in the 1920s.[3] A group of Protestant Christians were against scientific discoveries or hypotheses like Charles Darwin's evolution of the species because the hypotheses seemed to contradict the biblical account of creation. The supposition here is that the Bible is the revealed word of God and has to be literally true. They were happy to hold on to these "fundamentals" of their religion as revealed by God. Their opposition slowly spread from the theories

---

[2] For very helpful general surveys, besides the volume referred to in the previous note, see Lionel Caplan, ed., *Studies in Religious Fundamentalism* (London: Macmillan, 1987); Karen Armstrong, *The Battle for God: Fundamentalism in Judaism, Christianity, and Islam* (London: Harper Collins, 2000); Tariq Ali, *The Clash of Fundamentalisms* (London: Verso, 2002). I use information from these books throughout this chapter.

[3] Marty and Appleby, *Fundamentalisms Observed*, 1–65.

of science to atheistic communism and to relativistic liberalism of modern and postmodern times.

When political liberals sought to enlarge the framework of moral behavior to legitimize/legalize contraception, abortion, LGBT relationships, euthanasia, and so on, the fundamentalist groups vigorously opposed doing so. In a democratic framework they organized themselves and sought the support of likeminded "conservatives" from the mainline churches. This led to the emergence of the Moral Majority, which sought to influence the elections. There is no doubt that George W. Bush garnered this group's support successfully during the presidential elections. Though the Moral Majority itself suffered reverses because of the financial and moral scandals of its leaders, conservatives remain sizable enough to influence elections. Among these fundamentalist groups there have been smaller groups and individuals who have adopted violent methods like attacking abortion clinics and murdering doctors performing abortions.

Violent protests arising out of communalism and discrimination have characterized the conflict in Northern Ireland. Minority (Roman Catholic) communalism has responded to majority communalism (Protestants). In a majoritarian "democracy," violence may be one way in which the oppressed minority seeks to express itself. When Indonesia was freed from the military control of General Suharto, communal conflicts broke out. The majority Muslims attacked Christian groups and Christians in islands where Muslims are a sizable majority. It was not simply interreligious violence. The Christians whom the Muslims attacked were often ethnically Chinese and controlled the economy. Therefore, it was not only a religious but an ethnic and economic statement. In contrast, in the Philippines the Christian majority has resisted the demands of the Muslim minority in the south for freedom, leading to violence that arises out of an internal colonization of the Muslim minority by the Christian majority.

Today, at least some in the "Christian" or "post-Christian" Euro-America not only believe in a conflict of civilizations, but also look on the Muslims as their principal enemies, demonizing them. Muslims in Europe are expected to become French or Dutch socioculturally and keep their religion a strictly private affair. Visible signs of religious belonging are discouraged or forbidden. A post-Christian, secular, antireligious—or at least a-religious—cultural outlook is forced upon them. This can also be seen as a form of secular fundamentalism.

One of the problems we repeatedly come across in similar situations is the different yardstick with which the violence of the oppressed minority is judged as compared to the violence of the majority, which controls the state and military apparatus. The former are easily branded terrorists. Terrorism is basically the indiscriminate killing of the innocent. Every violent group indulges in it. Today's bombs are not selective but are weapons of mass destruction. I will come back to this issue later.

The Case of the Muslims

Muslim fundamentalism has to be understood in a colonial and postcolonial setting. Its dynamics can be explained rather simply and illustrated differently with reference to different countries. Since my aim is not writing history but promoting understanding, I describe simply the dynamics. Toward the end of the nineteenth century the Ottoman Empire was slowly crumbling. The colonial powers were trying to extend their influence in the Middle Eastern countries. They supported local princes against the Ottoman emperors in return for commercial concessions of all kinds, such as permission to build the Suez Canal and to exploit the oil reserves. They encouraged a small group of local people to be educated in Europe, thereby acquiring a taste for European culture and its values. These people tried to promote this new culture in their own countries.

After the First World War the colonial powers acquired responsibility for the political control of many of these countries. During this time religious leaders who were working closely with the local kings and chiefs felt progressively alienated. The poor common people could not care less for the European culture that the elite rich fancied. From the people emerged leaders who wanted to defend their cultural and religious identity and struggle against their exploitation. They were against the colonizers and joined independence movements. The colonizers were the hated other.

When these countries became independent after the Second World War, the secularized elite came to power and tried to impose modern, secular governments on the countries without preparing the people. The gap between the rich and the poor increased. The poor no longer had the colonizers to hate. They began to hate their own secularized and secularizing overlords. Popular leaders gathered and organized the people around their culture and religion, going back to the roots of their identity. There were also movements of religious revival. There were memories of great Muslim empires in the past, which made the experience of the present situation worse. Popular movements that were social and religious, engaging in educational and developmental activity, slowly began acquiring a political color. They wanted to go back to the traditional sociopolitical order governed by the Qur'an and Qur'anic law.

The secularized leaders saw these movements as a threat to their own power. So they sought to repress them, sometimes violently. Violence gives birth to more violence. Small groups of people took to forms of violent revolution. Such revolutions were directed not only against their current local overlords, but also against the Euro-Americans who were their backers. In a globalized world the Euro-Americans were not only guilty of spreading a secularized, godless consumer culture through their media and influence, but they also continued to exploit these countries in various ways, mostly through unjust commercial activity.

For those who wish to have historical references, here are a few names: Hasan al Banna (1906–49), Sayyid Qutb (1906–66), the Muslim Brotherhood leading the revolution against Nasser (1918–70) and Anwar Sadat in Egypt, Ayatollah Khomeini (1902–89) and Ali Shariati (1933–77) against Shah Muhammad Reza Pahlavi in Iran, and Abul Ala Mawdudi (1903–79) from India-Pakistan had a lot of influence all over the Middle East.

The Muslim identity is not so much nationalistic as transnational. The Muslim community—the *Umma*—transcends borders in principle and stands united against the external enemy. At the same time, it is against Muslim groups perceived as friends of the foreign enemy. In recent years there has been tension between different sects within the community: the Sunnis, the Shias, and the Kurds. With the radicalization of Muslim identity, they are now turning against the Christian minorities who belong to the same ethnic groups and share the same national and cultural identity and who have been living among them always.

In a sense, Muslim violence is directed against an external enemy perceived as oppressive. Muslims seek unity and strength in their religious identity. Violence starts as anticolonial and becomes communalistic and nationalistic. Then it discovers its roots and justification in religion. This focus on religion tends to become defensive and fundamentalist. It becomes violent only when it is suppressed and legitimate means of self-expression are denied. This violence is directed both against internal and external enemies. These people want to build society in terms of the Sharia or Islamic law, which will reduce non-Muslims to second-class status. I think that politics has more to do with Islamic fundamentalism than religion. That Islam does not separate religion from politics only complicates the situation. We hear about Al Qaeda or the Taliban. Are they religious fundamentalists? They are reacting to foreign cultural, economic, and military presence, direct and indirect, on their soil. They are also making use of their religious identity to provide motivation and force. We cannot simply focus on the religious aspect and ignore the other dimensions of the phenomenon if we wish to counter their influence on and support from the people.

The situation in India is different, dealing with a Muslim community that is a minority. Muslim emperors ruled large parts of India for nearly five centuries. Then the British gained control in the nineteenth century. As Indians started agitating for their freedom, the Muslims (more than 30 percent of the population) felt that they would be a minority in an independent India. So they proposed the theory of two nations, based on religious identity, and finally succeeded in getting the country divided into India and Pakistan. India is still left with 135 million Muslims. But the divisive impulse is not healed. Though India gives Muslims minority rights, they have not really merged into the national mainstream because of their poverty and marginalization. The tension between Hindus and Muslims goes on, nursed also by Hindu fundamentalist groups. Periodic violence erupts, leading to ghettoization, on the one hand, and a spiraling of violence, on the other. Today they may be receiving support from the global Muslim community. The violence in India is more sociopolitical than religious.

In Malaysia, Muslims, who are about 60 percent of the population, have managed to establish a dominant sociopolitical status for themselves. Their identity is communalistic and nationalistic. Indonesia, in spite of its Muslim majority, has remained a secular country, recognizing five official religions. There is a certain Muslim resurgence now and some violence, but the secular fabric is still surviving. What we note in the case of Islam is the close association between religion and politics or the state. Religion is an element of political and national identity. Fundamentalist attitudes therefore tend to be at once religious and political. The "other" who is resisted is not primarily the "religious other," but the "secularizing, materialistic economically and politically oppressive other" who includes dominant groups of compatriots. There is no doubt that religion is a unifying and energizing factor. But it is not the primary force, as it was in early Christian fundamentalism.

The Hindu Cultural Fundamentalists

The Muslim emperors ruled a great part of India for nearly five centuries.[4] They had enemies as well as allies among the Hindu princes. Unlike the early Muslim plunderers and later British colonizers, they stayed in India, married Hindu princesses, dialogued with Hindu (Indian) art, culture, and religion. Indian culture, especially music, painting, and architecture in the north of India, has been influenced by Islamic practitioners. The British took control of the country in the nineteenth century. When the Indians began their struggle for freedom, the Muslims and the Hindus had a common cause at first. But the Muslims did not relish the idea of being a minority in a freed India. They began to look after their own interests and proposed the theory of two nations, Hindu and Muslim. The British may have encouraged the process, following a policy of divide and rule. The Muslim League was founded in 1906.

The Hindus, however, followed their own development. A Hindu renaissance movement, led by people like Raja Ram Mohan Roy, tried to reform Hinduism socially. The Arya Samaj, founded by Swami Dayanand Saraswati, attempted to reform Hinduism by going to its Vedic roots. Spiritual leaders like Swami Vivekananda asserted the superior and integrating nature of the Hindus in the area of spirituality. In the early decades of the twentieth century the Indian National Congress that led the freedom movement sought to include all Indians of whatever religion. But it was obviously dominated by Hindus. Mahatma Gandhi even used his Hindu identity and Hindu symbols to mobilize the masses, although he also promoted ashrams open to all believers.

Side by side with this broad national movement we see emerging a Hindu national movement in the line of Dayanand Saraswati and Swami Vivekananda. Veer Savarkar spelled out its ideology (*Hindutva*, Hinduness).[5] It indicates, not primarily a religion, but a people practicing a culture (based on the Vedas and Sanskrit) and belonging

---

[4] On Hindu fundamentalism, see Christophe Jaffrelot and Thomas Blom Hansen, eds., *The BJP and the Compulsions of Politics in India* (Delhi: Oxford University Press, 1998); Thomas Blom Hansen, *The Saffron Wave* (Princeton, NJ: Princeton University Press, 1999); John Zavos, *The Emergence of Hindu Nationalism in India* (Delhi: Oxford University Press, 2000); David Ludden, ed., *Making India Hindu* (Delhi: Oxford University Press, 1996); Gerald James Larson, *India's Agony Over Religion* (Albany: State University of New York Press, 1995).

[5] V. D. Savarkar, *Hindutva*, 6th ed. (New Delhi: Bharti Sahitya Sadan, 1989; originally published in 1923).

to a territory (between the Himalayas in the north and the seas in the south) with millennial roots. They have a common and a specific identity rooted in history. India is their homeland. It is also their holy land, in which is rooted their religions (Hinduism, Buddhism, Jainism, Sikhism) and their rich culture. Muslims and Christians are invaders who do not have the same roots. Most of them are Indian converts and live in India. They have India as their homeland. But it is not their holy land. Their cultural and religious roots are in Arabia (for the Muslims) and Palestine (for the Christians). Hindus celebrate as their heroes leaders like Shivaji, who opposed Muslim hegemony. They would like to establish a Hindu state in India. They consider the Muslims and Christians as people with foreign roots. They can privatize their religion but have to submit to the Hindu cultural hegemony at the social and national level. The followers of the *Hindutva* were marginalized at the time of independence. They were even ostracized when one of them shot Mahatma Gandhi in January 1948.

When India became independent in 1947 and established itself as a democratic state in 1950, it chose to be secular. Its secularism is not antireligious. It is equally positive to all religions. It provides for religious freedom. It offers special rights to religious and linguistic minorities to live and develop their particular identity, while the fundamental rights of everyone are respected. The minorities initially were allowed to follow their own civil law. But the state was expected to evolve a common civil code, applicable to all citizens. Over the years the followers of *Hindutva* have gained political ground. They led the coalition government at the center for five years. They still lead the governments in some states. Here I am focusing only on their ideology.

The followers of *Hindutva* speak of Hindu nationalism, asserting that Indian identity is Hindu culturally, not religiously. Of course, this cultural identity is closely linked to Hinduism as a religion, but they are not identified. They make use of Hindu religious symbols to inspire the crowds. Their recent rallying symbol has been the Ram temple to be built in the alleged birthplace of Ram (one of the manifestations or *avatars* of Vishnu) over which a mosque had been built in the fifteenth century. They make use of Hindu festivals like *Ganesh puja* to make a statement of power against the Muslims by noisy processions through areas where Muslims live. They gather together groups of sannyasis to support their causes. But they seek to include and transcend caste differentiations focusing on religio-cultural unity. They oppose conversion movements and seek to reconvert people who have become Christian, Muslim, or Hindu. In a majoritarian democratic system the increase in numbers of one group is not merely a demographic fact but a political one. Hindu-Muslim riots have been a regular feature of Indian history from the early twentieth century. Recently, Hindus have started attacking Christians also. Without condoning such violence and without finding political expression, a certain anti-Muslim and anti-Christian ethos seems to be becoming increasingly common among educated, middle-class Hindus.

Are these people fundamentalist in a religious sense? No. The founder of *Hindutva*, Vinayak Damodar Savarkar (1883–1966) was not a practicing Hindu, and some of the present leaders are also non-practicing. Religious symbols are simply made use of as rallying points for the masses. They call themselves cultural nationalists. But religion is only a small part of that culture. Their culture has no place for Muslims and Christians. Though they are a majority in India, they feel that they are a minority globally compared with Christians and Muslims. They claim to have their roots in India and assert a certain ownership over the country as their holy land. Unlike Savarkar, they do not accept that they were also migrants into India, even though they came here more than three thousand years ago. Here we have a case of sociocultural fundamentalism that has turned communalistic or political and makes use of religion as a rallying point. It approaches fascism. It not only ghettoizes others but also seeks to control and destroy their economic resources. It promotes hatred as an ideology.

This is very similar to the cultural nationalism of many European countries that find it difficult today to integrate Muslims and other minorities. They may not be openly violent, but discriminations are not absent. They are cultural fundamentalists. Being secularized, they do not use religion as a source of identity and integration. Some are even aggressively secular, discouraging or forbidding any public manifestation of religious identity. But a vague religious identity seems to crop up when the Muslims are seen as "others." They cannot deny, either, that their culture has religious roots.

Buddhist Fundamentalists

Tamil Hindus and Singhalese Buddhists have been engaged in a civil war in Sri Lanka for more than twenty years.[6] The Singhalese majority (about 75 percent) consider Sri Lanka their nation. Having captured power through a democratic process, they have proceeded to

---

[6] Donald K. Swearer, "Fudamentalistic Movements in Theravada Buddhism," in Marty and Appleby, *Fundamentalisms Observed*, 628–90.

discriminate against the minority Tamils in a systematic way in the job market, higher education, and so forth. There has also been a process of systematic colonization of the Tamil north by settling Singhalese in new government projects of development. Tamil protests have led to a conflagration.

The Singhalese quest for a Buddhist national identity goes back more than a hundred years. The British colonial power more or less destroyed the socio-religious structures in which the Buddhist monks had worked closely with the kings. The monks were the main educators and animators of the community. There was a growing gap between the rich elite favored by the colonizers and the many poor. This provoked a revival. The leader of this revival was Anagarika Dharmapala, who founded *The Mahabodhi Society Journal* in 1891. He not only developed a modern rationalist (Protestant) Buddhism, but he also restored national pride in the Buddhist traditions of Sri Lanka. He built up a middle-class following. Profiting by this, S.W.R.D. Bandaranaike swept into power on a nationalist Buddhist ideology in 1956. He was also helped by a revived *Sangha* (assembly) of monks. It is not my intention to go into all the political developments and ramifications. This Buddhist majority has now been in power for fifty years. The Tamils are seen as intruders in a Buddhist land. As is the case of the Hindus in India, the majority Singhalese Buddhists in Sri Lanka perceive themselves as a global minority compared to the Hindu Tamils, who are also found in South India, Singapore, Malaysia, and other places. The Buddhist monks have been actively and aggressively supporting the war effort of the government against the Tamils and are one of the obstacles to any peace efforts tentatively made by the more practical politicians.

In what sense can the Buddhists in Sri Lanka be called fundamentalist? They are certainly not defending Buddhism, but rather their ethnic, religio-cultural identity, of which religion is only an element. But this religion is linked to their vision of their own "national" past, as in the case of the Hindus in India. It is more a question of imagined national identity than a strictly religious one. Buddhists certainly cannot justify violence in the name of Buddhism. Christians may talk about a "just war" and Muslims may invoke *jihad,* but there is nothing in Buddhism that encourages violence. Therefore, the fundamentalism is Sri Lanka is not religious. It is not Buddhist. It is ethnic and national, perhaps even fascist. Its real causes are economic and political. There may perhaps be a demonization of the Tamil enemy in the context of popular religiosity. Religion is only a marker of socio-ethnic identity.

Fundamentalism
and Terrorism

Fundamentalism is often associated with terrorism. Terrorism can be briefly described as indiscriminate violence on and killing of innocent and defenseless people. Fundamentalism need not be violent. It becomes violent only when it is self-defensive. But in a context of a divisive "we-they" situation, the other is demonized and aggressive violence and hatred justified in the name of God. People evoke the *jihad* in Islam, which seems to justify aggression in order to spread the Islamic faith. The Old Testament of the Bible is full of such violence. The Hindu epics, the Ramayana and the *Mahabharata,* are stories of wars of good against evil. But I wonder whether we can show any instances in the world today where violence is perpetrated to help spread religion. There are examples of individuals or small groups which engage in violence in the name of God.[7] But these are not normal people, and they are not supported by the normal religions. There is a certain fanaticism or even madness and irrationality behind it. But more often religious symbols and emotions are merely used to justify or even provoke violence that is primarily economic and/or political. It is communalistic. It is also a habit to identify as terrorism the violent actions of subaltern groups. The unjustified violence indulged in by the majority or by the state is not seen as terrorist. State terrorism is rarely identified as such. It is conveniently covered up by legal legitimation. Armies claiming to counter terrorism end up killing thousands of innocents. And yet they are not taken to task for provoking further terrorism by their indiscriminate killing.

In India, for instance, there have recently been widespread riots in cities like Mumbai and Coimbatore in which Muslims are targeted. Even the police may join the majority in the name of restoring order. Official enquiries are instituted. But usually there is no real follow-up. When the Muslims retaliate by bombings, they are immediately arrested and prosecuted, with even many innocents suffering in the process. Such blatantly partial behavior is bound to increase suppressed anger that will break out when an occasion offers itself.

---

[7] See Mark Juergensmeyer, *Terror in the Mind of God: The Global Rise of Religious Violence* (Berkeley and Los Angeles: University of California Press, 2000); Oliver McTernan, *Violence in God's Name* (Maryknoll, NY: Orbis Books, 2003).

Secular Fundamentalism

What is fundamentalism then? I have the impression that there is a presumption that it is always rooted in religion. I personally think that this is not so. As we have seen, group struggles may be primarily economic, social, political, or national. Religion is often taken on board because of its power to knit people together at a deeper, pre-rational level. Its link to the Ultimate may even give it an absolute character. But religion need not always be the main issue.

I also have the impression that fundamentalism is always seen as the contrary of liberalism in economics, politics, or religion. One takes for granted today that liberalism is the accepted modern way of looking at and doing things. Anything opposed to it is branded fundamentalist. But people can be conservative or traditional without being fundamentalist.[8] Conservatism can be a legitimate point of view in many circumstances. Liberalism is not always right. It may be good to avoid definitive value judgments in such ideological areas. There are also double standards, and they are sometimes glaring. It would be a very good thing if the world could be rid of nuclear weapons. But there seems no logic when the Euro-American powers, Russia, and China (and India, Pakistan, and Israel) have thousands of them but want to deny them to others. There is also the pretension that these countries are more responsible than the others—after the many wars that have been fought in the twentieth century. Their use of chemical weapons has exploded this myth.

Liberalism and secularism also can be made into dogmas and imposed on people in a fundamentalist manner. One example of aggressive and fundamentalist secularism is that of France, which recently forbade the use of all prominent religious symbols in the public sphere. Many European nations expect Muslim minorities to adopt their secular culture and do not tolerate any religious self-expression or manifestation in public. To appear impartial, they also impose such a ban on other believers, like Christians and Sikhs. Sikh children cannot wear their turbans in French schools. Christians cannot wear a visibly prominent cross, or Jews their skull cap. Recently, an employee at the London airport was suspended for wearing a prominent cross to work; the suspension provoked protest from Christian groups. Is this not secular fundamentalism?

---

[8] Andrew Sullivan, *The Conservative Soul: How We Lost It, How to Get It Back* (New York: Harper Collins, 2006).

It is now recognized that uncontrolled liberalism leads to widespread inequalities. Liberal capitalism encourages free competition. But free competition among groups unequal at the starting point is disastrous. The poor too have rights to the world's goods. While mere redistribution of wealth may not be the best solution, ways must be found of empowering the poor through affirmative action programs. Political liberalism is based on individual freedom; groups, including the state, are seen as voluntary and contractual. Natural, cultural, ethnic, and religious groups are not recognized. Today there is an increasing sensitivity to group rights.[9]

Apart from the religious fundamentalism in the United States, all other fundamentalisms have arisen in colonial and postcolonial situations as responses to various types of oppressions, exploitations, and impositions. We see them arising today also in the postmodern, liberal, and secularizing societies of Euro-America. The Muslim minorities in many European countries feel discriminated against and deprived and are becoming restive.

So, when we are faced with a particular situation, we have to look closely to see whether it is really fundamentalist in orientation, and identify the kind of fundamentalism it is, as well as the real causes for its origin and development. Otherwise our responses to it will be misplaced, inadequate, or one-sided.

Promoting Justice

How can we respond, then, to fundamentalism? Rather than trying to address each problem area, I make four general suggestions here. They are not in order of importance. One or another of them may be more relevant in a particular situation. But I think that we have to take all of them seriously at the global level.

The real root causes of fundamentalism in many areas are inequality, discrimination, and injustice experienced by poor and by the minorities. This started during the colonial period and continues now through unfair commercial transactions imposed by the multinational and international financial institutions on the poorer nations. This is

---

[9] See John Rawls, *Political Liberalism* (New York: Columbia University Press, 1993); Charles Taylor, *Reconciling the Solitudes* (Montreal: McGill University Press, 1993); Amy Gutmann, ed., *Multiculturalism* (Princeton, NJ: Princton University Press, 1994).

often done in collaboration with the local rich elite, who also control political power. So the conflict is both internal and external. Middle-class people are particularly sensitive to experienced or perceived inequality, social discrimination, and injustice. The only solution to this problem is constant sensitivity to poor people, made poor by unjust economic and sociopolitical structures, and the continuing promotion of social justice at all levels. This is obviously a tall order. Every national government as well as international agencies will have to be concerned about this. When there is a natural disaster like a tsunami there is a lot of international sympathy and response. But the daily poverty of the people does not seem to excite many.

It is also necessary to take a historical perspective. Many of the richer countries today in Euro-America have grown rich through colonialism, impoverishing the poor countries in the process. The exploitation continues even in the postcolonial period at the economic and commercial level. In such a situation we have to look not merely for justice, but also for restitution. Such talk may sound strange and impracticable to many. But we must understand that violence and terrorism are often the weapons of the weak who have been driven to the wall. They are aimed at drawing the world's attention to the poor, who are otherwise ignored. It is often the powerless poor who seek mutual support by organizing in terms of ethnicity or religion or language or nationhood. The powerful have to negotiate with them, not suppress them. Negotiations must lead to some efforts at doing justice.

The Middle East has been the playground of the great powers, often through proxy, for many decades. There are many authoritarian governments supported financially and militarily by richer countries. They will probably solve their problems if they are left alone. Israel would be obliged to recognize and respect the rights of the Palestinians and make peace with them if it were not supported economically and militarily by the West. Muslims in parts of India are being systematically ghettoized, denied their rightful place in society and polity as citizens. They are poor and underdeveloped as a community.

A Secular Consensual Democracy

The ideal political order is a democracy, which is described as government of the people, by the people, and for the people. This ideal actually does not exist anywhere. But many countries are striving for it. In light of our reflection on fundamentalism I would like to make suggestions to make democracy better. Today we have a Universal

Declaration of Human Rights accepted, at least formally, by most people. But these rights focus on individuals. We have to complete it with the rights of groups based on religion, culture, language, and so on. We have to accept that we are living in a pluralist world. Groups should have the right and the freedom to live, promote, and preserve their group identities. They have to be recognized, respected, and accepted by others. There must be formal equality among them in the public, political sphere. In the area of religion this would mean a secular political order. But the secularism will not be antireligious or a-religious, but rather equally positive to all religions. While there should be a strict separation between religion and the state, the state need not deny or discourage religious identities. At the level of civil society religious groups too can enter the discussion concerning national policies and programs.[10]

In a pluralistic situation there are bound to be majorities and minorities. In most democracies today, rule by the majority is prevalent. Where this majority is not really democratic but communalistic, built around ethnicity or religion, it can oppress minorities. This is what is happening in Sri Lanka, for example. Actually, it happens in most countries. It is better to move toward a democratic system where there are institutional checks and balances that protect minorities and enable them to play their rightful role in the polity. The Indian Constitution, with its special rights for minorities, tries to do this. But the ideal would be that the emphasis in policy and decision making at all levels focuses not so much on a majority, but on a consensus among minorities and majority. Democracy, then, would not be majoritarian but consensual. Every group must be represented in some way in bodies that discuss and make decisions. Of course, people may and will differ in economic and political ideologies. But religions should not be divisive. If everyone is really interested in the good of the people and there is open dialogue without hidden agendas, then consensus would be easily forthcoming.

In a pluralistic situation dialogue will become a way of life. This will be true also of religions. In modern times Christians have promoted interreligious dialogue. But most of them see it as an instrument of mission or as happening at the spiritual level. Dialogue must start at the sociopolitical level and later can rise to a spiritual and religious level. It should be active, then, at the level of civil society. People must discuss ideologies in the media, in the universities, in discussion groups of concerned citizens, and so on.

---

[10] For further development of these ideas, see Michael Amaladoss, *Making Harmony: Living in a Pluralist World* (Chennai: IDCR, 2003).

Most national boundaries were laid out by colonial powers. Modifications and readjustments may be necessary in particular cases. National boundaries may be dictated by geography, culture, history, language, and so forth. But with increasing migration of people today, pluralism of all kinds is present everywhere. While local culture and history have to be respected, they also have to open up to respect and accept others. On the other hand, history is ongoing and complex. It should not be simplified and homogenized in a narrow way. For example, in India there is a continuing cultural stream (Hindu) that has its origin more than three thousand years ago. But it has been influenced by various other streams—Buddhist, Jain, Sikh, and folk—in the course of history. Islam and Christianity have also contributed to it. Neither the roots nor the contributions need to be forgotten. Sri Lanka has a Singhalese majority and a Buddhist past. But Tamils have been on the island for centuries and have influenced the national culture and even the Buddhist religion in many ways. Migrations and invasions and consequent interaction among people are frequent in history and any claim to ethnic, cultural, or religious purity is suspect and ideological.

The Reform of Religion

Religion is an element in most instances of fundamentalism. Except in the United States of America it is used as a source of strength and unity for a group constituted on other grounds like culture, ethnicity, political ideology, aspirations, and so on. By radicalizing divisions between groups and sacralizing them, each group tends to demonize others. Violence against the "other" is then justified, even encouraged, although it may be presented as self-defense. But religions also speak about love, nonviolence, and peace. Each religion, therefore, needs to interpret and contextualize its sacred scriptures.

While religion should be respected at its own level, it needs also to be secularized. This means that there is a strict separation between religious institutions and the sociopolitical order. This has been happening in Europe, where science and economic and political structures slowly acquired their autonomy from the control of religion through hard struggle over many centuries. Hinduism and Buddhism never had that kind of control over the sociopolitical order. Muslims do not traditionally distinguish between religion and politics. But today, where they are in a minority they do so—in India, for example—they should move toward doing so even in the states where they are a majority.

Turkey is an example that could be imitated elsewhere. Obviously this cannot be imposed by outsiders, especially under cultural, political, or military pressure. It will be resisted. But left to themselves, they may eventually do so. Although the Qur'an can be and has been interpreted by any one after deep study, it has been completed by the traditions of the Prophet's sayings and doings as codified by later followers—the *Hadith*. Muslims tolerated in their kingdoms the other "people of the Book," namely, Jews and Christians. The tolerance came with a tax. I am sure that under contemporary circumstances such tolerance can happen without the tax and also include other religions.

The Healing of Memories

In our quest for a world free of fundamentalisms, we are not starting from zero. We have had a history of violent conflicts, and we are still having them. At some stage we have to make a clean break with the past. We have to think of the future rather than of the past. We have to look for restorative rather than retributive justice. We have to explore the way of forgiveness rather than vengeance. We have to speak of conflict resolution and reconciliation.[11] Forgiveness supposes the acceptance of guilt by the other and the willingness to restore justice. This can be a symbolic, social process rather than involve all the numerous individual cases. The only partially successful example of such a process is the Truth and Reconciliation Commission of South Africa under the chairmanship of Bishop Desmond Tutu, though there have been other such commissions elsewhere.[12] The commission listened in public to the stories of suffering told by victims and to the acceptance of guilt by the perpetrators of the violence. The bargain was that those who confessed would not be legally pursued and punished. Though it did not bring to book all those who were responsible for the violence, especially the masters and the brains behind the operations, it did have a cathartic effect at a social level and has enabled the community to go forward.

But such commissions have never touched an interreligious conflictual area, except perhaps in East Timor, where the conflict continues. As compared to economics, politics, or social structures, only religions

---

[11] See Raymond G. Helmick and Rodney L. Petersen, eds., *Forgiveness and Reconciliation: Religion, Public Policy, and Conflict Resolution* (Philadelphia: Templeton Foundation Press, 2001).

[12] Desmond Mpilo Tutu, *No Future without Forgiveness* (New York: Doubleday, 1999).

can promote the spirit of forgiveness. But true reconciliation can only be based on justice, though it should be restorative rather than retributive, as I have said above referring to the South African experiment. Bishop Tutu also warns that the justice, should not be victors' justice which is focused on revenge. It should be justice with forgiveness. This links to our first suggestion about the need to promote social justice.

Conclusion

Fundamentalism is a complex phenomenon. It is more economic, social, and political than religious. Religion is often used to further other ends. It is a pity, of course, that religions let themselves be used in such a way. We can respond to fundamentalism adequately only if we understand its real causes. On the one hand, we have to learn to look at it, not from the point of view of colonizing liberals, but from that of victims oppressed in many ways. On the other hand, we have to identify the political power games that seek to use religion as a pawn in their nefarious schemes. People should have the freedom to practice any religion of their choice, not only in private, but also in public socially. At the same time a strict separation must be maintained between religious and state institutions. Economic justice and political freedom must be assured. Historical wrongs should be righted. A healing of memories should take place. Forgiveness and reconciliation must be promoted. Our response to fundamentalism has to be as complex as fundamentalism itself. It remains an unmet challenge.

Chapter 7

The Utopia
of the Human Family

The phenomenon of globalization is certainly not welcome if it is to
be the globalization of a particular culture or country or ideology
or economic system. Such globalization aims at the subordination,
if not disappearance, of other cultures, ideologies, and so on. In the
contemporary world a consumer culture sustained by a liberal capitalist economic system is seeking to dominate the world, supported
by the media power, political strength, and armed might of the Euro-
American peoples. The other peoples of the world and their cultures
are marginalized. When they are not strong, their separate identities
tend to disappear. Thus, globalization becomes monochrome.

But globalization does not have to be monochrome. Factors that
favor globalization, like the global outreach and rapidity of the media
and means of communication, can also bring together various peoples
and their cultures into a global community that respects and protects
their different identities. Globalization can mean global solidarity and
mutuality in a context of democratic freedom and pluralism.

Both these aspects of globalization can be found also in the sphere
of religion. For instance, the church is said to be catholic or universal.
Paul's vision of the goal of history is the gathering of all things into a
unity (Eph 1:3–10; Col 1:17–20; 1 Cor 15:28). But the goal of mission
practice, especially in the period starting in the sixteenth century, seems
to be the globalization of Christianity in its Semitic and Greco-Roman
form. Even the much-talked-about project of inculturation aims at
translation rather than local creativity. We see a tension here between
two ideologies of catholicity. We can find this conflict between vision
and practice also in some of the other developed religions of the world.

A global vision is a consequence of belief in one Absolute as the
origin and/or goal of history. The Absolute may also have a negative

image and role as in the *nirvana* of Buddhism. But there is one inclusive perspective that embraces the whole of history. We do not find this in the tribal religions. These are, to the tribe, its life and its symbols. Other tribes are seen to have other guardian spirits. It is said that the tribals too have an idea of a supreme God. But this supreme God is in the background, not interfering in their normal life. For this they have to deal with various spirits. In some of their mythology their conflict with other tribes may be presented as a war between their guardian spirits.

Harmonious Nature

In the Confucian tradition we see that the supreme God, known as Heaven, is the guarantor of Nature and its Law that governs the universe. It is the *Dao* or the Way. This principle is further developed by Daoism, which, together with Buddhism, provides a religious dimension to Chinese culture. We see here a global vision.

> Up to the time of Confucius, the Supreme Power was called *Ti* (the Lord) or *Shang Ti* (the Lord on high) and was understood in an anthropomorphic sense. Confucius never spoke of *Ti*. Instead he often spoke of *T'ien* (Heaven). To be sure, his Heaven is purposive and is the master of all things. He repeatedly referred to the *Tien-ming*, the mandate, will or order of Heaven. However, with him Heaven is no longer the greatest of all spiritual beings who rules in a personal manner but a Supreme Power who only reigns, leaving his Moral Law to operate by itself. This is the Way, according to which civilization should develop and men should behave.[1]

Nature is not merely natural, but moral. It indicates not merely how things are, but how they ought to be. People have to live in conformity with Nature. The ideal of life is to be in harmony with the Way things are and ought to be.

The utopia of Confucianism is, therefore, a vision of the world where everyone and everything lives in harmony by following the Law of Nature. Nature itself is dynamic, animated by the complementary

---

[1] Wing-Tsit Chan, *A Sourcebook in Chinese Philosophy* (Princeton, NJ: Princeton University Press, 1963), 16.

principles of the *yang* (initiation) and the *yin* (completion). Life and death, growth and decline are caught up in a cosmic cycle. It is when people seek to control life that corruption and power games enter. Says Lao Tzu:

> Rid of formalized wisdom and learning
> People would be a hundredfold happier,
> Rid of conventionalized duty and honour
> People would find their families dear,
> Rid of legalized profiteering
> People would have no thieves to fear.
> These methods of life have failed, all three.
> Here is the way, it seems to me:
> Set people free,
> As deep in their hearts they would like to be,
> From private greeds
> And wanton needs.[2]

Nature is destined to live in harmony, and we are invited to live in harmony with nature.

One without a Second

Hinduism starts with a multiplicity of gods, some of whom are divinized forces of nature like the sun, wind, fire, and water. Deeper reflection leads them to awareness of the oneness of all being. Brahman is seen as the principle of the world. Atman is the self of persons. Brahman and Atman are not two, but one. This is the principle of *advaita* (not-two). This leads to a universal vision. The *Isa Upanishad* says:

> Behold the universe in the glory of God: and all that lives and moves on earth. Leaving the transient, find joy in the Eternal: set not your heart on another's possession. . . . Who sees all being in his own Self and his own Self in all beings, loses all fear. When a sage sees this great Unity and his Self has become all beings, what delusion and what sorrow can ever be near him?[3]

---

[2] "No. 19," in *The Way of Life According to Lao Tzu*, trans. Witter Bynner (London: Lyrebird Press, 1978), 37.

[3] *The Upanishads*, trans. Juan Mascaró (Hammondsworth: Penguin Books, 1965), 45.

To unite oneself with the Atman (Self) then becomes the goal of life. Through the Self one is actually uniting oneself with the whole universe. This universal communion is illustrated by the *Bhagavad Gita,* when it describes Arjuna's (the seeker) vision of Krishna (God in human form): "There, in the body of the God of Gods, the son of Pandu (father of Arjuna) then beheld the entire world, divided in manifold ways, all united" (11:13).[4]

Hindus look on this world as hierarchically ordered according to the caste system. People work out their salvation in this world according to the fruit of their *karma* (action) through a multiplicity of births. But the final goal is a communion in which all will be one. It is certainly not an earthly paradise or utopia, but a fullness that is rooted in yet transcends history.

We might be tempted to see this as an inward-oriented, otherworldly utopia. But Swami Agnivesh, a contemporary social activist struggling for the liberation of bonded laborers, writes:

> It is unthinkable to attain truth within, without simultaneously fighting the forces of untruth outside. Therefore the fight against untruth, bondage, and unjust social order based on violence and greed and usurpation become part and parcel of one's spiritual pursuit.[5]

For Mahatma Gandhi, inspired by the *Isa Upanishad* quoted above, the goal of life was to realize Truth or Being *(Sa)t,* though he was aware that this can be done only through a succession of partial realizations. But this is an ethical process of love and service. He outlines his utopia:

> I shall work for an India, in which the poorest shall feel that it is their country in whose making they have an effective voice; an India in which there shall be no high class and low class of people; an India in which all communities shall live in perfect harmony. There can be no room in such an India for the curse of untouchability or the curse of intoxicating drinks and drugs. Women will enjoy the same rights as men. Since we shall be at peace with all the rest of the world, neither exploiting, nor being

---

[4] *The Bhagavad Gita,* trans. Antonio de Nicolas (York Beach, ME: Nicolas-Hays, 1990), 84.

[5] Swami Agnivesh, "Vedic Socialism," *Seminar* 339 (1987): 21.

exploited, we shall have the smallest army imaginable. . . . This is the India of my dreams.[6]

This historical utopia is not the final communion with Truth that is Being. But it is a necessary and inevitable mediation. Though this vision has Hindu accents, Gandhi's ideal reached out to the whole world, as he found God in every being, particularly in the poor. He proposed interreligious harmony:

> I do believe that there is only one religion in the world, but I also believe that although it is one mighty tree, it has many branches. . . . And even as all the branches take their essence from one source, even so all religions derive their essence from one fountain-source (God).[7]

But this universal, inclusive tradition of Hinduism, lived by Gandhi and many other modern Hindus, is being negated by contemporary religio-political forces like the *Hindutva* (Hinduness), which is not only against all other religions, but also promotes a hierarchical domination by Brahmanism within the Hindu fold itself. The *Ram Rajya* (the kingdom of Ram, one of the "incarnations" of God) one evokes in this context is a kind of millennial vision that prolongs the existing social order freed of its enemies. Gandhi may have used it in a more acceptable sense from a political and economic point of view, but at the social level he was supportive of the caste system.

Inter-Being

Buddhism is often thought to be an individualistic religion, centered on the monk seeking his own emptiness *(nirvana)*. The Buddha's four noble truths affirm the reality of suffering, craving as the cause of suffering, and the possibility of overcoming this craving by following the eightfold path consisting of right awareness, action, and mindfulness. But modern commentators like Bhikku Buddhadasa of Thailand and Thich Nhat Hanh of Vietnam have developed a socialist vision from Buddha's teaching. One of the important teachings of Buddhism is the denial of an ego. What we experience is actually a chain of

---

[6] Quoted in Ignatius Jesudasan, *A Gandhian Theology of Liberation* (Maryknoll, NY: Orbis Books, 1984), 128.

[7] Ibid., 77.

interdependent phenomena. But one could argue that what is denied is not the ego as such, but the ego as an independent source of action. The ego is always caught up in a network of relationships. Contemplating this network, Buddhadasa affirms that reality is itself socialist. Thich Nhat Hanh speaks rather of inter-being. To be in this world is to inter-be. There is no other reality beyond this network of beings. Donald Swearer summarizes Buddhadasa's teachings in the following words:

> The individual is not-self. As such s/he is part of an ongoing, conditioning process devoid of absolute self-nature, a process to which words can only point. This process functions according to universal principles we call nature. It is the true, normative, and moral condition of things. To be a not-self therefore, is to be void of self, and hence, to be part of the normal, interdependent co-arising matrix of all things, and to live according to the natural moral law in a fellowship voluntarily restrained by other-regarding concerns.[8]

Such a vision is of course universal and inclusive. It is socialist. Buddhadasa says:

> If we hold fast to Buddhism we shall have a socialist disposition in our very being. We shall see our fellow humans as friends in suffering—in birth, old age, sickness and death—and, hence, we cannot abandon them.[9]

> Solving social problems is dependent on living in a socially moral way; acting in the best interest of the entire community by living according to nature's laws; avoiding the consumption of goods beyond our simple needs; sharing all that is not essential for us to have with others, even if we consider ourselves poor.[10]

The Mahayana tradition of Buddhism has the ideal of the bodhisattva, who, even after attaining enlightenment, lingers along in this world to help other suffering people. Traditionally, one speaks of the fourfold vow of a bodhisattva. The first of these is: "Living beings are innumerable: I vow to save them all." It is certainly a universal vision.

---

[8] Donald K. Swearer, ed., *Me and Mine: Selected Essays of Bhikku Buddhadasa* (Albany: State University of New York Press, 1989), 6.

[9] Bhikku Buddhadasa, *Dhammic Socialism* (Bangkok: Thai Interreligious Commision for Development, 1986), 102.

[10] Swearer, *Me and Mine*, 180.

In practice, Buddhism, though it had its origin in India, has spread across Asia by easily adapting itself to the different cultures and even religions found among different peoples. In this sense it has been more open to true globalization than other developed religions, which are tied to a particular culture, even when they claim to be universal.

The Universal Community

According to Islam, God has been manifesting Godself through various prophets in the course of history. Muhammad is the last prophet, and his message is for all peoples. The foundation for the universality of the message is that God is one. There is no other God. Therefore, God's message is for all human beings. Submission to God's directive is an obligation for every human being. Everyone who submits to God belongs to the community of the *Umma,* which is universal, transcending cultures and borders. Every Muslim is a vicegerent of God. All people are therefore equal.

Mawlana Sayyid Abul A'la Mawdudi of Pakistan, a widely known modern interpreter of Islamic tradition, speaks of "*theo*-democracy":

> The right to rule belongs to the whole community of believers. There is no reservation of special prerogative in favor of any particular individual, family, clan or class. Such a society cannot tolerate class divisions, and it will not permit disabilities for citizens on the basis of birth, social status, or profession. . . . All administrative matters and all questions about which no explicit injunction is to be found in the *shariah* are settled by the consensus among the Muslims.[11]

This is democracy, because all are equally responsible. It is *theo*-democracy because it is based on the sovereignty of God, not of the people, as in the modern democracies. All are subject to divine guidance. It is not theocracy because the religious leadership has no role in politics. The affirmation of political equality leads to a sense of justice, which is ready to tax the rich and to have special concern for the widows and the orphans.

This universal, democratic vision is not without difficulties. First of all, such equality is only for Muslims who affirm faith in the one God

---

[11] Quoted in John L. Esposito, ed., *Voices of Resurgent Islam* (New York: Oxford University Press, 1983), 110, 117.

and accept Muhammad as God's prophet and the Qur'an as God's revelation. All other believers are treated as second-class citizens who have eventually to be converted to Islam. Unfortunately a drive toward converting the others can take the form of a *jihad*, which does not exclude violent means. Second, in the Sufi tradition the religious leader has a dominant role in interpreting God's will. We see this phenomenon in Iran. Third, though in the past Islam had been adapting itself to the various peoples and their cultures across Asia, a certain Arabization is increasingly operative today. There has been no real effort to liberate God's message from its context in Arabic culture and history.

Conclusion

I have not explored the utopias of all the religions of the world. I have limited myself to four of the dominant religious traditions: Confucianism, Hinduism, Buddhism, and Islam. The affirmation of one God or one Absolute and the elaboration of a meaning system based either on revelation or on privileged experience encourage believers to bring everyone under the same God/Absolute and the corresponding meaning system. In this sense every religion is globalizing.

Confucianism, Buddhism, and Hinduism used to make space for other religions. Today, every religion is being politicized. This means that the globalization that the religions wish for today is not through the acceptance and promotion of equality and diversity, but through the domination of one particular perspective—their own. This may be the reason why they do not hesitate to get the help of political and economic powers.

I think that any search for cosmic or universal communion should be based on interreligious understanding. At that level every religion can contribute certain universal perspectives. A dialogue among them can lead to mutual understanding, enrichment, and collaboration. Globalization based on such foundations will certainly lead to cosmic harmony.

Chapter 8

Ethics in a Multireligious Context

The role of ethics is to offer us guidance about what to do in the different circumstances of our lives. It has to particularize the general principle: Do good and avoid evil. In a community it governs our relationships with one another. It also helps us in acting together when we are pursuing common goals. There are many situations in life in which it is not easy to specify what is good and what is evil. One such situation is the multireligious context in which we are living today. Each religion has its own way of looking at life and reality. Of course, this situation is not peculiar to us. Most of the world is today pluralistic. Even in countries dominated by one religion, there are small minority groups belonging to other religions. Within the majority religious group itself there may be people who are secularized, agnostic, or nonbelieving. There may also be differences between personal and public life. At the level of economic and political life people may be guided by various ideologies. This context is very sensitive precisely because of the intimate relationship that exists between ethics and religious belief. Religious pluralism, therefore, involves ethical pluralism.

Generally speaking, two kinds of attitudes are possible in the face of ethical pluralism. The first is to deny it. We cannot, of course, deny the fact of pluralism. But we can simply assert that our own convictions are right and that whoever disagrees with us is wrong. So there are no alternatives to choose from. If we have the power, we may try to impose what we consider right on everyone. The second approach is to recognize and accept the pluralism and search for ways of adjusting with one another so that we can still live and act together, at least in what concerns the whole community, even when we are faithful to our convictions in our personal life and in the group to which we belong. No one would seriously advocate the first way of proceeding. There may, however, be differences in the manner in which the second way is understood and practiced.

In the following pages I start with the Christian tradition. I am not going back into history, but just seeing how the Second Vatican Council handled pluralism. It did not speak about ethical pluralism but did address the question of religious pluralism. But what it said had ethical implications, as I try to show. Then I move toward a more general theory that may be acceptable to everyone.

Error Has No Rights

Christians did pass through a stage when they denied the existence of pluralism. This was based on the supposition that our religion is the true one, revealed by God. Every other religion is false. People who belonged to them were in error. As the popular axiom went: Error has no rights! This meant that where and when we have the power, we can impose our truth and morality on others, if necessary by force. When there emerged a distinction between sacred and secular power, the sacred power demanded the help of the secular arm to impose the truth. Those who refused to accept the truth could be done away with. They were often burnt at the stake in the Middle Ages. Those who were not Christians not only missed salvation in the next world but did not have rights even in this world. Until new areas of the world—like Sub-Saharan Africa, the Americas, and South and East Asia—were "discovered" by the people from Europe and the Mediterranean, they took for granted that the gospel had been preached everywhere.

Those who had not become Christian were guilty of not obeying God's call. And so they deserved punishment. The Jews were considered guilty of murdering Jesus. So they were marginalized and persecuted in various ways. Crusades were organized against the Muslim infidels. When the people in the Americas and Africa were "discovered," they were considered subhuman. Colonizers felt free to enslave them, appropriate their land and property, as well as treat them as human commodities and use them as cheap labor. Many of these poor natives would consider themselves lucky to soften, if not fully escape, such treatment by embracing Christianity.

Many indigenous groups do not enjoy their full rights even today. They live in reservations. The Australian Aborigines were not citizens in their own land till about forty years ago. Many Euro-American countries that pride themselves as paragons of human rights and democracy, often limit their benefits to their citizens. Migrants are expected to adopt the local culture. The local religion is not imposed on them only because the local people themselves are not very religious. The human rights that they claim in their own countries are not recognized for people in faraway poor countries who can be imprisoned and disposed of at will. They can be freely exploited by unjust commercial and economic policies.

Affirmation of Civil Liberties

Dignitatis Humanae (Declaration on Religious Liberty) of the Second Vatican Council came as a big change in attitudes, though it referred only to the practice of religion in the civil sphere. At the council some still held to the position that error had no rights. So the right to religious liberty was based not on the rightness or wrongness of the religions, but on the dignity of the human persons who professed them. The religions themselves were not judged right or wrong. The declaration only defended the right of humans to follow their conscience, right or wrong. What was affirmed, therefore, was the freedom of people to practice any religion of their choice at the civic level, so that no state could coerce them in religious matters. They can exercise this freedom both individually and collectively. So the religions were accepted as social groups. It is instructive to look at these texts.[1] Religious freedom is a human right:

> The right to religious freedom is based on the very dignity of the human person as known through the revealed word of God and by reason itself. This right of the human person to religious freedom must be given such recognition in the constitutional order of society as will make it a civil right. (DH 2)

Please note that the dignity of the human person can be known by reason itself, that is, by everyone. As human persons all are free and responsible to seek the truth. Therefore, they should be free from any external coercion, by the state, for example. The only condition is that public order is assured. Since humans are social beings, their search can also be social:

---

[1] See Keith J. Pavlischek, *John Courtney Murray and the Dilemma of Religious Tradition* (Kirksville, MO: Thomas Jefferson University Press, 1994). Murray was one of the chief architects of the declaration. Pavlischek's book throws light on the declaration from Murray's point of view.

The search for truth, however, must be carried out in a manner that is appropriate to the dignity of the human person and his social nature, namely by free enquiry with the help of teaching or instruction, communication and dialogue. (DH 2)

This social right involves many other rights. The religious communities are free to profess, practice, and propagate their religious convictions. They can administer themselves, select and train their leaders, own buildings and property, control means of communication. They can have "educational, cultural, charitable and social organizations" (DH 4). Parents are free to bring up their children in any way they like and to send them to a school of their choice. Any freedom also involves responsibility:

In availing of any freedom men must respect the moral principle of personal and social responsibility: in exercising their rights individual men and social groups are bound by the moral law to have regard for the rights of others, their own duties to others and the common good of all. All men must be treated with justice and humanity. (DH 7)

Natural–Human–Divine Law

While trying to root the principle of religious freedom on the dignity of the human person, the Declaration also enunciates another principle, namely, that of the natural-divine law. Let us see how it spells it out:

The highest norm of human life is the divine law itself—eternal, objective and universal, by which God orders, directs and governs the whole world and the ways of the human community according to a plan conceived in his wisdom and love. God has enabled man to participate in this law of his so that, under the gentle disposition of divine providence, many may be able to arrive at a deeper and deeper knowledge of unchangeable truth. (DH 3)

Let me draw your attention to the adjectives used in this section to qualify the divine law: besides being divine, or because of it, it is true, eternal, objective, universal, and unchangeable. How do people know this divine law?

It is through his conscience that man sees and recognizes the demands of the divine law. He is bound to follow this conscience faithfully in all his activity so that he may come to God, who is his last end. (DH 3)

Conscience, of course, has to be educated (DH 8). While the church does this for Christians (DH 14), we are not told who is responsible for this for other people. Of course, predictably, the church offers its services.

The role of conscience is further elaborated by *Gaudium et Spes (Pastoral Constitution on the Church in the Modern World)*. This text is interesting because it relates human dignity to conscience:

Deep within his conscience man discovers a law which he has not laid upon himself but which he must obey. Its voice, ever calling him to love and to do what is good and to avoid evil, tells him inwardly at the right moment: do this, shun that. For man has in his heart a law inscribed by God. His dignity lies in observing this law, and by it he will be judged. His conscience is man's most secret core, and his sanctuary. There he is alone with God whose voice echoes in his depths. (GS 16)

The problem, of course, is that conscience can be more or less correct.

In this whole discourse, the declaration does not use the term *natural law*. But the ethical tradition of the church often uses this concept when it seeks to dialogue with and convince people of other religions and ideologies.

A Commentary on the Natural Law

As a matter of fact, *Gaudium et Spes* can be seen as an extended commentary on the "contents" of natural law. On the one hand, the church claims a deep solidarity with people. On the other hand, it claims the special guidance of revelation that throws light on natural law. It is addressed to all peoples. It seems particularly interested in people who consider themselves atheists. So, though it occasionally cites scripture, it tries to speak a language that is accessible to everyone—the language of reason—but rooted in its faith.

And that is why the Council, relying on the inspiration of Christ, the image of the invisible God, the firstborn of all creation, proposes to speak to all men in order to unfold the mystery that is man and cooperate in tackling the main problems facing the world today. (GS 10)

The document covers a vast area. It starts with a brief analysis of the "hope and anguish" of contemporary society. It is significant that pluralism is not one of those elements. The first chapter speaks of the dignity of the human person. Then themes like interdependence, common good, equality and social justice, responsibility and participation, and finally solidarity are evoked around the theme of community. This is followed by a section on the rightful autonomy of earthly affairs and on human work in the world:

By the very nature of creation, material being is endowed with its own stability, truth and excellence, its own order and laws. These man must respect as he recognizes the methods proper to every science and technique. (GS 36)

I suppose that this principle would also apply to humans and their natural (God-given) cultural and religious structures. A section on the dialogue between the church and the modern world concludes the first part.

The second part talks about some more urgent problems. These include the marriage and the family, culture, economic and social life, the political community at national and international levels, and peace. The document concludes with a call to dialogue at all levels: within the church, with the other churches, with the believers of different religions and with all people of good will. There is a final affirmation of hope:

Since God the Father is the beginning and the end of all things, we are all called to be brothers; we ought to work together without violence and without deceit to build up the world in a spirit of genuine peace. (GS 92)

The Present Situation

Taking these two documents together I have the impression that the church is jockeying, knowingly or unknowingly, for its position and role in the modern world. It recognizes the prevalent religious and ideological pluralism as a fact, especially in the post-revolutionary, postcolonial, and postmodern world. It realizes that it is no longer a dominant force in society, even in countries where the majority still professes to be Christian. It is very clear about the ethical principles that its own members have to follow. Where Christians are in a majority, it still tries to promote among them faithfulness to its moral principles. Where Christians are not in a majority, it claims to be a spokesperson for basic human and social ethics. So it takes refuge in the traditional idea of the natural law, based on reason, which applies to everyone, since each one's conscience witnesses to it. Since conscience needs occasional enlightenment, the church offers the light of its revelation, of course in a dialogical manner. It is significant that in recent years, the church frequently claims to be a "specialist" on what concern the human—also because God became human in Jesus. Since, because of historical reasons, the pope and the Vatican City State have an international status, the pope makes use of this status to enunciate what he considers universal moral principles.

Two further changes in the awareness of the situation must be mentioned, though they have not affected the church's official position basically. But they have given matter for serious reflection for some Christians. First of all, the church's attitude to other religions has been changing. As we have seen above, Vatican II's *Dignitatis Humanae* affirmed the civil liberty of people to follow any religion of their choice according to their conscience, but it did not say anything about the status of these religions. Even *Nostra Aetate (Declaration on the Relationship of the Church to Non-Christians)* finds in them "good and holy elements" and encourages dialogue with them (NA 2). But they are considered human and natural. As Pope Paul VI writes in his apostolic exhortation *Evangelii Nuntiandi*:

> By virtue of our religion a true and living relationship with God is established which other religions cannot achieve even though they seem, as it were, to have their arms raised up to heaven. (EN 53)

John Paul II's encyclical *Redemptoris Missio* is the first official document that recognizes the presence and action of the Spirit of God in other religions and cultures (RM 28–29). Even then they are set in a framework of "preparation-fulfillment" in relation to the church. Asian bishops and theologians, however, accept other religions as significant elements in the plan of God. They look on them as co-pilgrims toward the kingdom. The Indian bishops in their document preparatory to the Synod of Bishops on Asia write:

As God's Spirit called the Churches of the East to conversion and mission witness (see Rev 2—3), we too hear this same Spirit bidding us to be truly catholic, open and collaborating with the Word who is actively present in the great religious traditions of Asia today. Confident trust and discernment, not anxiety and over-caution, must regulate our relations with these many brothers and sisters. For together with them we form one community, stemming from the one stock which God created to people the entire earth. We share with them a common destiny and providence. Walking together we are called to travel the same paschal pilgrimage with Christ to the one Father of us all (see Lk 24:13ff., *NA* 1, and *GS* 22).[2]

If the other religions are taken seriously in this way, then their moral positions, if they are different from those of the church, cannot simply be dismissed out of hand. We have to dialogue with them.

Second, the claim of the church to be teaching an unchanging moral law is also being increasingly questioned. On the one hand, historians have shown that the church's moral teaching has been changing in the course of history.[3] On the other hand, there is no consensus in the church today on every aspect of moral law. The church's teaching about contraception is one example. This situation has made us aware that, while God and Truth are absolute, the church's understanding of that Truth may be conditioned by historical and cultural circumstances and human limitations. This is also true of other religions.[4] Even if the church claims to be teaching what it considers natural and unchangeable, believers of other religions may refuse to accept it. The light that the church offers is being questioned by the lights that are projected by other resurgent religions and revolutionary ideologies. The question, then, is whether the church should be open to dialogue in such matters.

To add to the complexity of this situation, cultural and religious pluralism have become increasingly conflictual.[5] Postmodernism has

---

[2] See Peter C. Phan, ed., *The Asian Synod: Texts and Commentaries* (Maryknoll, NY: Orbis Books, 2002).

[3] Sean Fagan, *Does Morality Change?* (Dublin: Gill and Macmillan, 1997).

[4] See Michael Amaladoss, *Making Harmony: Living in a Pluralist World* (Chennai: IDCR, 2003), 91–116.

[5] See Mark Juergensmeyer, *Terror in the Mind of God: The Global Rise of Religious Violence* (Berkeley and Los Angeles: California University Press, 2000); Sudhir Kakar, *The Colours of Violence* (New Delhi: Viking, 1995).

challenged the certainties of reason and its dominant meta-narratives.[6] It is not my intention here to go into the reasons of this development. I am just acknowledging it and exploring its implications for ethics in a multireligious society. As far as the official church is concerned, it can continue to offer its moral directives to its members and to the world. Its own members will have to consider them seriously and educate their moral conscience accordingly. But it cannot impose its directives on other people. Similarly, every other religious and cultural group should be free to follow its moral principles without imposing them on others. But without imposing, one can seek to persuade through example and argument.

What happens when different religious groups live together as a community, locally, nationally, and internationally? What moral principles govern their interrelationships and their common action?

Moral and Legal

At the practical level a distinction is usually made between what is moral and what is legal. The moral is seen more as inspirational and ideal, whereas the legal is more practical and governs public behavior in a particular country or region. At the universal level, for instance, we have the Universal Declaration of Human Rights. Most countries have accepted this. But it is also criticized for being too individualistic and liberal. There have been efforts to supplement it by the International Covenant on Economic, Social, and Cultural Rights. The United Nations' conventions on women and ecology have also come up with nonbinding declarations. Such documents have inspirational value. They are not accepted by every country or religion. They may also be differently interpreted by different groups.

At the legal level, most countries are guided by written constitutions that spell out fundamental rights and obligations. They are subject to interpretation by the courts. The lawmakers enact laws within the framework of the constitution. It is inevitable that the Constitutions conform to the perspectives of the majority. Some Muslim countries enshrine Sharia law in their constitutions. In such situations the expectation today is that it is not imposed on the minorities. India allows the different religious groups to follow their own civil laws, though

---

[6] See Paul Lakeland, *Postmodernity: Christian Identity in a Fragmented Age* (Minneapolis: Fortress Press, 1997).

the aim is to move toward a common civil law. The concern is that the common civil law should really be *common* and not the imposition of the law of the majority on everyone. Relationships among countries are governed by international law. This comes through tradition. But not all countries accept it. They are often guided by self-interest. The United States, for instance, has refused to accept the jurisdiction of the International Court. Recently it has been flouting international law regarding war, treatment of prisoners, and so on. The European Union is trying to work out a uniform law code that will govern the people who belong to it.

People who observe a law normally consider it as corresponding to moral principle. But they do not translate every moral principle into a legal obligation. Therefore, what is moral need not necessarily be legal. What is legal is usually moral. But a kind of behavior accepted as moral by one group may be considered immoral by another. What happens, then, when different groups of people living together in a community subscribe to different moral codes, dictated by their various cultures and religions?[7] Because the moral code is based on religious faith,[8] it acquires an objective, universal character. So we have a clash of different moral absolutes, corresponding to different religious absolutes. There is no problem in each religious group following its own moral law in private and in particular group behavior. Its members have the freedom and the right to do this, following their conscience. Even in this case it should not harm public order. Every group is also welcome to persuade and convince others that its moral code is the true or perfect one. But it cannot impose it on others. It has to respect the religious convictions and commitments of others. It is on this problem that I focus here. What does moral principle mean in a context of dialogue among different religions and ideologies? We explore this dialogue at two levels.

Ethics in a Multireligious Context

First of all, an attitude of and openness to dialogue presuppose that we recognize that our perspective may be limited. This is not easy. Every religious and moral commitment tends to be absolute. But a certain

---

[7] See Bhikku Parekh, *Rethinking Multiculturalism* (London: Macmillan, 2000). He discusses issues like female circumcision among African peoples.

[8] At the level of cosmic religiosity there is no difference between culture and religion.

consciousness of historical evolution will teach us that convictions that seemed absolute at one time are open to reinterpretation and change under different circumstances. Or to put it in another way, while a broad principle like "do good and avoid evil" is absolute, decisions about what is concretely good or evil in a particular situation is open to interpretation and discernment. We do this constantly.[9] Every religion has different schools of interpretation. Even the Muslims have four hermeneutical traditions. What needs interpretation is not relative. Rather interpretation is a concrete application of an absolute principle. So we should not speak here of the absolute and the relative, but of the general and the particular, the abstract and the concrete, the ideal and the possible. At the level of the concrete and the possible there may even be many options to choose from. If we are aware of this tension between the ideal and the possible, the general and the particular, we will be open to other groups who think differently from us. Their choices need not be ours. But we can respect them and to try to understand their reasonableness.

Second, such openness to the others may eventually be a source of challenge and conversion. It makes us look at situations in a new perspective. We may look more critically at our own choices. Intercultural and interreligious interaction has been constant in history. Even religions have undergone change. Elite Hinduism abandoned animal sacrifices and became nonviolent under the influence of Buddhism. Sikhism emerged out of an interaction between Hinduism and Islam. Islam was inculturated in many parts of Asia under the impact of Sufi saints, who were in turn influenced by the bhakti traditions of Hinduism or other popular religions. The Christian theological and legal tradition owes more to Greek philosophy and Roman law than to its Jewish roots. The Wisdom tradition in the Bible is indebted to the wisdom of the peoples in the Middle East. The social teaching of the church owes much to the challenge of Marxist and socialist ideologies. The human rights tradition has been developed less by the church than by various fringe groups in Christianity or rationalist groups opposed to Christianity that drew their inspiration from the humanism of the Greek tradition. The struggle to abolish the practice of slavery was led by the Quakers. Many of the movements for human, feminist, ecological, and migrant rights are led today by various nongovernmental organizations rather than by official religious groups, though a certain religious inspiration need not be ruled out.

---

[9] See Thomas Dean, ed., *Religious Pluralism and Truth* (Albany: State University of New York Press, 1995).

Third, when different religious groups are living together in a community, they have to collaborate for the promotion of the common good. The ideal way for this to happen is not to search for some common perspective based on reason, but for each religious group to look for inspiration and motivation from its own resources, and, through ongoing dialogue, search for consensus regarding common goals and plans of action in which all can collaborate.[10] Actually a survey of liberation theologies in various Asian religions has shown that this is possible.[11]

Mahatma Gandhi had an interreligious ashram where he trained people belonging to different religions as volunteers for his programs of *satyagraha* and civil disobedience. Even today feminist and ecological programs are interreligious in character. Moreover, campaigns for Dalit and tribal liberation cross religious boundaries. Transcending religious boundaries brings a new perspective, richness, and dynamism to these programs. Techniques like the "ideal speech situation" of Jürgen Habermas[12] and the "fusion of horizons" of Hans-Georg Gadamer,[13] developed under different circumstances, can be usefully employed to facilitate interreligious dialogue focused on common praxis. The ideal speech situation supposes that we are honest in discussion, that we do not try to deceive the other, that there is a possibility of free speech, and that all questions are answered to the extent possible. The fusion of horizons concept supposes that everyone makes an effort to look at the situation from the point of view of others. Such a discussion will help us to reach a consensus on what is desirable, possible, and achievable in a given situation without hurting the sensibilities of anyone. It will also show limits that cannot be crossed.

A final question is the kind of criteria that have to be used in discerning the correct choice. Reason is no longer useful. No one religion or ideology can be used as an ultimate criterion in a pluralist society. In such a situation the criteria could be whatever protects life of all kinds (including the earth), whatever respects the dignity of human persons, and whatever promotes community and solidarity. These are practical, not theoretical, criteria.

---

[10] See Michael Amaladoss, "Liberation: An Interreligious Project," *East Asian Pastoral Review* 28 (1991): 4–33.

[11] See Michael Amaladoss, *Life in Freedom: Liberation Theologies from Asia* (Maryknoll, NY: Orbis Books, 1997).

[12] Jürgen Habermas, *The Theory of Communicative Action*, vols. 1 and 2 (Boston: Beacon, 1984, 1987).

[13] Hans-Georg Gadamer, *Truth and Method* (London: Sheed and Ward, 1975).

Conclusion

A common interreligious project of this kind is possible only under certain conditions. I mention some of them, without claiming to give an exhaustive list.

First of all, we must avoid any form of individualistic liberalism. Our context is the community and our goal is the promotion of the common good, that is, the good of each one and of the community as a whole.

Second, every effort must be made to avoid fundamentalism of any kind in religion. Fundamentalists are beyond argument. Fundamentalism closes us to any conversation. While our convictions may be rooted in our religious beliefs, we should be able to show others their reasonableness. This does not mean rational and logical proof. But it may be based on arguments of fittingness, probability, proportionality, and possibility.

Third, where there has been conflict, every effort must be taken toward promoting forgiveness and reconciliation, aiming at restorative rather than retributive justice.[14] Our desire must be to build community, in spite of the difficulties, rather than to settle scores. This supposes that we are ready to overlook some tensions and difficulties in the interests of the common good.

Fourth, there must be a general atmosphere of friendliness and dialogue among the various religious groups. This means that every effort is made to clarify misunderstandings and prejudices through the informal contacts of common life that avoids ghetto formation. Occasional common celebration of festivals at a social level and common prayer services on the occasion of catastrophes may promote community integration. Recent studies have shown that the roots of interreligious community and understanding lie in the bonds of economic and political collaboration.[15] When people's productive lives are interlinked, they tend to defend those bonds.

---

[14] Desmond Mpilo Tutu, *No Future without Forgiveness* (New York: Doubleday, 1999).

[15] See Ashutosh Varshney, *Ethnic Conflict and Civic Life: Hindus and Muslims in India* (Delhi: Oxford University Press, 2002).

PART II

RESPONDING TO RELIGIOUS PLURALISM

THE OPPORTUNITIES AND CHALLENGES OF INTERRELIGIOUS ENGAGEMENTS IN ASIA

Chapter 9

God of All Names and Interreligious Dialogue

Another world is possible. But it is only possible through a trans-formation of this one. Such a transformation involves the integral liberation of humans and of the world, which cannot happen without transformation in the fields of cultures and religions. The transformation of religions is complex. Religions tend to be both legitimating and prophetic. In their attempt to become relevant to a particular situation, religions get socially and politically contextualized. They justify existing economic and sociopolitical structures. Slavery, apartheid, the caste system in India, and other socioeconomic inequalities have been justified in this way. At the same time, in the name of deeper values or of the Transcendent they witness to, the religions also challenge people and their living situations and structures to change. Every religion, in this sense, has both oppressive and liberative characteristics. They may be represented by different groups within the religion. Institutions tend to be conservative, while charismatic persons or movements tend to be prophetic. The prophetic and liberative dimensions of religions seek to remake the world. They are animated by hope. Not only do they affirm that a new world is possible, but they claim to offer ways of attaining it. Hinduism quests for freedom from the burden of the cycle of births in this world by promoting righteous action without attachment. Buddhism seeks to transcend a life of suffering by rooting out desire or clinging. Christianity searches for liberation from sin and its oppressive structures by love and selfless service of the others. Islam aims at promoting universal justice and community by obedience to God's law.

One would have thought these religions could collaborate in freeing people of their sufferings in this world and usher in a new one.

But a look around the world shows us that religions, as a matter of fact, seems to be part of the problem. Flashpoints like Iraq, Palestine, Bosnia, Northern Ireland, Sudan, Kashmir, the Philippines, Indonesia, and even Thailand point to underlying interreligious tensions all over the world that have created an atmosphere of self-defensive fear. Religious pluralism, therefore, is not merely a fact, but a problem. For the metacosmic religions it is not merely a social and political problem; it is also a religious one, if they think of themselves as the only true religion. Among Christians, however, there has been an increasingly positive appreciation of other religions and a desire to dialogue and collaborate with them in building a new world. This new theological outlook has not yet gained wide acceptance, at least in official circles, and needs still to be explained and defended. But it is crucial for any efforts at building another world. I would suggest that all religions need to develop such a positive outlook toward other religions. Before I outline this new theology, let us look a little more closely at the situation that has given rise to it. All theology is, after all, contextual.

Religions in Conflict

The fact of religious pluralism in the world needs no demonstration. That today their mutual relationships are in a conflictual mode, more or less hostile, if not violent, is also obvious.[1] A glance at history shows that interreligious conflict has always been there. When we are the victims, we call them persecutions, which produce martyrs. Why should religions be in conflict? I think that there are two sorts of interrelated reasons.

The first reason is that *religion is used as a political tool*.[2] Politics has a social base: a group, a nation, an empire. The source of unity

---

[1] See Samuel P. Huntington, *The Clash of Civilizations and the Remaking of World Order* (London: Touchstone Books, 1996); Sudhir Kakar, *The Colours of Violence* (Delhi: Viking, 1995); Mark Juergensmeyer, *Terror in the Mind of God: The Global Rise of Religious Violence* (New York: Oxford University Press, 2000); R. Scott Appleby, *The Ambivalence of the Sacred* (Lanham, MD: Rowman and Littlefield, 2000); Veena Das, ed., *Mirrors of Violence* (Delhi: Oxford University Press, 1995).

[2] Bipin Chandra, *Communalism in Modern India* (New Delhi, 1984); S. Arokiasamy, ed., *Responding to Communalism* (Anand, Gujarat: Gujarat Sahitya Prakash, 1991); Achin Vanaik, *Communalism Contested: Religion, Modernity, and Secularization* (New Delhi: Vishtaar, 1997); Peter van der Veer, *Religious Nationalism: Hindus and Muslims in India* (Delhi: Oxford University Press, 2002).

of such a group can be *external*, like political or military domination, or simply territory or *internal,* like language, ethnicity, culture, or religion. When empires collapse and nation states emerge such principles of identity and unity are particularly in demand. Ancient Egypt and Rome had state religions where the ruler was divinized. People who did not pay homage to the ruler were considered strangers, even enemies. When the Roman emperors became Christian, they used Christianity as a unifying force, even calling ecumenical councils to ensure this. Islam does not make a distinction between religion and politics. Even today, where Muslims are a majority, Islam is the religion of the state. Christianity enjoys a quasi-official role in Euro-America—in spite of the recent European Constitution. Nepal is a Hindu kingdom. Sri Lanka, Thailand, and Burma are Buddhist states. Japan is Shinto. In most countries minority religious groups are tolerated. The impact of a certain brand of Christianity on the recent elections in the United States is too well known to need comment.

Religion is therefore used as a source of identity and community building, besides justifying the existing situation. Rooted in ultimate, even transcendent, dimensions of life it is perhaps the strongest force for social cohesion. Politicians consciously use religion as an easy means of bringing and knitting people together into a group. Such a unity embraces and transcends even economic and sociopolitical inequalities. People who belong to the same religion are made to feel that they share the same economic and political interests. Even where individual rights are affirmed, social relations are governed by group identities.

In a majoritarian democracy the religion of the majority is privileged. Recent stories centering around crucifixes in the classroom, both in Germany and Italy, are illustrative. In India, which has a secular constitutional framework, a Hindu party has been seeking, unsuccessfully, political domination by a simplistic identification of culture, religion, and nationality. The Islamic community or *Umma* seeks to transcend national boundaries. In such situations, though the real causes for interreligious conflict are political, supported by economic interests, religious symbols are used to motivate the masses. It may even be that the leaders of such movements are not themselves believers in the religion that they make use of as a political tool. But they certainly play with the simple faith of the masses.

The second reason for interreligious conflict is that metacosmic religions, claiming to be based on a special revelation of God or on the privileged experience of a founder, consider themselves the unique or the better way to achieve the goal of human life, however it may be described.[3] Christianity claims that Jesus is the only savior and that everyone who is saved is related in some way to the church. Islam thinks that everyone is born a Muslim, because it is the natural religion. Buddhism stresses that the only way to *nirvana* is the path that has been shown by the Buddha. Hindus believe that whatever practices various religions may follow, their goal is experiential, nondual oneness with the Absolute.

The religions are open to others, but on their own conditions. Even such limited openness disappears when they become political tools. They further radicalize the sociopolitical division. The conflict is interpreted in the context of an ongoing cosmic conflict between good and evil. One identifies oneself with God, while the others, the enemy, are identified with the devil. The others are then demonized and violence against them is deemed a virtue. Religions with a sacrificial tradition can also justify most violence as having a sacrificial significance. So we have the crusades, the *jihads*, and the holy wars. At that stage people no longer feel guilty killing the religious other; they may even consider it a sacred duty. One is even ready to sacrifice one's own life in fulfilling it.

Any theology developed in this context will have a double role. On the one hand, it has to help in the purification and transformation of religion itself into a truly liberative force. On the other hand, it has to make religion into a collaborative force rather than a cause for conflict and violence. In this essay, taking the first necessary step for granted, I focus on the second dimension of interreligious relationships.

Search for a Method

There are two ways to approach the phenomenon of religious pluralism. The first is to see them as if from the outside. One may claim it to be an "objective," "scientific," or "philosophical" approach. The other is to see them from within one's own religious tradition in which one believes and to which one is committed. I think that this is the proper theological approach. Let me illustrate.

---

[3] Karen Armstrong, *The Battle for God: Fundamentalism in Judaism, Christianity, and Islam* (London: Harper Collins, 2000); Lionel Caplan, *Studies in Religious Fundamentalism* (London: Macmillan, 1987); Leo D. Lefebure, *Revelation, the Religions, and Violence* (Maryknoll, NY: Orbis Books, 1988).

Some look at religion in an abstract manner as an effort to apprehend and reach out to the "Real" or as a way to human liberation.[4] Religions are obviously many. This pluralism is then approached with a readymade framework: exclusivism, inclusivism, and pluralism. A religion is said to be exclusive if it claims to be the only way. It is inclusive if it tolerates other religions but on its own conditions. It is pluralistic if it accepts many ways. Interreligious conflict can be avoided only if a pluralistic position is adopted. At first sight such a framework looks like a useful tool to classify theologies of religion. If we look at Christian theology, for example, some claim that the church is the only way to salvation. These are the exclusivists. Others accept a certain role for other religions but suggest that Christianity is the best way or has the fullness of the means of salvation. They are the inclusivists. The pluralists affirm that Christianity is one true way to salvation, but that there can be other equally true or effective ways. If all religions are not the same, at least they play the same role in human society. Some philosophers may even suggest cynically that the really "Real," if it exists, is after all beyond all these human efforts to understand and express it.

This framework of "exclusivism, inclusivism, pluralism" has been dominating the field of reflection on religious pluralism in recent years. Theologians of religion seem to feel obliged to take a stand in relation to it. Even theologians who refuse to adopt the scheme are forced into it. The problem is that this is a "liberal" view. Few believers in any religion will feel comfortable with such a scheme. I do not think that this framework is a useful tool for theological reflection. We cannot have a universal theology of religions.[5]

Liberation theologians, more than others, are aware that the starting point of theological reflection is faith commitment. This has two elements. One is the experience of life with its sufferings, problems, and questions. The other is a faith vision, which helps one to confront and live this life. Theological reflection is a correlation between these interlinking elements. Such a correlation can lead to mutual transformation. We seek to transform life in the light of our faith commitment.

---

[4] Paul F. Knitter, *No Other Name? A Critical Survey of Christian Attitudes to World Religions* (Maryknoll, NY: Orbis Books, 1985); idem, *One Earth, Many Religions: Multifaith Dialogue and Global Responsibility* (Maryknoll, NY: Orbis Books, 1995).

[5] Cf. W. C. Smith, *Toward a World Theology* (London: Macmillan, 1981); Leonard Swidler, ed., *Toward a Universal Theology of Religion* (Maryknoll, NY: Orbis Books, 1987).

On the other hand, our understanding and expression of faith may also change in the light of our experience and struggles. Today, we experience religious pluralism not only as a fact but as a problem. If we wish to adopt a positive, dialogical approach to other religions, then we must find a space for other religions within our theological world. Every religion must make a similar effort to make space for other religions within its own theological framework.[6] Only then can the religions dialogue at the level of faith. I think that it is at this level that one can speak of real interreligious dialogue. Not just any kind of interreligious encounter qualifies as interreligious dialogue. Let me explain.

Collaboration and Dialogue

In a society where there are many religious groups, people have to live together. This can be done in various ways. A first model is that of a religion-free public social order.[7] It refuses to give religion any kind of public, social role. Religion is privatized, so to speak. This happens in countries like China and France. People are free to practice any religion of their choice. This freedom is a human right. So long as the exercise of this right does not interfere with the right of others to practice their religion and does not upset public order, the state must respect and protect it. Collaboration among religious groups at the secular level is possible and necessary. But religions do not enter the scene. For example, Vatican II's *Dignitatis Humanae* on religious freedom did not go beyond this level. It demanded freedom for religions in civil society. But civil society itself should be free of any religious elements. Communist states seek to impose such a religion-free social and political order. Secular states like France try to do the same as can be seen in the recent case of Muslim girls wearing the head scarf in state schools.

This model, however, encounters two problems. First of all, the multireligious community must agree on economic and sociopolitical

---

[6] For example, see Michael Amaladoss, *Making Harmony: Living in a Pluralist World* (Delhi: IDCR, 2003), 123–34.

[7] Rajeev Bhargava, ed., *Secularism and Its Critics* (Delhi: Oxford University Press, 1998); Neera Chandhoke, *State and Civil Society: Explorations in Political Theory* (New Delhi: Sage, 1995); Keith J. Pavlischek, *John Courtney Murray and the Dilemma of Religious Tradition* (Kirksville, MO: Thomas Jefferson University Press, 1994).

values that it wants to pursue. If religions are to be kept out of the picture, on what principles can these values be based? The French would advocate reason. The Chinese would advocate ideology. The question is whether everyone would agree on reason and/or ideology as adequate sources for a social vision and values. Many would believe that only religion, insofar as it speaks of ultimate questions in life, can be the root of such vision and values. They would say that in this case reason and ideology are functioning as quasi-religions. The second problem is that no true religious believers would agree that their religious faith should control only their private life and should have nothing to say about their social and public life.[8] I am sure that liberation theologians would be particularly sensitive to the attempt to reduce religion to the purely private sphere.

An alternate model would be that each religious group seeks to develop its own vision and values for social life. In a multireligious situation, different religious groups seek, through dialogue, to arrive at an "overlapping" consensus regarding visions and values that they wish to pursue together in collaboration.[9] The religions therefore are allowed a certain public presence and role in civil society. Religious groups enter into discussion, mutual persuasion, and consensus formation in the public, civil space in discussion groups, in the written and spoken media, in the universities, and so on. Accepting other interlocutors and working toward consensus supposes equality between religions at a formal level, irrespective of numerical strength and political power. Theological questions start right here.

A particular religion may have difficulty in recognizing the other religions as equals. It may privilege its own ethical perspectives as better or even nonnegotiable. Such disagreements can happen even within religious groups as, for example, in the United States with regard to contraception and homosexuality. It can very well happen among religious groups. The status of women, for instance, seems to be a sore point between different religious groups. Religious groups, therefore, have to dialogue with one another at this level. Such dialogue may lead to a change in perspectives within each religious community. Hinduism, for instance, had a period of reform and renaissance under

---

[8] Cf. Neera Chandhoke, *Beyond Secularism: The Rights of Religious Minorities* (Delhi: Oxford University Press, 1999); T. N. Madan, *Modern Myths and Locked Minds: Secularism and Fundamentalism in India* (Delhi: Oxford University Press, 1996).

[9] John Rawls, *Political Liberalism* (New York: Columbia University Press, 1993).

the impact of Christianity and British culture at the end of the nine-teenth century.

Beyond this dialogue at the sociopolitical level, religions can also encounter one another in the strictly religious sphere. Interreligious dialogue in this sense supposes that the other religion is recognized, respected, and accepted as a valuable partner in dialogue. This means that one hopes not only to give, but also to receive. One feels ready to be challenged to change at the religious level. Dialogue becomes mutual prophecy. It is here that interreligious dialogue becomes a theological problem. The theological question, then, is what space do we make for other religions within our own religious vision and how does this affect other aspects of this vision? In Christian terms this would ask what is our theology of religions and how does it affect our ecclesiology, Christology, and eschatology? This is where a new theology, which favors interreligious dialogue, emerges.

A New Theology of Religions

Christian theology had always recognized that people belonging to other religions could be saved by God if they are true to their con-science. What is new is that today we believe that God is reaching out to the people, not in spite of their religions, but in and through their religions.[10] The roots of this change of perspective are found in the Second Vatican Council, though it did not affirm this positively. In *Gaudium et Spes*, its constitution on the church in the modern world, the council made a strong assertion of the universal salvific will of God (GS 22). The decree on other religions, *Nostra Aetate,* accepted God as the common origin and goal of all peoples and found "good and holy elements" in other religions (NA 1–2). The decree on mis-sion, *Ad Gentes,* rooted the mission of Jesus Christ in the mission of God that embraces the whole universe and the whole of human and cosmic history (AG 2). The council however did not say anything positive about other religions as such. Theologians like Karl Rahner affirmed that if God reaches out to other believers, given their human and social nature, it must be through the beliefs, symbols, and rituals of their religions, through which they are trying to reach out to God.[11]

---

[10] Jacques Dupuis, *Toward a Christian Theology of Religious Pluralism* (Mary-knoll, NY: Orbis Books, 1999). This book has a large bibliography.

[11] Karl Rahner, *Theological Investigations*, vol. V (London: Darton, Longman and Todd, 1969), 128.

Asian Bishops and theologians also developed a similar perspective.[12] Such a positive appreciation of other religions received a symbolic confirmation when John Paul II invited the leaders of other religions to come together at Assisi to pray for world peace. As authoritative commentators pointed out at that time, this gesture of John Paul II recognized the other religions as legitimate, since the other believers can pray—that is, be in touch with God—through their rituals and, secondly, their prayers will be heard by God. A more formal confirmation of the presence and action of the Spirit of God in other religions came in his encyclical *Redemptoris Missio* (RM 28–29).

Such a positive appreciation of the other religions in God's economy of salvation is integrated into Christian theological tradition in two different ways. A group of Indian theologians have described this as a paradigm shift.[13] The first paradigm is a linear one. History starts with various religions. Even if the Spirit of God is present in them, it is only in a limited manner. Then God reveals Godself to Abraham and Moses. Jesus Christ is the final and ultimate word. All other manifestations of God find fulfillment in him. The church has the fullness of the means of salvation.

The second paradigm is more complex. God has a plan: to share God's life with everyone. God also wishes to gather all things in harmony. God sends the Word and the Spirit into the world and reveals Godself to various peoples in various ways. God's self-revelation provokes a human response of faith. This divine-human dialogue is always salvific. Part of God's plan is to become personally involved in the process. God chooses the Jews to prepare God's coming and the Word of God becomes flesh in Jesus. Jesus and the church are the symbols and servants—sacraments—of God's plan. God chooses to do this in a humble, kenotic, dialogical way. The different manifestations of the Word are not opposed to one another, even if the Word incarnate has a special role and mission. But this role is to bring all things together. Fulfillment itself is eschatological. We do not know how this would happen. We are but humble servants who are called to dialogue with all people of good will. The Spirit who is present everywhere is the animator of this process of reconciliation and communion.

---

[12] See Theological Advisory Commission of the Federation of Asian Bishops' Conferences, "Theses on Interreligious Dialogue," in *Being Church in Asia*, ed. John Gnanapiragasam and Felix Wilfred (Manila: Claretian, 1994).

[13] Thomas Malipurathu and L. Stanislaus, eds., *A Vision of Mission in the New Millennium* (Mumbai: St. Paul's, 2001).

The Church and the Reign of God

How does one relate the other religions to the church? Starting with the affirmation that the church is necessary for salvation, some affirm that all the people who are saved are related to the church in some mysterious way. I think that it is better to set the other religions in the context of the reign of God. Jesus proclaims and inaugurates the reign of God. Jesus sends the church into the world as the symbol and servant or the sacrament of the reign of God. There are, however, two ways of looking at the reign of God. Some, while accepting that the church is the beginnings of the reign and is not identical with it, see the reign of God as the future of the church. The church will grow into the reign. Others see the reign of God as wider than the church and present wherever God's grace is operative. The reign of God may also be operative in and through other religions. The church therefore relates to other religions as collaborators in the project of realizing God's reign in this universe. In the ongoing struggle between God, on the one side, and Satan as the personal power of evil and Mammon as the social power of evil, on the other, the religions are on the side of God and of the church. They are allies rather than enemies. The church's own role is not one of domination but of service to the reign of God, wherever and however it is being realized.

The reign of God is an eschatological reality. It is not purely other-worldly, waiting to be realized at the end of history. It is not going to be fully realized in this world either. God has not promised us that. But the reign is constantly being realized as human communities of freedom, fellowship, and justice are being built up. The people may be economically poor and politically powerless. Yet they are slowly realizing the reign of God in their lives and their communities, praying "your kingdom come" and hoping for its full realization at the end of times. It is this hope that keeps people struggling, finding joy and peace in the midst of their struggle. It is in this context that another—a very different—world seems possible and is being realized by people of good will, of whatever religion or ideology, working together and energized and empowered by the Spirit of God.[14]

Jesus, the Liberator

What is the role of Jesus Christ in the process? Most Christians confess that Jesus is the only savior. So they seek to relate everyone who

---

[14] John Fuellenbach, *The Kingdom of God: The Message of Jesus Today* (Mary-knoll, NY: Orbis Books, 2002).

is saved to him, if not through explicit faith, then by implicit faith. Implicit faith refers to a system that is operative without the conscious awareness of the people who are its beneficiaries. Some, however, think that Jesus is one among the saviors. The people of other religions are saved in other ways. In technical terms they say that the role of Jesus in the salvation of others is "representative," not "constitutive."[15] Of course, it is difficult to see what Jesus represents to people who do not recognize or acknowledge him. The problem, once again, is that the argument is abstract, a priori.

Perhaps a closer look at the New Testament will throw some light. The disciples encounter Jesus, listen to his proclamation of the reign of God, and witness to his initiation of its realization. His violent death at the hands of the Jewish and Roman authorities shattered their dreams. But his resurrection makes them realize that Jesus was no ordinary human being and that the reign of God he inaugurated was eschatological—already present and yet reaching out to fulfillment beyond history. First they say that God has raised him up. Then they slowly realize that this ascent follows a descent. Deeper reflection on this mystery leads them to assert the pre-existence of Jesus in their early hymns. Paul sees God creating everything in Christ and also gathering up all things in him (Eph 1:3–10). John sees Jesus as the incarnation of the Word, who was with God in the beginning, in whom everything was created and who is enlightening everyone coming into the world (John 1:1–14).

What happens here is that what God does in the humanity of Jesus is related to what is happening in eternity. What Jesus does, therefore, should not be isolated. Nor should it be reduced simply to a historical manifestation or symbol of an eternal mystery. Eternity is being played out in cosmic history, and what happens in history is relevant to eternity. The descending and ascending of Christ is not simply playacting. The divine involves itself in history and transforms it. But the principal actor here is God: Father, Word, and Spirit. The Word that became human in Jesus has been active in various ways all through history.

The different religions may be seen as expressions of the different manifestations of the Word through the Spirit. What God does through the Word cannot be reduced to what God does through Jesus, though they are obviously interrelated. Jesus is a special manifestation insofar as he is the incarnate Word. But he comes as a self-emptying servant, not to assert his superiority, to dominate, or to control. So when we confess Jesus as the only savior, we are using the principle of

---

[15] Paul F. Knitter, "Commitment to One—Openness to Others," *Horizons* 28 (2001): 255–70.

the "communication of the idioms." God—Father, Word, and Spirit—is the only savior. God is working in the world in various ways. The Word becoming flesh is God's work. But it does not monopolize God's work; it is at its service. Jesus as the Word of God is the only savior. The Word made flesh is the sacrament—or symbol and servant—of this mystery. Its service consists precisely in entering into history and in collaborating with the many ways in which God is active in it.[16]

To confess, therefore, that Jesus is the only savior is to acknowledge that the mystery we name Jesus is present and active everywhere, not to claim any kind of superiority for Jesus. This very mystery calls us to collaboration among the various ways it is manifested in history. The incarnate manifestation of the Word is not its only manifestation, though it is a special one. But its specialty is humble service. Its role is one of being at the service of the mystery and its many manifestations. The service that it envisages and demands is one of dialogue.

A Call to Dialogue

This dialogue, however, is not simple because every divine manifestation involves a human response. Both God's self-manifestation and the human response are free. While God's manifestations are interrelated, God is not obliged to repeat Godself. The human response is also conditioned by history and culture as well as by the sinfulness of humans. This is true also of the church. It is because of this pluralism of God's manifestations and human responses that the dialogue can be mutually prophetic, purificatory, and enriching.

While God and God's reign are points of convergence, pluralism of religions is not only a value, but inevitable, given the diversity of divine manifestations, of history and cultures, and of human groups themselves. The biblical vision of history is one of bringing together, of gathering, not of making one, so that "God may be all in all" (1 Cor 15:28). It is harmony and communion rather than unity, certainly not uniformity. This supposes freedom and equality, justice and solidarity. Thus a theology of dialogue can be supported by a theology of pluralism and harmony.[17] The Muslim *Umma* (universal community),

---

[16] Michael Amaladoss, "Jesus Christ as the Only Saviour and Mission," *Japan Mission Journal* 55 (2001): 219–26.

[17] See Theological Advisory Commission of the Federation of Asian Bishops' Conferences, "Asian Christian Perspectives on Harmony," FABC Papers, no. 75, in *For All the Peoples of Asia, Vol 2: Federation of Asian Bishops' Conferences*

the Buddhist inter-being, and the Hindu *dharma* confirm this vision of harmony.

Openness to the other is not against the affirmation of one's own identity. Dialogue becomes a problem only when the different identity of the other is denied or downgraded. The theology through which one seeks to justify to oneself the possibility of dialogue is itself not the object of dialogue.

Intrapersonal Dialogue

Interreligious dialogue may start as collaboration in the pursuit of agreed upon human and spiritual values at the economic, social, and political levels. At some stage religions encounter each other as religions. Faith encounters faith. At a basic level there is an effort to know and understand the other religion. Ignorance and prejudice will have to be overcome. The attempt to understand leads to comparative study, because one's point of reference is one's own religion. Understanding may lead to appreciation. We believe that God has spoken to them, and that they have devised ways of experiencing God or the Ultimate. God may have spoken to them in a way different from the way in which God has spoken to us. Still, insofar as it is God who has spoken, we feel that what God has manifested to them is not totally irrelevant to us. It may even be complementary.

Some people then read and are nourished by the scriptures of other religions. Others may seek to experience God or the Ultimate following the *sadhana* or spiritual practices of another religion. We know Hindus who have sought to be disciples of Jesus and follow his teachings. There are Christians who practice Hindu yoga or Buddhist systems of meditation like Zen or Vipassana. They have been spiritually enriched. Some seem to succeed in integrating such methods and experiences with their Christian context and identity. There are others who do not succeed in such integration. They seem to feel that they are different, but equally valid experiences of the Absolute. These people may offer experiential support to the experience of religious pluralism.

The fact that God is the common origin and goal of all the religions and that it is the same Spirit of God who is present and active in all the religions does not mean that all religions are the same and have the same religious or spiritual experience. People who are open to the

Documents from 1992 to 1996, ed. Franz-Josef Eilers, 229–98 (Manila: Claretian, 1997).

spiritual experience of other religions are often accused of syncretism. Syncretism is an indiscriminate mixing of religious meaning systems. People who are engaged in interreligious dialogue at the level of spiritual experience are not being syncretistic. It is an intrapersonal process. They are rooted in their own faith, while being open to other faith experiences. When no integration is possible, there is a dialectic. It is mutually challenging and creative. I am not indulging here in hypothetical considerations, but trying to make sense of reported experiences.[18]

Dialogue as Reconciliation

Where there has been interreligious conflict no true dialogue is possible without conflict resolution and reconciliation. So we also need a theology of reconciliation. The starting point for reconciliation is, of course, the recognition that something unjust has been done and people have been hurt. There is an acknowledgment of guilt or at least of responsibility, either individual or collective, or both. People want to rebuild community based on justice. The justice they look for is not retributive, based on revenge, but restorative, based on forgiveness. Revenge can often lead to a spiral of violence. Forgiveness promotes reconciliation and community. Forgiving need not mean forgetting.

As a matter of fact, memory may remain a useful warning signpost for the future. But memories too have to be healed. Restorative justice involves an attempt to restore to people what they have lost during the violence. People, of course, cannot be brought back to life. But means of livelihood can be provided. The sense of human dignity that one loses when treated as an object can be regained when the stories of one's sufferings are listened to. The Truth and Reconciliation Commission that the South African Government established after the end of the Apartheid regime was a pioneering effort in this area.[19] Such efforts could be imitated elsewhere.

The theological bases for reconciliation are found in the life and death of Jesus. Jesus witnessed to the forgiving love of the Father, healing people by forgiving them. His new commandment of love goes hand in hand with the demand that they forgive each other. Both God and Jesus are held up as models of forgiveness. The prayer "forgive us

---

[18] Dennis Gira and Jacques Scheuer, eds., *Vivre de plusieurs religions: Promesse ou illusion?* (Paris: L'Atelier, 2000).

[19] Desmond Mpilo Tutu, *No Future without Forgiveness* (New York: Doubleday, 1999).

our sins as we forgive those who sin against us" sums up the attitude. Asking pardon can be as hard as forgiving. The church itself had the courage to ask pardon for its misdeeds, not without some quibbling, only in recent years.

Dialogue and Conflict

While pluralism by itself need not lead to conflict, struggle may be inevitable when pluralism leads to division, domination, and injustice. Unjust structures do not change by themselves. Is a spirit of dialogue opposed to conflict in such circumstances? The horizon of all our actions and struggles is the community of the reign of God. Any struggle must be set in that context. This would mean that the necessary struggle would be nonviolent and lead to negotiation and progressive change. Violent revolution may occasionally succeed in throwing out a dictator. But it hardly ever brings peace and justice. Jesus himself is the model of nonviolent struggle. Following his example, leaders like Mahatma Gandhi, Martin Luther King, Jr., Dom Hélder Câmara, and Nelson Mandela have shown its contemporary relevance.[20] Where struggles and violence are frequent, structures to promote conflict resolution may have to be set up.

Dialogue, conflict resolution, and reconciliation can be analyzed in terms of social psychology. Theology, however, is involved when we are exploring interreligious conflicts. Religion also gives a depth to the process of repentance, forgiveness, and reconciliation. Religions that do not speak much about sin may not also talk about forgiveness. But all understand the need for reconciliation and peace.

Prophetic Dialogue

I have suggested that each religion has to develop its own theological perspectives with regard to its relation with other religions. It is not meaningful to speak of a universal theology. We tend easily to accuse others of being fundamentalist, unforgiving, and so on. Christianity has been fundamentalist until recently. Our openness to dialogue is still halfhearted and often has a hidden agenda. Even today Asians with their living experience of other believers seem more open to dialogue than Euro-Americans. We began asking forgiveness for our

---

[20] For Gandhi, see George Pattery, *Gandhi, the Believer* (Delhi: ISPCK, 1996).

past misdeeds only a few years ago. Hindus have shown themselves more open to dialogue than Christians in India. Therefore we need not rush to judge others. Theological dialogue with other believers may provoke others to reflect and develop their own theological traditions and to become more open to dialogue. We have seen this happening among Asian theologians of liberation of all religions.[21] Every religious tradition is trying to make space for other religious traditions within its own religious context and is open to dialogue and collaboration not only in the sociopolitical sphere but also in the religious one.

Dialogue with Ideologies

We have been talking so far about interreligious dialogue. Much of what we have said will also apply to our interaction and collaboration with people who are not particularly religious but follow an ideology. They may be nonbelievers, agnostics, or marginal believers. But they may believe strongly in an ideology and follow it with commitment. If our aim is to achieve harmony among human beings we cannot ignore ideologies. We have to collaborate with their followers too. They too can be fundamentalist and violent, having blind faith in their ideologies. They may not believe in God. But we believe that God is working also through them. When Jesus evoked the picture of the final judgment he conferred blessedness, not on people who were faithful practitioners of religious ritual, but on people who were close to the poor and the suffering, who were compassionate and helped those who were in need. It is significant that the World Council of Churches has a sub-unit for dialogue with faiths and ideologies. Ideologies are quasi-religions. Their followers attribute certitude and absoluteness to them. They shape their vision and values.

Conclusion

A new world, then, is possible. All people have to build it together. Even if some struggle is inevitable, it can be nonviolent, leading to justice through negotiation and reconciliation. Religions and ideologies need not be obstacles to such collaboration. All religions can make space for such interreligious collaboration, based on their experience

---

[21] Michael Amaladoss, *Life in Freedom: Liberation Theologies from Asia* (Maryknoll, NY: Orbis Books, 1997).

of pluralism and their belief in one God. This is true today also of Christians. A new theology of religions and of mission and a new practice of dialogue are emerging among them. This new awareness brings new challenges and new possibilities for faith-praxis.

This is perhaps the moment to rethink part of the title of this chapter. The phrase "God of all names" may make it appear that the different religions are only different names for one-and-the-same God. This image does not take seriously the identity and difference of the various religions. Every religion is an interplay of divine and human freedom (RM 28–29). They are different experiences and expressions of divine-human encounter. God is neither a common denominator nor the great Unknown. God is the source of richness and diversity. God manifests Godself in various ways to various peoples at various times in various cultures under various historical circumstances. God is the inexhaustible source of this diversity. Pluralism, therefore, has to be acknowledged, accepted, and respected. But this pluralism is not chaotic. There is one God, and this God has a plan for the universe which is working itself out in history. We believe that this plan includes also an incarnate manifestation of the Word of God, besides the universal presence and action of the Word and the Spirit. But it is meant to be sacramental. God's goal is to create a new world:

> See, the home of God is among the mortals.
> He will dwell with them as their God;
> They will be his peoples,
> and God himself will be with them;
> he will wipe every tear from their eyes.
> Death will be no more;
> mourning and crying and pain will be no more;
> for the first things have passed away.
> And the one who was seated on the throne said, "See,
>   I am making all things new." (Rev 21:3–5)

It is our task to discern God's action in history and through peoples and to collaborate with God and with others in realizing the new world. This collaboration will have to take place at all levels: economic and political, personal and social, cultural and religious. Interreligious dialogue is only one element of this collaboration. But it is a crucial one because it provides meaning, motivation, and inspiration in an ultimate context. That is why dialogue among religions is interesting and necessary. Such dialogue will lead to cosmic harmony where "God will be all in all" (1 Cor 15:28).

Chapter 10

Changing Dialogue—
From Religions to Ideologies

When we speak about dialogue, we think immediately of interreligious dialogue. In the Christian discourse interreligious dialogue itself is set in the context of mission. Asian bishops and theologians often speak about evangelization as a threefold dialogue with the poor, the cultures, and the religions. Interreligious dialogue is seen either as an integral dimension of evangelization or as a preparation for proclamation, depending on one's theological orientation. This orientation follows the manner in which one evaluates the other religions. Paradigms like exclusivism-inclusivism-pluralism are used to understand the relation among the religions. In the following pages I suggest that it is time that we broadened the activity of dialogue to include ideologies. This is not totally new. The Dialogue sub-unit of the World Council of Churches always speaks about dialogue with "living faiths and ideologies."[1] But I am not sure how seriously this is being taken in practice. The matter becomes complicated when many followers of ideologies may not be ready to dialogue with religions.

In the modern world, especially in Euro-America, the process of secularization is gaining ground. The majority of the people do not practice any religion. Those who practice a religion seem to be becoming exclusivist, almost as a defensive reaction. Any project of interreligious dialogue in such a situation will reach out to a small minority, largely ineffective in a sociopolitical sense.

There are also many movements for an alternative world. The fourth World Social Forum brought thousands of people from all over the world to Mumbai, India, in January 2004. Many of these people

---

[1] The Vatican used to have a Secretariat for Dialogue with Non-Believers, which was later merged with the Pontifical Council for Culture.

belonged to nongovernmental organizations and were not flaunting any religious affiliation. They may even be wary of it. Many of the active social movements across the world struggling for human rights, the liberation of women, and the preservation of the earth are not inspired by religion. But for some, the values they fight for may substitute for religion. Many of these people may even be critical of religion—at least institutional religion—as being obstacles to their liberation movements.

A Changing Context

For some years I have been associated with a center for interreligious dialogue in Chennai, India. The center had a tradition of bringing together believers of different religions for ongoing conversations regarding their scriptures and religious experiences. Sometimes groups came together for a whole day—or days—to "live together" in an atmosphere of prayer and faith interaction. They also prayed together on these and other occasions. This was certainly spiritually enriching for everyone concerned.

In recent years, however, there have been increasing instances of interreligious violence in India, as elsewhere. The phenomenon of interreligious violence is not new. Hindu-Muslim riots have been going on for over seventy years, at least in some parts of the country. The Hindu-Sikh violence, after the Indian army entered the golden temple at Amritsar and Indira Gandhi was assassinated, is well known. More recently, anti-Christian violence has also started. A rising Hindu fundamentalism is certainly the cause of this. What is new, however, is the justification and political support that such violent acts are increasingly evoking even among the educated middle class. People who will not themselves indulge in such activity will not openly condemn it either. Their criticisms will often be muted with many *ifs* and *buts*.

When an effort was made in our center to discuss themes like "religions and violence" and to explore the causes of religious violence, the ready interlocutors in such a discussion were not the "religious" people who used to dialogue with us, but others who were on the margins of the religious institution or even out of it. Only these were ready to be critical of their own religion. When dialogue tried to focus not merely on sharing of religious experience but on active collaboration for social transformation, then again it is the "nonreligious"—the secular activists—who have been willing partners in conversation and common action.

Reflecting on this experience I conclude that we have to widen the goal and practice of dialogue to include ideologies. This may involve some rethinking regarding our traditional ideas on interreligious dialogue.

Ideologies and Religions

We can start with a clear understanding of what we mean by ideology. Aloysius Pieris describes ideology in the following way:

(a) a worldview,
(b) essentially programmatic,
(c) about a this-worldly future to be realized, not without struggle, in the socio-political order,
(d) with the aid of certain tools of analysis or a method of discernment based on its own (that is, ideological) premises,
(e) and requiring by its own intrinsic nature to be transcended by the Truth it seeks to articulate.[2]

Pieris then compares ideology to religion. He says that they differ with regard to their concept of the future.

Religion, *primarily* and *normatively* (but not exclusively), points to an Absolute Future, a Totally Other, so that the horizon of final liberation is given a metacosmic ultimacy. . . . But, contrary to a widespread misconception, religion does emphatically teach that the Absolute Future has to be anticipated here in this life not only through the spiritual achievements of individual persons but also through visible structures in human society. . . . It is usually the case that a religion, in incarnating the Absolute Future here on earth, makes use of visible social structures, strategies and institutions that (this-worldly) ideologies provide.[3]

Religions, therefore, though they have a transcendent or metacosmic goal, cannot function without a this-worldly ideology. While the religious vision is the result of revelation in some form, the ideology emerges out of human and social experience.

---

[2] Aloysius Pieris, SJ, *An Asian Theology of Liberation* (Maryknoll, NY: Orbis Books, 1988), 24.
[3] Ibid., 25.

Cosmic and Metacosmic Religion

It is interesting to compare this correlation between ideology and religion with another correlation that Pieris also makes between cosmic and metacosmic religion.

> The cosmic . . . religiosity consists of revering nature and its forces, either in the form of a nominal being or a nominal complex of being who is/are, nevertheless, so much part of the world as to be encountered in the context of an ecological spirituality.[4]

Cosmic religiosity is different from metacosmic religion.

> The metacosmic . . . religions . . . posit the "existence" of an immanently transcendental horizon, . . . Which/Who is salvifically encountered by humans, through liberating knowledge (gnosis) and redemptive love (agape) respectively.[5]

Pieris goes on to point to their interrelationship by using the analogy of a helipad (cosmic religion) and a helicopter (metacosmic religion).

> Their encounter is one of mutual fulfillment, as they are complementary. Hence there is no radical conversion from one to the other. Thus, "inculturation" means none other than a metacosmic religion finding its natural point of insertion in a cosmic religion.[6]

Putting together these two correlations between religion and ideology and cosmic and metacosmic religion we see a complex and at the same time a simple picture. Just as metacosmic religions do not function without an ideological base to express their this-worldly relevance, they do not function without a relationship to one or the other cosmic religion either. Such a comparison of these two correlations leads me to suspect that there is a correlation between ideology and cosmic religiosity, at least at a functional level.

My hypothesis at this stage is that, for some people, ideology replaces cosmic religiosity. That is why ideology has a quasi-religious function. It commands a certain commitment and loyalty. It offers a total explanation of reality, though the totality is this-worldly and not

---

[4] Aloysius Pieris, SJ, *Fire and Water* (Maryknoll, NY: Orbis Books, 1996), 66.
[5] Ibid. See also Pieris, *An Asian Theology of Liberation*, 71–74.
[6] Pieris, *Fire and Water*, 66.

transcendent. People whose religious life has been largely at a level of cosmic religiosity easily abandon it to embrace an ideology. This is one reason for the phenomenon of rapid secularization. Reason, science, and technology can easily destroy cosmic religiosity by offering alternative explanations and justifications for cosmic phenomena. But they cannot touch the transcendent dimensions of metacosmic religion. They can, however, coexist and even integrate with it.

The integration of cosmic religiosity or ideology with a metacosmic religion is never a neat fit. There is always a tension and an ambiguity. On the one hand, cosmic religiosity/ideology tries to adjust itself to metacosmic religion. On the other hand, metacosmic religion may allow itself to be conditioned in various ways by cosmic religiosity/ideology. The tension will, and probably should, never disappear. Metacosmic religion has to be relevant to life in the world. Otherwise it will become "pie in the sky" or an "opium." It has to be sensitive to cosmic religiosity/ideology. At the same time, cosmic religiosity/ideology may be easily conditioned by existing circumstances and it needs to listen constantly to the prophetic call of metacosmic religion if it does not wish to be stagnant.

It is here that we may see a distinction between cosmic religiosity and ideology. While cosmic religiosity is happy to let things be as they are and reconfirm existing structures through ritual, ideology—at least in its original inspiration—seeks to be transformative and move toward a goal, even if this goal is not transcendent.

Metacosmic religion is therefore a complex structure. It has its feet in cosmic religiosity and ideology. Various elements of these are often in tension. The tension is ongoing. It could be creative. But it could also be destructive. My purpose here, however, is not to delve into the complex interrelationship among these various elements but to suggest that interreligious dialogue should take this complexity seriously in planning its strategies and activities.

Metacosmic Is Not Otherworldly

A popular description of religion suggests that it seeks to answer ultimate questions especially dealing with life and death, the problem of evil, unmerited suffering, and so on. Metacosmic religions offer answers to these questions in the context of a Transcendent Reality or World. This Transcendent is often perceived as otherworldly. The focus of religion then becomes otherworldly. It is not interested in life in this world.

I think that this is a misunderstanding of religion. In their search to give meaning to life, people do ask ultimate questions. But the answers that they seek are supposed to tell them, not how to live in another world after death, but how to live in this world. Even when this world is seen in the context of another world, the focus is on this world. Religion is for life. Even when it has its eyes on an ultimate consummation, it is asking how it can be reached by an appropriate way of living in the here and now. Its speculations on another world are meant to orient life in this one. Some people, of course, may misunderstand this tension between this world and the other and choose to focus on the other. They seek to deny and escape this world, even literally running away into the forest or to the mountain. Abandoning this world may have a symbolic value as an affirmation of its passing and relative nature. But giving it up as something evil can only be alienating. What true religion asks is not to deny the world but to transform it in the light of the Transcendent. This world has a deeper or transcendent dimension. But this dimension is not something apart, but rather within. It asks us not to run away from or abandon the world, but to look at it in a new way in the context of the transcendent within. This is what leads to a transformation of life in the world.

Cosmic religiosity may not speak of transcendence in the same way as metacosmic religion. But it does seek to go beyond the self and the present by setting them in the context of a community of ancestors and spirits.

The main point here is that religion is for life here and now. It seeks to show us how to live. Religion is necessarily linked to an ethic—a way of life. The Buddha was very clear about it by refusing to speak about God or the other world. For Hinduism, religion was spelled out in terms of *margas* or ways of life. The five pillars of Islam spell out a pattern of living. Jesus spells out his ethic in the Sermon on the Mount.

The this-worldly and otherworldly dimensions of religion can be—and often are—characterized spatially as horizontal and vertical. Normally the two orientations should be in a healthy tension. But it often happens that the vertical dimension is emphasized one-sidedly and the horizontal one is ignored, even when it is not denied.

If religions are for this life, then they cannot do without a worldview, a system of values, and a code of action. These can be supplied by a culture or an ideology or a cosmic religious system. Often there may be a mixture of all these. As a matter of fact, it may not be easy to distinguish between a culture and its cosmic religiosity except in a formal way.

In a multireligious situation it may be that more than one meta-cosmic religion are rooted in the same cosmic religiosity. Similarly, in the same socio-economic-political context religions may also share the same ideology. A mutual adjustment between the religions, on the one hand, and the cosmic religiosity and ideology, on the other, does not take away a commonality that is shared. In the same way, one metacosmic religion may relate to many cosmic religiosities and ideologies. As it moves from one cosmic religiosity to another, it may not totally give up one and take on another. It may carry with it some elements while integrating new ones. While Buddhism has spread all across Asia, it has not lost certain basic elements of the Indian worldview as expressed by the yogic psycho-physical system and its method of concentration. Islam has carried with it everywhere many elements of Arab culture. Roman Catholic ritual practices and community organization are still rooted in Roman and Germanic cosmic religiosity and culture.[7]

In such a situation the religions identify themselves, not in terms of what they share with other metacosmic religions, namely, their cosmic religiosity or ideology, but what is specific to them, namely, their metacosmic dimension.

Interreligious Encounter

What happens, then, when different religions encounter one another? Normally there is a hierarchical order and power relationship in which one religion dominates the others. I am not going to explore this situation here. Let us take for granted that the religions feel the need to encounter one another as more or less equal. For example, the Second Vatican Council speaks about the need for interreligious dialogue in a context in which God is recognized as the common origin and goal of all peoples. This means that all religions belong to a common divine economy, though this may be understood in different ways. Similarly, in a particular country the religions may feel the urge to dialogue with each other when the country chooses to be secular, treating all religions equally.

When we speak about interreligious dialogue, we think of a formal interaction between two groups of people who belong to different

---

[7] James C. Russell, *The Germanization of Early Medieval Christianity: A Sociohistorical Approach to Religious Transformation* (New York: Oxford University Press, 1994).

religions. Cosmic religions are very much part of a culture or an ethnic group. When they encounter each other there is an interaction and mutual influence. There is no formal exchange. But when metacosmic religions encounter each other there is a formal exchange. Moreover, they tend to focus on the metacosmic dimension of each religion. This means that their discourse is often limited to the transcendent or otherworldly dimension. The consequence is that interreligious dialogue is often limited to spirituality and finds expression in events like common prayer. Dialogue at this level is certainly interesting and necessary. But I think that it is not enough. It can even be alienating, because it is not focusing on the direct and immediate purpose of religion, which is precisely life in this world here and now. Religions in dialogue must encounter one another at all levels: the metacosmic, the cosmic, the cultural, and the ideological. There can be pluralism at all these levels. Pluralism can lead to conflict under certain circumstances.

When we speak about the various ways of dialogue—of life, of common action, of intellectual exchange, and of experience—the first two refer more to the horizontal, this-worldly level, while the other two refer rather to the vertical, otherworldly level. Formal dialogue often takes place only at the latter level. In situations of interreligious conflict this seems quite inadequate.

Cosmic religions are not usually in conflict as they are limited to a tribe or a specific social group. The groups may be in conflict, but this is not seen as a religious conflict. They tend to be pluralist. Metacosmic religions, on the contrary, tend to be exclusivist or inclusivist. In the face of other religions, while they may aggressively proselytize, they do not normally indulge in violence, unless they are politicized. However, they tend to legitimate the cultures and ideologies in which they are rooted. At the same time some groups in them also tend to be prophetic in the name of the Transcendent that they confess. Differences and conflicts among religious groups arise also at the level of the this-worldly dimension of religions. At this level ideologies and a quest for power in the name of an ideology come into play. The religions are often pulled into conflicts insofar as they legitimate the ideologies.

It happens that different groups of people who are believers in the same religion may follow different ideologies in practical life, just as the same religion can be rooted in different cultures. Christians can be capitalists or socialists. Both groups will seek to justify their ideologies from the Bible or theology. Correspondingly, people who differ at the level of religion may converge at the level of ideology. Their ideological fellowship may be more important than their religious differences. Pieris, in his writings, often refers to the Workers' Fellowship in Sri

Lanka, in which Christians and Buddhists come together to celebrate their fellowship.[8] What makes their interreligious friendship possible is precisely their togetherness at the level of ideology. Community of ideology facilitates interreligious encounter.

Dialogue among Ideologies

What I suggest here is that today we cannot talk about dialogue between religions without exploring the dialogue between ideologies. What makes this dialogue between ideologies interesting and challenging is the fact while some ideologies may have occasional backing by one or other religion, other ideologies may claim neutrality with regard to the various religions, while some others may be vigorously antireligious. Some ideologies may be even religious, like *Hindutva* or Islamic fundamentalism. While religious fundamentalism is basically a religious phenomenon, it can become ideological by assuming cultural or political identities. That is why I think that we cannot talk about interreligious dialogue without talking about dialogue between ideologies.

Ideologies may tend to be as convinced about their truth and as exclusive of others as religions used to be. However, ideologies tend to dialogue in practice. Capitalism and socialism may be seen as mutually exclusive ideologies. But we know that there has been a lot of interaction between these ideologies. There are many intermediary ideologies that are being tried out by various groups and countries. We have different types of capitalism and different kinds of socialism. Ideologies need not be exclusively economical. Apartheid was a social and racist ideology. *Hindutva* in India claims to be cultural nationalism. It is a political ideology that uses religio-cultural identity as an element of unification. Islamic fundamentalism is also a politico-religious ideology.

It is not my intention here to explore the intricacies of inter-ideological dialogue in itself. I want to look at it, in a limited way, as an integral element of interreligious dialogue. If the ideological dimension of religion is not taken seriously, then interreligious dialogue may be alienating and fruitless in practice; though, limited to a few, it may have a certain meaning at the strictly religious level. One might, of course, wonder whether this is authentic religion.

---

[8] Aloysius Pieris, "The Workers' Mass at a Factory," *Christian Workers' Fellowship* (1997), 107–12.

Religion and Ideology

With reference to religion we seem to have three ideological positions. There are some ideologies that are vigorously *antireligious*. Marxism as interpreted by Lenin and Stalin was antireligious. The secularism or *laicité* of some of the French republicans is also aggressively antireligious. The controversy of the "Islamic scarf" or *hijab* in France in 2003–4 is widely known. While some Muslims see the wearing of the scarf as a religious duty, some French secularists think that allowing the scarf or similar religious symbols (a big cross or the Jewish skull cap or even the Sikh turban) is against secularism. Not all Muslim women across the world see the scarf as a necessary part of their dress. Wearing it, therefore, may be an ideological gesture. On the other hand, forbidding it as a violation of secularism may also be an ideological gesture, since secularism in many other parts of the world would accept, or at least tolerate, individuals using symbols to manifest their religious or other identity.

Other ideologies may be *neutral* with regard to religion. For example, most Christians in Europe today (85–90 percent) are non-practicing. A majority of these are not antireligious. They just ignore religion. But they do have ideological convictions at the social, economic, and political levels. There are also many movements and nongovernmental organizations interested in various projects like human rights, the liberation of women, the defense of indigenous peoples, the protection of the earth, the promotion of the oppressed and marginalized groups of people, like the Dalits, that are not religious. If religious believers have this-worldly goals, like the promotion of justice in all its dimensions, then they cannot ignore this group today. Interreligious dialogue that is limited to religious believers would leave this vast majority outside.

The third kind of ideology includes those that receive *some sort of religious legitimation*. If religions claim to be dialoguing with each other, they cannot ignore these, because these are often the cause of violence between religions. A dialogue with these ideologies may be urgent and even prior to any authentic and fruitful interreligious dialogue. Is it meaningful, for instance, to promote Hindu-Christian dialogue without any reference to the ideology of *Hindutva*, especially when you have reasons to suspect that many of the Hindus who are your dialogue partners have some, at least hidden, sympathy with some of the ideas and goals of *Hindutva*? I am not passing any value judgment here on the ideology of *Hindutva*. I am only saying that we have to engage it in dialogue. A simple condemnation of it is not a dialogical attitude. This may mean that we are limiting our attention either to a small group of fervent Hindus who are in a mode of "public denial" of the extreme acts of *Hindutva* or to a few secular, perhaps non-practicing Hindus. It may be an interesting activity. But it is not socially beneficial and does not meet the goals of interreligious dialogue, since it does not challenge the legitimating aspects of religion. Similarly, we cannot dialogue with Muslims while ignoring some of Islam's ideological elements. We would then be limited to talking to some "secularized" Muslims. This may be interesting and necessary, but it is not enough.

Dialoguing with Ideologies

Dialogue with these three kinds of ideologies will be different. Dialogue with antireligious ideologies should focus on freeing them from their prejudice regarding religion. But this supposes that religion divests itself of any hegemonic intent in society. Dialogue should lead to a development of a secular, democratic order in which religious and ideological pluralism is respected. Such ideologies tend to be philosophical rather than social or economic. In dialoguing with them it is freedom of religion that has to be defended. Freedom of religion would involve not only the liberty to practice the religion privately but also to express and practice the religion socially and publicly without, however, any domination or offense to anyone. Religious freedom in this sense would also include the freedom to hold any ideology.

The focus of dialogue with the second position, an a-religious ideology, would be collaboration in building up a community of freedom, fellowship, and justice. It would be necessary to develop a civil space in which different ideologies can be active and, through dialogue, arrive at common goals and perspectives that the community can pursue, even if each religion and ideology finds inspiration and justification for them in its own tradition.[9] Search for consensus, not at the level of ideology, but at the level of action programs, would be the motive for dialogue. Pluralism of ideologies is respected. The transcendent dimension of religion remains a concern of the believers. But they should try to develop an ideology that would mediate between their religious vision and conviction and the economic and sociopolitical reality of the actual world. Religions may not need to develop totally new ideologies. They may work with existing ideologies but adapt

---

[9] Michael Amaladoss, *Making Harmony: Living in a Pluralist World* (Chennai: IDCR, 2003), 52–53.

them in the context of their own religious and prophetic vision. Any prophetic impact that the religions may have in such a situation is not direct but comes through the ideological options that they have developed as worthy of pursuit in the given situation. The contact with this-worldly ideologies will also be a prophetic challenge to the religions to examine the otherworldly legitimations that they may be offering certain ideologies without much refection and experience in the field. It would also help them realize that they are for life in this world before they focus on life in the other one. Religion becomes a praxis more than a theory or vision of a Transcendent, though the former is rooted in the latter.

Dialoguing with religious ideologies is perhaps the most difficult. At a basic level the dialogue has to make every religion respect the freedom of people to follow any religion of their choice. This will have to start with civil freedom. But at some stage the recognition of other religions as legitimate leads to the respect and acceptance of other religions. This used to be a characteristic of at least some forms of Hinduism. Buddhism has focused on practice, remaining open to different religious visions. Christianity has been going through a process of conversion and reorientation after the Second Vatican Council. I think that Islam has still to begin the process of opening up. An active dialogue with other religions and an authentic knowledge of other believers can certainly help in achieving such openness and in giving up ignorance and prejudice.

Interreligious Dialogue

I think that it is when religious freedom and pluralism are accepted at the social and civil level that dialogue between religions at the metacosmic level becomes socially meaningful. Nothing stops two believers from coming together and dialoguing at the level of belief and experience. But it does not become socially significant in an atmosphere of tension and conflict. I am not, of course, talking of a temporal sequence here. It is possible that dialogues at different levels are taking place simultaneously and are interacting with, challenging, and enriching one another in a creative, meaningful way.

Dialogue of religion at the metacosmic level happens at two levels. At one level the focus is this-worldly. Religions too may interact when different ideologies are interacting at their own level. Religious interaction may be supportive of ideological interaction. In the process their legitimating tendencies may be challenged and their prophetic creativity may be released.

At another level the focus may be otherworldly. In every religious tradition there have been people who have withdrawn from this-worldly involvement and have focused on the pursuit of the other-worldly Transcendent. Some may suggest that this is not authentic religion. But there have been such people in every religious tradition. They may embrace the whole world in their vision. But they are not actively involved in building up a just society and they are not con-cretely opting to struggle with the poor. They have a symbolic value, because the "other world" transcends "this world." They keep remind-ing people that the kingdom of Christ is not of this world. I am think-ing of people like Swami Abhishiktananda, who abandoned even life in an ashram and chose to live alone in a hermitage. He was not out of touch with the world. He quit the hermitage frequently and kept in touch with many people through his contacts and writings. But his pursuit of the advaitic experience was solitary.[10] Such people help us to relativize all ideologies and affirm the many ways of experiencing God. Focused on the Transcendent, they affirm the pluralism and rela-tivity characteristic of life in this world. They play, therefore, a useful, symbolic role. However, focus on his kind of life as authentic religion and his kind of dialogue as the only form of authentic dialogue is to do injustice to religion and to dialogue. Dialogue is more urgent and important in "this world." That is why interreligious dialogue should include inter-ideological dialogue.

Conclusion

I began with my experience in a center for dialogue. I conclude with my experience in the academy. Much of the discussion deals with what are called world religions, which are metacosmic religions. The focus is on "truth," "salvation," and spirituality. The context is "otherworldly." One plays with paradigms like exclusivism-inclusivism-pluralism. One forgets that religion is for life. While the goal may be transcendent, the way to it leads us through "this world." Religions lead us to freedom and liberation in "this world," even if they may find fulfillment only in the "other world." I have consistently used the term *other world*

---

[10] Swami Abhishiktananda, *Ascent to the Depth of the Heart* (Delhi: ISPCK, 1998).

rather than *next world* because the other world is a deeper and transcendent dimension of this world. We may live and share in the "other world" here and now, though our life will continue after death. Any attempt to isolate religion from life should be resisted. One way of avoiding such isolation is precisely to pay attention to and dialogue with ideologies, whether they are part of religions or independent of them. Ideologies will keep us grounded on life and on the earth.

Such a shift in perspective has been taking place in the past few decades. Aloysius Pieris has been playing a pioneering role in this, trying to root religion in life. This explains his search to root the criterion to evaluate religion in the *humanum*, which is in advaitic union with the Transcendent. These should be neither separated nor identified but held in tension. Paul Knitter also has sought to focus on the earth as a common concern of all religions.[11] In a previous book I have drawn attention to the leaders of various religions who have developed the this-worldly and liberative perspectives of their religions.[12] In a phenomenon like the World Social Forum different ideologies come together in dialogue. It is a pity that in this search for an alternative world order the religions do not find a place. This suspicion of the religions can be understood if we look at the past record of religions with regard to their metacosmic focus, or to their opposition to ideologies, or to their supporting religious ideologies. Only a dialogue with ideologies can free the religions from this bind.

Interreligious dialogue is changing both with reference to its focus and to its praxis. Its focus is now life-in-this-world, and its praxis is engaging the various ideologies, religious and nonreligious, that seek to promote that life.

---

[11] Paul Knitter, *One Earth, Many Religions* (Maryknoll, NY: Orbis Books, 1995).

[12] Michael Amaladoss, *Life in Freedom: Liberation Theologies from Asia* (Maryknoll, NY: Orbis Books, 1997).

Chapter 11

Do We Need Borders
between Religions?

A REFLECTION ON IDENTITY
AND DIFFERENCE

In his book *The Clash of Civilizations and the Remaking of World Order*,[1] Samuel Huntington suggests that in the future the world will be divided up according to the dominant civilizations and that world peace will depend upon the ability of these civilizations to tolerate one another and live side by side. He wants the United States to become the center of the Western civilization based on Christianity and renounce any attempts either to become multi-cultural or to impose its own civilization on the rest of the world. What is significant in this vision is not only the division of the world according to civilizations, but the identifying of these civilizations with particular cultures and religions. The West will be Christian, Russia will be Orthodox, South Asia will be Hindu, the East will be Confucian, and the Middle East will be Islamic, leaving on the fringe Africa and Japan.

Such a view of the world that sees conflicts mainly as civilizational (cultural and religious) will certainly be opposed by others who see the reasons for conflict as primarily economic and political and only secondarily and derivatively cultural and religious. These analysts see cultural and religious identity instrumentalized for economic and/or political gain.

---

[1] Samuel Huntington, *The Clash of Civilizations and the Remaking of World Order* (London: Touchstone Books, 1996).

Religious Identities

As we look at the many conflicts around the world today, it is obvious that the causes are always complex. Reductionism in either direction—economic-political or cultural-religious—is not helpful. While economic and political considerations are never absent, we have to recognize that cultural and religious identities also play a role. In Northern Ireland, in the Balkan countries, in the Middle East, in Africa, in South Asia, in Indonesia, and in the Philippines, religions, cultures, and ethnicities contribute to the ongoing conflict. Ethnic and religious tensions exist even in affluent Western Europe and America, though there is no overt conflict. People in this part of the world speak about the problems of multiculturalism. Even in democratic societies people seek to build the unity of the nation around a dominant religious culture. The demands of a religio-cultural nationalism may be explicit and strong in India and Sri Lanka and in the Islamic countries. But they are not absent elsewhere. Christian identity does play a dominant and unifying role in the West. Therefore religious identity is a source of tension and conflict.[2]

In the rest of this chapter I focus upon religious identity. At the same time I suggest that religions need not be causes of conflict. Religious groups do not need to build walls around themselves to protect and defend their identity. They should define their identity positively in terms of what they are and not negatively in terms of what they are not. When they transcend their historical and cultural conditionings to reach out to the Ultimate, they also cross their borders and reach out to other religions as collaborators in a common cosmic project rather than as enemies or rivals.

Respecting Difference

When people speak about community among religions they tend to focus on the lowest common denominators. They say: All religions are the same, or all religions lead to the same God as all rivers lead to the sea. Ramakrishna says that the same water is called by people by different names in different languages. Such a view may seem irenic. But it does not take seriously the differences among religions. It may be true that all religions speak about liberation from evil and

---

[2] Michael Amaladoss, "Difficult Dialogue," *Vidyajyoti, Journal of Theological Reflection* 62 (1998): 567–79; idem, "Dialogue as Conflict Resolution: Creative Praxis," *Vidyajyoti, Journal of Theological Reflection* 63 (1999): 21–36.

sin, peace, detachment, prayer, love of the other, and service. But the frameworks in which these values are talked about are different. Real community must recognize and integrate differences without downplaying them.

Precisely because of such serious differences it is not possible to adopt a superior point of view that talks about and compares the religions from a "higher level." Such a higher level does not exist. Our outlook on the other religions is conditioned by the religion or ideology which we follow. Therefore a higher, neutral point of view is not maintainable. So I am speaking here as a Christian. But I would argue that as a Christian I do not see the need for any borders between religions. Authentic dialogue is a crossing of borders that eventually makes such borders unnecessary. It would be very tempting to look at this theme from a Hindu point of view, given the reputation of Hinduism's tolerance toward other religions. But I would prefer a Hindu to speak about it. The only exception to this principle will be people who claim to be liminal persons, situating themselves on the borders between religions like Hindu-Christians, Buddhist-Christians, and so on.[3] I think that even these people have their roots somewhere, even when they feel free to pass through borders. I do claim to be a Hindu-Christian. But my roots are in Christianity.

I also limit my remarks to the Indian situation. Of course, I do hope that what I have to say will also be applicable to other situations. But it is good to focus one's reflections on a particular historical context, and my context is Indian.

Conflict or Communion?

The Indian multireligious context today offers us two kinds of experiences. The borders between religions seem to be both firm and porous. Let me focus on them.

Analyzing the conflictual situation between Hindus and Muslims in Hyderabad, Sudhir Kakar, an Indian psychoanalyst suggests that religious identity runs deep in the psyche.[4] The child imbibes its

---

[3] Dennis Gira and Jacques Scheuer, eds., *Vivre de Plusieurs Religions: Promesse ou Illusion?* (Paris: L'Atelier, 2000).

[4] Sudhir Kakar, *The Colours of Violence* (New Delhi: Viking, 1995); idem, "Some Unconscious Aspects of Ethnic Violence in India," in *Mirrors of Violence*, ed. Veena Das (Delhi: Oxford University Press, 1990).

socio-religious identity from the family and the wider religious group of which the family is part. This identity is interiorized through the lifecycle and seasonal rituals and festivals. The religious identity is also a social identity. According to Kakar, the child is rooted in this identity firmly by its school-going age. Part of this rooting is emotional and unconscious. Since it deals with ultimate questions, it can be experienced as very deep and mysterious. Because of this it cannot be easily changed by merely rational reflection. When the child meets other children belonging to other religions, they are experienced not merely as different but as inferior. In a conflictual situation, placing oneself on the side of God, the other can easily be demonized. Kakar thinks that the group tends to project onto the other the emotions and attitudes that are not acceptable in oneself.

Such an adversarial relationship tends to get radicalized by historical memory. Where interreligious conflict has become a tradition, everyone will have someone—a father, a mother, a brother, a sister, a son, or a daughter—who has been harmed in earlier encounters and who cries out for revenge. Such suppressed emotions can be unleashed in a moment of mass frenzy, uncontrolled by reason or good sense.

Conflict also leads to ghettoization when people who have been living in mixed colonies seek the security of special areas peopled by members of their own religion. Psychological and mental borders have now become walls that separate one self-defensive group from the other. Even missionaries tend to settle new converts in new colonies around a church or temple or mosque, both to build up their group solidarity and to protect and defend them against hostile neighbors belonging to other religions.

Such a walled-in mentality is behind the movement against conversions led by the *Hindutva* brigade. A change of religious allegiance can be seen not merely as a change of social and political loyalty, but also as a critical comment on the inadequacy of one's own religion to its declared aim of leading people to prosperity in this world and to ultimate liberation.

Side by side with such reinforcing of borders we have other phenomena in which people seem to cross religious borders easily. Pilgrim centers with miraculous powers, like the shrine of our Lady of Health at Vailanganni, shrines of popular Saints like St. Antony of Padua, or prayer services focused on healing, attract people belonging to all religions. Christians too search out ritual specialists like exorcists belonging to other religions. What seems important at these moments is an experience of sacred power that responds to the human need for health and well-being.[5]

Religions are distinguished as cosmic and metacosmic. Cosmic religions find in cosmic powers an explanation for ultimate questions that refer to life's needs, the problems of suffering and evil, and eventually death. Metacosmic religions root these explanations in realities beyond the cosmos. Cosmic religions are normally limited to a particular group of people at a particular place and time. Metacosmic religions, on the contrary, spread across different places and reach out to different peoples and cultures. People have remarked that as metacosmic religions spread, they do not totally displace the local cosmic religions but rather integrate them. This may not be so at the official level. But this is very much so at the poplar level. It is through cosmic religions that metacosmic religions are rooted in a particular people and culture. Where such a rooting is not accepted by the metacosmic religious system, people start independent religious movements or churches. This seems to be a common phenomenon in Africa. Cosmic religiosity is variously forbidden, tolerated, or even accepted by the representatives of metacosmic religions. What is clear from these experiences is that, at least at the popular level, religious borders seem rather porous. Religion has a more functional than an institutional role in life, and people feel free to traverse borders without losing a sense of identity. In many villages the annual festival used to be the affair of the village community and even the members of other religions played a role in celebrating it.

Swami Abhishiktananda was a French Benedictine monk who felt attracted by the advaitic tradition of India and gave himself up to intense *sadhana* to attain a true advaitic experience of the Absolute. The diary of his personal experiences witnesses to his success in achieving an advaitic experience and to his ongoing struggle to reconcile it with his Christian experience. In spite of being an advaitin he was faithful to the Eucharist and to the psalms till his last day. In the last few months of his life he seems to have transcended this tension between his advaitic and his Christian experience, though he does not tell us how. He would certainly call himself a Christian-Hindu.[6] Other Christians have had a similar deep encounter with Buddhism and Taoism.

---

[5] Thomas Bamat and Jean-Paul Wiest, eds., *Popular Catholicism in a World Church* (Maryknoll, NY: Orbis Books, 1999).

[6] Henri Le Saux (Swami Abhishiktananda), *La montée au fond du Coeur* (Paris: O.E.I.L., 1986).

Correspondingly, many Hindus, like Keshub Chandra Sen or Mahatma Gandhi, considered themselves disciples of Jesus Christ, though they did not belong to any of the official churches. Though Brahmabandhab Upadhyay made a distinction between *samaj dharma* (social order), according to which he was a Hindu, and *sadhan dharma* (religious practice), according to which he was a Christian, toward the end of his life he seems to have been a Hindu-Christian at the level of *sadhana*.

These examples show that religious borders seem to be porous, that people can cross over to other religious experiences and integrate them with more or less success without losing their religious identity. This may seem a logical or philosophical impossibility. But it seems possible experientially. One could raise a question whether it is also a theological/religious impossibility. I do not think so. But as a matter of fact, such interreligious experiences will be branded syncretistic by many Christians today. Though there was an integration of Hindu devotionalism in the Islamic Sufi traditions in India, contemporary fundamentalist Islam seeks to "purify" itself of all such extraneous traces. Scholars of the history of religions suggest that the "prophetic" religions, like Judaism, Christianity, and Islam, have more rigid borders than the Eastern "mystic" religions, like Hinduism and Buddhism. While the former focus more on doctrine, the latter pay more attention to practice. Christianity is also heavily institutionalized, so that political factors may come into play in the question of identity and borders.

I have presented above two sets of experiences. In the first, identity seems protected by impermeable borders. In the second, the borders are more porous and permeable. Unfortunately, at the moment religions seem to discourage actively the second type of experiences and strengthen the first type. Hindu temples are keener on forbidding the entry of non-Hindus into the temple. The bhakti tradition in Indian Islam is now discouraged and non-Muslims are excluded from entering Islamic holy places like Nagore. Tamil is being replaced by Arabic as the language of worship and celebration. Festivals in which even members of other religions had a part to play to indicate the community nature of the celebration are now becoming sectarian. I think that this development is due to a wrong appreciation of identity and difference in the field of religion. Religions do not need borders; rather, they are called to dialogue with each other leading to mutual enrichment and collaboration. This is true also with regard to Christianity, which is thought of as one of the religions that tend to have strong boundaries and to exclude others. Interreligious conflicts have their true origin in a misunderstanding of religious identity and the instrumentalization of religions by politics.

Experiencing Identity

I would like to show in the following pages that both at the psycho-sociological and at the theological levels difference in religion need not lead to conflict. I try to do this by analyzing the experience of identity. The identity of persons and groups is not something given, as with material things. Persons and groups construct their identities. They do this not totally creatively from within, but in dialogue with significant others. Therefore, an identity is always in relationship. It is not protected by borders. The presence of borders indicates that the relationship has become unfree and distorted owing to power factors. Let me now unpack these summary statements.[7]

When we look at a thing, we ask what it is. The answer will indicate the elements that it is made of. It may also state the use to which it may be put. Human persons, too, may be instrumentalized or identified as objects. They may be designated by a name or a place in society. They may be described in terms of weight and height, color and shape. These details do not identify them as human persons.

At the other extreme, a person may lose any identity and find his or her roots in the Absolute. When spiritual seekers went to Ramana Maharishi of Tiruvannamalai, he posed them only one question for their reflection: "Who am I?" The search would normally lead the person to transcend all worldly identity to find his or her roots in the Absolute. At the phenomenal level, all that one can say about identity is *neti, neti*—not this, not this. At the moment we are not exploring identities at this depth.

Philosophers may tend to define human identity in terms of what are seen as its special characteristics. The human person is described as a rational animal. At the theological level one could speak of the human person as the image of God. In Christian discourse the human rights tradition is based on the perception that humans are in the image of God. While these descriptions do point to what is human as different from what is nonhuman, they focus on what is common to all human beings. They do not point to particular characteristics that differentiate one person from another. Every human person is born with some basic qualities and capacities that are common to all, like intelligence, emotions, and so on. But a person builds up his or her identity by making use of these capacities while relating to significant others.

---

[7] Though the formulations are my own, I am inspired in what follows by the following two books: Charles Taylor, *Sources of the Self: The Making of Modern Identity* (Cambridge, MA: Harvard University Press, 1989); Alistair I. McFadyen, *The Call to Personhood* (Cambridge: Cambridge University Press, 1990).

Identity in Relationship

As a child grows up, it becomes aware of itself as an individual precisely when it is in communication with others. In this communication it can be the sender or the receiver. But the communication is made possible through the medium of language. Language is not something personal, but social. It belongs to a group. But it is only a means of communication. What is communicated depends on the context. Persons live and become aware of their identity when they respond to others. A multiplicity of such responses cumulatively makes a pattern that determines a particular individual. Being a response to another, it engages the person's freedom and as such acquires a moral connotation. In such a situation of communication there is a mutual recognition of identity. When I am responding to the other, I perceive the other as an "I" who is engaged in freely interacting with me. The other is not an object on which I act. The other is an "I" with whom I interact. My own sense of identity and agency is confirmed when the other acknowledges me as an "I." What marks my identity is not that I am separate from the other. I am different. But I am in a communicational relationship with the other. If I am all alone, there is an identity that is merely material and physical. It becomes human only when it engages another in interaction. I become what I am in response to another. The interaction, to be authentic, must be mutual. Interpersonal communication therefore involves a "co-intending."

Such interpersonal interaction may not always be symmetrical. The relationship between a mother and her child is not symmetrical. Sometimes a person may interact with a group of elders. When there is freedom on both sides, such asymmetrical interactions lead to personal growth and strengthen identity.

Such an experience of identity does not suppose borders. The identity has roots in the person. But it becomes real and actualized precisely in the relationship of interaction. The interaction is a true dialogue: two people talking to each other. There is a free passage in both directions. There are two poles in a dynamic interrelationship.

Distorted Relationship

Unfortunately, relationship between two persons is not always of this ideal kind. It can be distorted in various ways. It can be antagonistic. The communication is negative. Rather, there is no real communication at all. The other is simply an object to whom one does not relate at all. One seeks to build walls around oneself to avoid any kind of contact. The walls need not be material, of course. But they can be emotional, linguistic (use of special codes, for instance, for communication), ideological, and even physical.

The relationship between persons can also be one of domination. One enslaves the other. The domination can be economic, political, or social. In the caste system the other is seen as a servant. In this case the communication is one-sided. The person who dominates is protected by a wall in terms of purity/status, riches, or power. The other is less than human. In such a situation one cannot really speak of a human, personal identity. It is an imposed identity. It is like a label that can be peeled off. There is no real communication. The people who are oppressed can assert their personhood. But this is not done by building walls around themselves to protect their "identity" behind a secure border. They have to assert their agency and freedom and force the other to acknowledge them and dialogue with them. That is to say, they assert their true identity precisely by breaking down the barriers and walls that exclude them and by relating to their dominators as equals. The restoration of their identity will not be complete till they are recognized as equals in a mutual relationship.

The presence of borders, therefore, indicates a distorted relationship. Such distortions are all too real in the world. But their reality and frequency are not to be taken as the norm to understand the nature of personal identity.

Group Identities

I have been talking so far about personal identity in a group. I have tried to show how it is built up in the context of free, communicational relationships with others. These principles regarding the formation and exercise of identity are also true with regard to groups. In the normal course of events, an individual is necessarily socialized into a group in the process of becoming an adult person. Inter-human relationships are inevitable. But the relationship between groups is not necessary. Tribal groups keep mostly to themselves. They may have economic contact with outsiders. They tend to limit social contact to the members of the group. But migrations of peoples and interactions among groups have been common in the course of history. Social scientists talk about these questions in their discussions on multiculturalism in many contemporary societies.[8]

When two groups interact, one group may tend to impose its identity on the other. Insofar as this action is successful, the dominated group loses its separate identity. It gets absorbed in the other group. Its culture and language as separate identities disappear. Some vestiges may remain as folklore. Some elements may be absorbed by the dominant group. The process of absorption may be tense or peaceful. There is no question of borders here.

In a second scenario there is again a relationship of domination between two groups. One is dominant, and the other is afraid of losing its identity. But in this scenario it seeks to protect itself. The tendency is to build walls around itself in order to safeguard its identity. But walls can only aggravate the problem, leading to conflict rather than harmony.

In a third scenario the groups interact with each other peacefully. There is a process of dialogue. There is mutual interaction. They retain their identity. But they grow and modify themselves as they succeed in living together. Their identity is dynamic. They do not need boundaries to protect themselves.

The ideal is that every group is recognized and accepted. The strategy, once again, is not to protect a dominated group by walls and borders, but to promote mutual relationship that is nonthreatening and nonreductive. Just as persons relate to one another in the context of a community that transcends them and integrates them, different groups can dialogue with one another only in the context of a wider unity. The principle of this unity today would be political and national. Different cultural groups relate to one another precisely because they share common economic and political interests as part of a nation. Underlying these common interests are a common territory that they inhabit and a common history that has brought them together.

Religious Identities

We have seen that authentic personal identity, while rooted in the person, reaches out to the other. It is in relationship that it emerges and grows. Borders are not necessary to protect identities, except when

---

[8] Amy Gutmann, ed., *Multiculturalism* (Princeton, NJ: Princeton University Press, 1994); David Theo Goldberg, ed., *Multiculturalism: A Critical Reader* (Oxford: Blackwell, 1994).

the relationship is distorted by factors of power. When such borders do come up, then the identity itself is distorted. It can become authentic again only when it can free itself from the domination of power and learn to dialogue with the other in freedom and creativity. In a community, identity and difference suppose each other dialectically. Borders do not help this dynamic tension but destroy it. Identity then becomes static. Borders, therefore, are not necessary in human and social relationships.

We can now apply these principles to the problem of religious identities and conflicts. We have seen above that religions-in-conflict seem to thrive on borders. On the other hand, there are people who feel free to pass to and fro from one religious tradition and another. I think that religious identity does not need borders to define and defend it. On the other hand, it can be enriched through dialogue with other religions.

In contrast to group identities like culture and ethnicity, religious identity is based on a relationship with God or the Ultimate. The social context in which religious identity is affirmed is not merely the interrelationships among the people who make up the social group, but their collective relationship to a self-revealing God or Ultimate. The collectivity of their relationship does not in any way restrict the personal identity and relationship each one has in relation to God or the Ultimate. Each one's identity is finally determined by the free interplay of divine call and human response as it happens in the life of every person.

When different religions meet, they are experienced as a threat to each other usually when their relationship is distorted by political factors. But, as we have seen, sometimes the religions see others as not merely different but as enemies at the religious level itself. I hope that my analysis of personal and group identity above can show that difference need not be a denial of identity. On the contrary, difference can be a source of enrichment for one's identity, without in any way being detrimental to it. One could say further that difference is even necessary to highlight one's identity more sharply.

The Divine Economy

An interplay of identities is possible only when there is a common context. I think that this is what is missing in our approach to other religions. (Here I would like to speak as a Christian, leaving the members of other religions to speak for themselves.) It has become traditional to classify Christianity's attitude to other religions as exclusivism, inclusivism, or pluralism. Exclusivism refuses all relationship because the others are not even recognized as real religions. Inclusivism affirms a distorted relationship of domination, reducing other religions to an inferior position. Pluralism affirms difference that does not require, much less demand, a relationship. What we need, I think, is an affirmation of community that does not negate but integrates different identities.

From a Christian point of view this demands a twofold attitude. We have to accept, first of all, that divine-human encounter is happening in each religion. I think that this is being accepted more and more today. The recognition of the presence and action of the Spirit of God in every religion (RM 28) assures us of the divine-human encounter in them and enables us to respect the freedom both of humans and of the Spirit.

Second, all religions belong to one common plan of God, the same divine economy of salvation. This supposes that they are in some way mutually interrelated and interdependent. Here we move beyond mere pluralism. We also destroy all the borders between them that may have been constructed by shortsighted humans, while affirming the different identity of each religion. Such interdependence is not merely affirmed a priori. It has to be experienced and be made operative through dialogue.

At the moment, however, this view of the divine economy of salvation is not yet very common in the official circles of the church.[9] The divine economy is still seen in a unilinear fashion. All the religions are seen as preparations for Christianity, which comes as their fulfillment. Christianity, therefore, once present, simply replaces them. This view has to be challenged. The Bible is the narrative of God's self-revelation to a particular people, namely, the Jews. God becomes a visible and human part of this story in Jesus Christ. But this does not authorize Christians to judge the extent and depth of God's action in other religions, especially because the self-manifestation of the Word in Jesus was kenotic or self-emptying. The church claims to respect the freedom of the Spirit of God active in other religions and the freedom of humans responding to the Spirit. If this is true, then the authentic Christian attitude is to bow down before the mystery of God's presence and action and seek to comprehend at least some aspects of it in humility, dialogue, and contemplation. We are entitled

---

[9] See Congregation for the Doctrine of the Faith, *Dominus Iesus* (August 6, 2000).

to witness before the world how God has been prodigal in God's self-manifestation to us. We have no right to presume to judge how God has been active in the lives of others, though we can permit ourselves a certain appreciation of the fruits of holiness that we see in them. There is no high ground from which we can look down on and compare all the religions. We do not experience them from within. We possess no criteria to evaluate their merits and demerits except as outsiders. Since we believe that God is the common origin and goal of all peoples, we can affirm a priori a mutual interdependence and convergence in the working out of the divine economy of salvation. But we can discover and appreciate the details only a posteriori, through listening to the others in whom God is present and active.

Conclusion

Dialogue and collaboration is the way of actualizing this interdependence and mutuality. We appreciate the identity of all religions, and we celebrate their call to community. Borders have no place here. They are not needed. We do not transcend borders. We should rather try to pull down the borders that have been put up by people either as an expression of their own uncertainties and fears or as a manifestation of ulterior economic and/or political motives.

Religious conversion will then be seen, not as crossing borders, but as answering a special call of God. Religions can start dismantling some of the institutional structures that were thought necessary to protect their identities. We could be more sympathetic to people who claim liminal identities as Hindu-Christian or Christian-Buddhist. We could appreciate the creative integration of popular religiosity and be more sparing of accusations of syncretism. We could be more accommodative of differences within the church and be less quick in excommunicating dissenters, that is to say, sending them outside the borders.

Living in an interdependent religious world without borders, we could look for a metaphysical foundation that would see reality itself, not as a monad or a collection of monads, but as inter-being—a mutually dependent network of beings.[10] "To be" is to be in relationship in all directions. In such a dynamic network of beings, who needs borders?

---

[10] See Thich Nhat Hanh, *Interbeing* (Berkeley and Los Angeles: Parallax Press, 1993). I am not developing this relational ontology here. One can root it both in Buddhist and advaitic thought.

Chapter 12

Double Religious Identity

A REFLECTION
FROM AN INDIAN EXPERIENCE

In many parts of the world today people are fighting and dying to affirm and defend their religious identity as the deepest element of their personhood. People also seem to feel that in order to assert their identity they have to oppose or degrade the identity of the other. There is an element of fundamentalism here. They see these identities also as socially conflictual, because religion is also used to weld a group of people together into a political force. In such a situation, getting people of different religious identities to live together in peace is already a great challenge. Speaking then of double religious identity may seem either an academic or a provocative exercise.[1]

On the other hand, in my Indian city, Chennai, if I walk on a Tuesday to the Church of St. Antony, there will be long queues of people to honor him and seek favors from early morning to late at night. I am sure that half of them are members of other religions. In my own parish in a small town, on feast days like Christmas, there may be more than a thousand people at the Eucharist. Among them, fifty to one hundred may belong to other religions. In spite of official public announcements, many of them will walk up for communion with great

---

[1] I have treated this topic earlier. See Michael Amaladoss, "Double Religious Belonging and Liminality," *Vidyajyoti, Journal of Theological Reflection* 66 (2001): 21–34. See also Dennis Gira and Jacques Scheur, eds., *Vivre de plusieurs religions: Promesse ou illusion?* (Paris: L'Atelier, 2000); Catherine Cornille, ed., *Many Mansions: Multiple Religious Belonging and Christian Identity* (Maryknoll, NY: Orbis Books, 2002); Peter C. Phan, "Multiple Religious Belonging: Opportunities and Challenges for Theology and Church," *Theological Studies* 64 (2003): 495–518.

devotion. If we dismiss these experiences as popular religiosity, let me evoke a list of serious scholars. Keshub Chandra Sen (1838–84) and Mahatma Gandhi (1869–1948) would have considered themselves Christian-Hindus. Brahmabandhab Upadhyay (1861–1907), Swami Abhishiktananda (1910–73), and Vandana Mataji would have thought of themselves as Hindu-Christians. Raimon Panikkar has written: "I 'left' as a Christian, I 'found' myself a Hindu, and I 'return' a Buddhist, without having ceased to be a Christian."[2] I am only evoking well-known names who have written about their experiences. We have no time here to go into their detailed stories.

Familiarity with such experiences already answers one of the questions evoked in the title of this chapter—Is double religious identity possible?—in the affirmative, at least partially. Of course, we will have to understand how this is possible. This is what I try to do in this chapter. I am not raising an abstract question. I am attempting to understand an experience with which I am familiar as an Indian and as a Christian.

Identity and Belonging

I should also make clear at the very beginning that I am speaking of *double religious identity* and not *double religious belonging.* Identity is something personal. Belongingness involves a community or institution to which a person belongs. A community may excommunicate a person. I want to distance myself from such a focus on the institution and concentrate rather on the individual and his or her experience. Of course, one cannot cut off an individual from a community. Humans are social beings. But an individual's link to a community takes various forms and can be more or less close. So I would like to look at this link from the individual's side and not from the side of the community. Besides, my belonging to a community determines my identity only secondarily, especially at the religious level. I am a Christian primarily because I am believer in and a follower of Christ, not because I belong to a church.[3] As a matter of fact, we have a variety of churches around. I can even start my own church. Institutional identity becomes

---

[2] Raimon Panikkar, *The Intrareligious Dialogue* (New York: Paulist Press, 1978), 2.

[3] See Raimon Panikkar, "On Christian Identity," in Cornille, *Many Mansions*, 121–44.

secondary in religion because I relate to the Transcendent. Religious identity is more fluid in religions like Hinduism and Buddhism that do not have a strong institutional base or clear borders. For example, Gandhi was a Hindu. But it would be difficult, if not impossible, to place him with any known group of Hindus. He felt free to interpret and live Hinduism in his own way.

Religion and Culture

When I am speaking of double identity, I am not referring to the process of inculturation. As an Indian Christian I can express my faith in an Indian language and culture. But culture is closely linked to religion. In a predominantly Hindu context, the terms I use to express my Christian faith may have a Hindu resonance. For example, some of us use the syllable *OM* as part of our prayer. But we give it a Christian meaning, seeing it as a symbol of the Trinity manifested by its sound structure: $a + u + m$. Hindus themselves would admit that it is a sound symbol of the Absolute, prior to any particular determinations that could be called Hindu. The symbol is also used by Buddhists. I am not a Hindu-Christian because I pray in an Indian language, even if some of the words are also used by Hindus in their own religious context. Such a freedom to reinterpret does not extend to symbols that are associated with a religion's historical-mythical structure. For instance, Christians would not feel free to use symbols like Rama and Krishna.

Cosmic and Metacosmic Religions

By double identity I do not mean what one may call cosmic-metacosmic religious integration. Aloysius Pieris has distinguished between cosmic religion that remains at the level of cosmic forces and metacosmic soteriologies that reach out to metacosmic principles or forces. He suggests that metacosmic religions, as they spread across different areas, do not do away totally with the local cosmic religion, but adjust themselves to it and integrate it at a lower level. This is particularly noticeable at the level of popular religiosity. When people in search of healing, for example, seem to have no problem crossing cosmic religious boundaries, visiting shrines or ritual specialists, I think that there is an element of double religiosity involved that cannot be easily dismissed as syncretism. Sometimes people speak of this as parallel religiosity.

Religious Identity

How do we determine religious identity? Pieris analyzes religious structure in terms of three levels: the core or foundational or *primordial experience* that is at the origins of a religion; the *collective memory* that stores up that experience in texts, symbols, rituals, and beliefs which help to evoke and relive that experience; and the *interpretation* of that experience in philosophical and theological terms.[4] To these I would add the *institutionalization* that is evolved to protect and transmit the collective memory, including the official interpretation. People attracted to a religion may use aspects of collective memory to reach out to the primordial experience while distancing themselves from the institutional framework.[5] For example, Gandhi read the New Testament and sang hymns to the crucified Christ without submitting himself to the sacramental discipline of any of the churches.[6] One cannot be a Christian without somehow getting to know and committing oneself to Christ. But does one need to be linked to an institution? In India, K. Subba Rao (1912–81) claimed to have had a vision of Christ and became his disciple without any links to any of the known Christian churches. He refused such links. He has a group of followers.[7]

Speaking of mystical experiences, sometimes commentators suggest that the core experience is the same, though it is differently interpreted and explained by different religious traditions. But it seems more likely that persons engaging in mystical forms of prayer do so following a particular tradition. This conditions not only their practice, but also their attitudes and mental-spiritual framework, and finally their experience.[8] A Canadian Christian doing Zen in Korea, for example, claims to have experienced Jesus arising out of the emptiness of Zen.[9]

---

[4] Aloysius Pieris, *Love Meets Wisdom: A Christian Experience of Buddhism* (Maryknoll, NY: Orbis Books, 1988), 120.

[5] Pieris calls this *communicatio in sacris* (see ibid., 122–23).

[6] Panikkar distinguishes more simply between *faith*, which is personal commitment, and *beliefs*, which are rational expressions and explanations of faith (*The Intrareligous Dialogue*, 17–22).

[7] See H. L. Richard, *Exploring the Depths of the Mystery of Christ: K. Subba Rao's Eclectic Praxis of Hindu Discipleship to Jesus* (Pasadena, CA: William Carey Library, 2005); Herbert E. Hoefer, *Churchless Christianity* (Pasadena, CA: William Carey Library, 2001).

[8] See Livia Kohn, *Meditation Works in the Hindu, Buddhist, and Daoist Traditions* (Magdalena, NM: Three Pines Press, 2008), 2.

[9] See Bernard Senécal, *Jésus le Christ à la rencontre de Gautama le Bouddha* (Paris: Cerf, 1998).

If specifying an identity is so complicated, how do we envisage double identity? Trying to understand the interactions among religions, Pieris speaks of three kinds: syncretism, synthesis, and symbiosis. When elements of two systems are thrown together in some unsystematic way, characterized only by the preference or convenience of a person or a group, it is *syncretism.* What is called New Age is said to be syncretistic. Syncretists are people who are searching for an identity.[10] People who are intellectual may try to bring two religious systems together and integrate them in an original, systematic way, giving birth to a third system. Such a process is called *synthesis.* And sometimes there is an interaction at the level of collective memory. One tries to understand the other from within on his or her own terms. Pieris describes this as *symbiosis.*[11] It is collaboration in common liberative action, rooted in one's own religious tradition but in dialogue with others. I think that we cannot yet call this double religious identity. What is it then? Let us explore briefly the experience of Swami Abhishiktananda.

Swami Abhishiktananda

Abhishiktananda was a Benedictine monk who came to India to witness to the contemplative dimension of Christianity, hoping to attract Hindus to it.[12] His first book, *Saccidananda,*[13] started with the advaitic or nondual experience of Ramana Maharishi and tried to show that it can find fulfillment in the Christian trinitarian experience. But as he himself got deeper into the advaitic experience, he was no longer able to see it as a preparation for the Trinitarian experience but as different. He was not able to integrate them intellectually, and perhaps also at the level of *sadhana* or spiritual practice. Sometimes he seemed to think that the advaitic experience was beyond all "name and form," that is, all religious determinations, without necessarily rejecting them. When his disciple Marc was initiated into renunciation or *sannyasa,*

---

[10] Syncretism is an accusation easily thrown at people claiming double religiosity. For clarification, see Chapter 14 in this book, "From Syncretism to Harmony," as well as my earlier essay, "Syncretism and Kenosis: Hermeneutical Reflections in the Indian Context," in *The Agitated Mind of God*, ed. Dale T. Irwin and Akintunde E. Akinade, 57–72 (Maryknoll, NY: Orbis Books, 1996).

[11] Aloysius Pieris, *Fire and Water* (Maryknoll, NY: Orbis Books, 1996), 161.

[12] For what follows, see Abhishiktananda's diary, *Ascent to the Depth of the Heart* (Delhi: ISPCK, 1998).

[13] Abhishiktananda, *Saccidananda*, 2nd ed. (Delhi: ISPCK, 1997).

he celebrated it as a joint initiation given by him together with a Hindu guru, Swami Chidananda, the head of Sivananda ashram at Rishikesh.[14] After a heart attack some months before his death, which seems to have been also a moment of advaitic experience, he gained inner peace. I think that he had come to realize that both the Hindu and the Christian ways were leading to the same Absolute. He affirmed his experience of oneness beyond all name and form. But this did not prevent him from continuing to read the Upanishads or celebrate the Eucharist. He could move from one to the other form of experience without attempting an artificial integration.[15] I would even say that reversing his original perspective he interpreted Christianity from an advaitic point of view. The question that we should ask with reference to Abhishiktananda is not whether the Christian and/or Hindu community or institution thought that he belonged to it, but rather what identity he himself experienced.

I have so far tried to clarify the terms of our discourse and point to people who experience double religious identity. So, at a practical level such an identity seems possible. How can we understand this theologically? But before exploring this, I would like to distance myself from a recent paradigm in the theology of religions.

A Recent Paradigm

We are aware of the recent paradigm: exclusivism-inclusivism-pluralism. The starting point is that religion brings salvation. If I think that Christianity alone is salvific, then I am an exclusivist. If I assert that salvation is primarily found in Christianity, but that it is also accessible to others insofar as Christ is found in hidden and limited ways in other religions, then I am an inclusivist. If I maintain that all religions are salvific, then I am a pluralist. Gavin D'Costa suggests that inclusivists and even pluralists are really exclusivist, insofar as they pretend that the other religions are salvific, but on their own terms.[16] People like Jacques Dupuis are classified as "pluralist inclusivists."[17] I think that

---

[14] Abhishiktananda has explained this in *The Further Shore*, 2nd ed. (Delhi: ISPCK, 1984).

[15] See Shirley du Boulay, *The Cave of the Heart: The Life of Swami Abhishiktananda* (Maryknoll, NY: Orbis Books, 2005), 229–42; Odette Baumer-Despeigne, "Cheminement spiritual d'Henri Le Saux. Textes inédits," *La vie spirituelle* 144 (1990): 531–43.

[16] See Gavin D'Costa, *The Meeting of Religions and the Trinity* (Maryknoll, NY: Orbis Books, 2000).

[17] See Phan, "Multiple Religious Belonging," 504.

this paradigm is inadequate to explore a theology of religions. It is an abstract logical exercise that equates religion with the way to salvation and then evokes different logical possibilities in a situation where there are many religions. It is a rational, essentialist, and philosophical view, not a theology. It claims to have exhausted all logical possibilities with its types so that, if you are doing theology of religion, you must belong to one type. The cases of D'Costa and Dupuis show that the logical distinctions are not adequate. I also know many Asian theologians who refuse to use these categories.[18]

A Theology of Divine-Human Encounter

I think that what we need is not a theology of religions but one of God salvifically reaching out to people in various ways. We can call it a theology of divine-human encounter that focuses on God and humans, trying to reach out to each other. Theology, after all, is about God, not about religions. Let us look at this encounter, first, from God's point of view and then from that of humans.

I think that all would agree that *it is God who saves, not the religions.* The whole discussion whether religions are salvific or not seem misplaced. God can save people with or without religion. When the primordial experience of divine-human encounter finds expression in human and historical terms, it does so in text, symbol, ritual, and institution that constitute a religion. This is true also of Christianity. What exactly is the role of such a religion in the salvific divine-human encounter? Can it be called a mediation? No, if the term *mediation* is used in a strong sense, as when we say that Jesus Christ is the mediator. The church is not comparable to Jesus Christ. But the Latin, as different from the Greek tradition, sacralizes and absolutizes its ministers and sacraments by use of formulas like "I absolve you!" and by claims that speak of "divine right" for its ministerial and sacramental structures. In this way some religious groups tend to attribute to themselves the absoluteness of God.[19] This is what we call today fundamentalism. The primary agent of salvation is God, and it is to God that a person responds in freedom with or without the symbolic

---

[18] See Michael Amaladoss, *Making Harmony: Living in a Pluralist World* (Delhi: ISPCK, 2003), 134–37. I can mention Aloysius Pieris and Felix Wilfred.

[19] For such an absolutization of religion and the culture of its first self-expression, see C. Cornille, "Double Religious Belonging: Aspects and Questions," *Buddhist-Christian Studies* 23 (2003): 43–49. Compare with this the view of Claude Geffré, "Double Belonging and the Originality of Christianity as a Religion," in Cornille, *Many Mansions,* 100–101.

structures provided by a religion. *Facilitation* may be too weak a word to indicate the role of religious structures. Expression and *celebration of a mystery* may be more adequate, but these should not be identified with the mystery. A further point is that divine-human encounter may take place in secular, nonreligious settings, when, for instance, a Christian encounters Christ in the poor and the marginalized (cf. Matt 25).

God reaches out salvifically to every human being. The Second Vatican Council, in *Gaudium et Spes (Pastoral Constitution on the Church in the Modern World)*, affirms this, though it adds "in a way known to God" (GS 22; see also AG 2). But John Paul II, in his encyclical *Redemptoris Missio*, accepting that the Spirit of God is present and active in all cultures and religions (RM 28), implies that these "unknown" ways of God may actually correspond to the various cultures and religions. Where God is present and relating to humans God's presence and action are salvific. We cannot quantify God's presence or salvation in the various religions.

We believe that God is one and has one plan for the universe. While God may call and reach out to people in various ways, the goal to which all are called is one. Paul tells the Corinthians, the Ephesians, and the Colossians that God's plan is to gather all things together until God is "all in all" (1 Cor 15:28; Eph 1:3–10; Col 1:18–20). Paul also refers to this goal as the "fullness of Christ." But this fullness is eschatological and in the future, not in the past. In the meantime God is working with people in various ways, not only through the mediation of Jesus and the church, but also through other "participated mediations," as John Paul II suggests (RM 5). This means that humans are collaborators with God and with one another in realizing God's one plan for the universe. Paul indicates to the Romans that this gathering includes also creation (Rom 8:22).

God is Absolute. But God's self-manifestations and human responses are conditioned by human, historical, and cultural limitations. At this level there is a legitimate pluralism. Such pluralism is enriching and is not relativism in the sense that humans create their own truth, conditioned by their limited circumstances, in relation to an unknowable Absolute that they are searching for.

In reaching out to humans, *God is free to manifest and communicate Godself to them in any way God likes. To this divine freedom corresponds the human freedom to respond creatively.* This interaction is lived in the person and in the human community and the world before being symbolically celebrated in religious ritual. Otherwise the ritual will be meaningless. God and humans can use any appropriate means to reach out to each other. We could even say that God graciously adapts God's way to the conditions and desires of humans searching for a God-experience. Francis Clooney quotes a beautiful song of Andal, a ninth-century Tamil devotee, who considers herself the bride of Vishnu and goes to his temple for the betrothal. To her friends, who laugh at her pretensions of being God's own bride, she says:

> Whichever form pleases his people, that is his form;
> Whichever name pleases his people, that is his name;
> Whichever way pleases his people who meditate
>   without ceasing,
>   that is his Way,
> That one who holds the discus.[20]

Clooney shows that this is not only Andal's personal view but belongs to the tradition of the community. He compares this to a similar perspective in St. Ignatius of Loyola. In the contrary direction God is also free to manifest Godself to people in any way and to the extent that God chooses, though God will consider the human, historical, and cultural conditions of the people to whom God relates. This interaction of divine and human freedom is affirmed even today in the freedom of the individual conscience.

The Human Pole

We can now move to the other pole of the encounter, namely, humans. *God may call people in various ways. But I am committed to the way in which God has called me.* It is a special vocation—a choice made, not by me, but by God. For me God is the Absolute for whom I am searching. But God has also spoken and has called me in a particular way. The world, then, is not a supermarket of religions where I can go around choosing my favorite brand or a bar where I can make my own salad with various ingredients. But this does not prevent me from being open to the ways in which God has called others and learning from them. What God has manifested to the other is not totally irrelevant to me. On the contrary, I am called to dialogue with others in view of collaborating toward the realization of God's plan for the universe, which is to gather all things together.

---

[20] Francis X. Clooney, "God for Us: Multiple Religious Identities as a Human and Divine Prospect," in Cornille, *Many Mansions*, 45.

While I can positively witness to the wondrous ways in which God has been active in me and in my community, I cannot arrogantly presume to judge the presence and action of God in other people a priori, especially setting my own experience as the criterion and norm. It is a mystery between God and the other. I can learn from them by listening to them speaking of their experience. I can also judge their claims, but by the fruits of their behavior, not in terms of my own experience. Their experience may be very different from mine. Comparing the different ways—God's ways, not human ways—I should use terms like convergence rather than complementarity, which has a static, quantitative connotation. Normally, the different experiences cannot be contradictory, since God is one, though I should not jump to such a conclusion before a careful examination and dialogue.[21]

As a matter of fact, most religions, while affirming their own particular God-experience, acknowledge the fact that God reaches out to all peoples. I offer here only some brief indications. John affirms a universal perspective when he says that "the true light, which enlightens everyone, was coming into the world" (John 1:9). Reflecting in the context of God's covenants, Paul says: "God will render to every man according to his works. . . . There will be glory and honor and peace for everyone who does good, the Jew first, but also the Greek. For God shows no partiality" (Rom 2:6, 11). In the *Bhagavad Gita* Krishna tells Arjuna: "In whatever way men approach me, in the same way they receive their reward" (4:11). "Even those who, devoted to other Gods, sacrifice filled with faith, even they sacrifice to me alone" (9:23). The Virashaiva poet Basavanna of the twelfth century says: "God is but one, but many his names. The faithful wife knows but one Lord" (613). The Qur'an says: "To each of you God has prescribed a Law and a Way. If God would have willed, He would have made you a single people. But God's purpose is to test you in what he has given each of you, so strive in the pursuit of virtue, and know that you will all return to God (in the Hereafter), and He will resolve all the matters in which you disagree" (5:49; cf. 11:118). The Sufi master Jalal ud-Din Rumi says: "Ways of worshiping are not to be ranked as better or worse than one another. Hindus do Hindu things. The Dravidian Muslims in India do what they do. It is all praise, and it's all right. . . . Though the ways are various, the goal is one. Do you not see that there are

---

[21] See my discussion in Chapter 3 of this book, "Which Is the True Religion? Searching for Criteria."

many roads to the Kaaba?" Buddhism looks on all religions as "skill-ful means" or *upaya*.

A Christian Perspective

For a Christian, God is trinitarian. *God, the Word, and the Spirit are present and active in history. God becomes incarnate in Jesus Christ to launch the final, eschatological stage in the realization of God's plan in history. But God continues to be active in the major-ity of humanity through other participated mediations.* Christian theologians can continue to discuss how they can reconcile, to their own satisfaction, this fact of experience with their belief in Christ being the only savior.[22] We do not have to take a position on this here to accept the fact that today God is reaching out to humans "in many and various ways" (Heb 1:1). In ecclesiological terms there is widespread acceptance today that the reign of God is wider than the church. Wherever God is present and active, there is God's reign. Not only the church, but other religions too belong to this reign. The church may claim a special relationship to the reign of God. But it is the service role of a sacrament, that is to say, being symbol and servant. One of the services that it can do is precisely to help bring all things and peoples together according to the plan of God, without pushing itself forward.

It is from this point of view *of promoting collaboration among peoples of all religions that God seems to call some people to be on the borders between different religious communities, showing in their lives not some abstract idiosyncratic integration, but community-in-difference.* I am a committed Christian or Hindu. But my situation and my experience may lead me to become aware that, while my way is adequate to help me to encounter God, it is also humanly, culturally, and historically limited. I may feel called, not to abandon my way, but to explore also other ways through which divine-human encounter can happen. Such people may be called *liminal* people, on the borders, but showing possible ways of being together in God's presence. Such exploration may be a means of bringing people of different religions to live and work together while remaining loyal to their own religious tradition. In the process one's own experience of God is enriched. Mystic experience need not be the only level at which this can be done.

---

[22] See Michael Amaladoss, "Other Religions and the Salvific Mystery of Christ," *Vidyajyoti, Journal of Theological Reflection* 70 (2006): 8–23.

People can also live, pray, and work together, not only formally, but normally and intimately.

Double Religious Identity in Practice

Double religious identity, therefore, is also possible theologically. It may be God's call at least for some people. How can it be really practiced? Once again I do not wish to speak in the abstract, but to refer to actual practices in India. I refer to three of them here: reading the scriptures of other religions, using methods of prayer from other religious traditions, and praying and worshiping together.

In 1974, Indian theologians had a seminar to discuss whether we can consider the scriptures of other religions as inspired. Their answer was yes. Their theological foundation was the idea of three covenants, namely, cosmic or natural, Judaic, and Christian. They even suggested that on a Sunday we could have three readings on the same theme from the three covenants, showing a progression. Collections of texts were made from other religious scriptures. But the practice was disallowed in official liturgy, though it forms part of prayer services in many ashrams and in private piety even today.[23] We have Jesuits who preach eight-day retreats based on the *Bhagavad Gita*. Contemporary theology of religions would further strengthen the arguments supporting these practices. We can distinguish two ways of doing this: a Christian, individually or in community reading the scriptures of other religions and interpreting them in the Christian context, as we do, for example, with the Judaic scriptures; and a multireligious community reading together the scriptures of different religions searching for common inspiration and prayer. Both are happening today and are spiritually nourishing people.

Many Christians in India (and elsewhere) are serious practitioners of Hindu and Buddhist methods of meditation like Yoga, Vipassana (insight meditation), and Zen. There was a time when one spoke of Christian Yoga and Christian Zen. There is not much talk about them today. A condemnation of such practices by the Congregation for the Doctrine of the Faith twenty years ago (1989) does not seem to be hindering any one. Zen masters have authenticated the Zen experience of their Christian disciples. Zen and Yoga are not just physical and

---

[23] See D. S. Amalorpavadass, ed., *Research Seminar on Non-Biblical Scriptures* (Bangalore: NBCLC, 1974); my discussion in Chapter 4 of this book, "The Scriptures of Other Religions: Are They Inspired?"

psychological techniques. There is a worldview and anthropology behind them that is different from the Greco-Roman view that underlies traditional Christian practice. The Christian practitioners of Yoga and Zen whom I know seem to feel no crisis of identity.

In 1987, Indian theologians also had a seminar on sharing worship. Once again they were positive. Their argument was that God is one and can be worshiped in various symbolic ways. At that time I objected to this argument, saying that symbols belong to a community and its history and that this sociohistorical dimension should not be ignored. Scandalizing weak believers also used to be a strong argument against such practice. But reflecting later in the context of inviting other religious believers to participate in the Eucharist, I realized that what are important are a basic faith in what is being done and a sense of fellowship with the community that is doing it.[24] This experience of community need not be institutional. In India the traditional Hindus do not have a strong sense of borders. We also come across people who are believers in Christ, but who do not wish to join the Christian community for sociological reasons.[25] People who are engaged in a common social project or in regular dialogue and prayer sessions may develop a sense of community that transcends religious borders. I have been at many interreligious prayer meetings in India where we have not merely come together to pray, but have prayed together.

I would like to suggest again that the focus here is not belongingness to a community, which is a sociological category, but identity, which I define primarily in terms of a person's relation to God and to others in the presence of God. Let us go back to the four levels of religion that we have distinguished above. At the institutional level, I cannot belong to two religious institutions at the same time. At the level of interpretation, I am free to interpret at least some common religious symbols like *OM*. At the level of collective memory, I think that a temporary presence to another community is possible on the occasion of a collective experience of community during an interreligious event or during common prayer or collaborative action over a longer period, or at a common symbolic celebration. At the personal level, I think that God is open to any symbols and ways that I use to reach out to God, though there would be a preference for me to the

---

[24] See Paul Puthanangady, ed., *Sharing Worship: Communicatio in Sacris* (Bangalore: NBCLC, 1988); Michael Amaladoss, "Eucharistic Hospitality," in *Beyond Dialogue: Pilgrims to the Absolute* (Bangalore: Asian Trading Corporation, 2008), 79–98.

[25] See Richard, *Exploring the Depths of the Mystery of Christ*; Hoefer, *Churchless Christianity.*

particular way in which God has called me. But by calling me to encounter other believers God may also be calling me to cross symbolic
boundaries occasionally.[26]

Is Double Identity Necessary?

So I now come to these questions: Is double religious identity possible?
I know many people who live it. Is it necessary? One can live and die
happily in a particular religion. Every religion is adequate to reach its
goals. But sometimes there are people who feel called to cross religious
boundaries in pursuit of the Absolute. It is not a total conversion to
another religion. We would not speak of double identity. It is an opening up, a passing to and back, having two experiences in tension. I
think that they are playing a liminal role in society. They are models
of possibility. I know Christians in India who feel that they need not
abandon the religion of their ancestors since God is also active and
present there. I remember a student of mine, a convert from Buddhism,
who told me that though he was happy being a Christian, he felt that
he had not really abandoned his Buddhism. Increasingly today, in a
world divided by interreligious conflicts, people of different religions
come together to realize and celebrate their togetherness as seekers
and worshipers of the one God through a multiplicity of symbolic
manifestations. These groups have a necessary and symbolic role in
society in bringing peace and promoting fellowship. They are making
an effort to make the borders between religions porous. Today, we
also have the phenomenon of interreligious families. They also have a
liminal role in society. A community identity, which is necessary both
for the parents and the children, can be an open one, facilitating a fellowship, not only at the social, but also at the religious level. Joseph S.
O'Leary speaks of a couple meditating together every morning, he as
a Buddhist-Christian, she as a Christian-Buddhist.[27]

Conclusion

The Asian religio-philosophical traditions have frameworks that may
be more helpful in thinking about such experiences than the Greek

---

[26] See Chapter 11 of this book, "Do We Need Borders between Religions?"

[27] See Joseph S. O'Leary, "Toward a Buddhist Interpretation of Christian
Truth," in Cornille, *Many Mansions*, 29.

philosophical tradition that cannot go beyond the principle of non-contradiction. The mystics speak of the "coincidence of the opposites." But it does not enter into our usual way of thinking. The Mahayana Buddhists speak of the "Two Truths." The advaitins or nondualists of the Sankara School speak of the Saguna and Nirguna Brahman—the Absolute with and without qualities. The Vishistadvaitins or qualified nondualists of the Ramanuja School evoke the *paratva* and *saulabhya* of Brahman—God far and near. The Absolute that seems far can manifest itself to us in a multiplicity of ways, all of which lead us to the one Absolute. The ways to the Absolute cannot be absolutized. Their affirmations regarding the Absolute may be true, but limited. Therefore, one cannot really speak of the clash of absolutes at the level of religions. If we have such a perspective of "pluralism-in-unity," double religious identity will not be a problem, but rather a welcome call and opportunity to experience the richness of God.

Chapter 13

Hindu and Christian—
Conflict or Challenge?

Indian and *Christian*. To put these two words together and say "Indian Christian" would be problematic today. There are at least some Indians—mainly under the *Hindutva* umbrella—who think that Christians are not Indians. What is surprising is that some Christians would agree with this. While there is still talk of the need to indigenize Christianity in India, implying that it is not fully Indian, others say that there is nothing that can be called "Indian." Successive invasions and migrations over the centuries have left India a multicultural country, with some cultures in conflict. So there is little that is "Indian" with which Christians can identify, especially if they belong to subaltern groups. Many scholars today hold that "India" is the creation of the colonial powers that once ruled the region and what is said to be "Indian" is really the dominant culture, thus marginalizing or subordinating the subaltern cultures. So a Dalit or a Tribal, for instance, will revisit the dominant "Indian" culture. In a culturally pluralistic situation, Christians add one more culture to the mix. I propose that it is possible to be Indian politically, without being so culturally and/or religiously. Today, personal and social identities seem to be shifting under the influence of globalization—thanks to large-scale migration, the homogeneity of the global markets, and the media. Increased incomes, the liberation and earning capacity of women, and intercultural and interreligious marriages all serve to blur social identities.

If being an "Indian Christian" is problematic, being a "Hindu-Christian" is more so. Today we come across people of other religions who call themselves "devotees of Christ" or Christu bhaktas, across different classes in society. There are people living in Christian and

173

other ashrams who claim to be Hindu-Christians.[1] Raimon Panik-kar famously said: "I 'left' as a Christian, I 'found' myself a Hindu, and I 'return' a Buddhist, without having ceased to be a Christian."[2] It is not merely a problem of personal and social identity. Given the present conflict, sometimes violent, between fundamentalist religious groups, it is a religious question. In the face of seemingly incompatible views about God, humanity, the world, and the project of salvation/liberation among the different religions, it becomes also a theological question.[3]

Ultimately, as adults, we construct our own identities, and being a Hindu-Christian is primarily a personal issue. A person like Panikkar has constructed a special religious identity for himself. While being a Christian, he has integrated Hindu and Buddhist elements in his spiritual way so that he can call himself a Hindu-Buddhist-Christian. He did not live this as a conflicting experience, but it must certainly have been a challenge. Panikkar explained himself in an interview which he gave in 2000. Let me quote it because it is keeping with the orientation of my essay:

> I was brought up in the Catholic religion by my Spanish mother, but I never stopped trying to be united with the tolerant and gen-erous religion of my father and of my Hindu ancestors. This does not make me a cultural or religious "half-caste," however. Christ was not half man and half God, but fully man and fully God. In the same way, I consider myself 100 percent Hindu and Indian, and 100 percent Catholic and Spanish. How is that possible? By living religion as an experience rather than as an ideology.[4]

To the casual observer this may seem not merely challenging but conflicting. Being a Christian or a Hindu is not just about personal

---

[1] For more information about these groups, see Ciril J. Kuttiyanikkal, *Khrist Bhakta Movement: A Model for an Indian Church? Inculturation in the Area of Community Building* (Berlin: Lit Verlag, 2014); Jerome G. Sylvester, "The Khrist-bhakta Movement: A New Paradigm of Faith in Christ Jesus," *Vidyajyoti, Journal of Theological Reflection* 27 (2013): 345–59 (Part 1) and 443–56 (Part 2); and Herbert Hoefer, "Jesus, My Master: 'Jesu Bhakta' Hindu Christian Theology," *International Journal of Frontier Missions* 19, no. 3 (2002): 39–42.

[2] Raimon Panikkar, *The Intrareligious Dialogue* (New York: Paulist Press, 1978), 2.

[3] See Chapter 12 of this book, "Double Religious Identity: Possible? Neces-sary?"

[4] Raimon Panikkar, "Interview," *Christian Century* (August 16–23, 2000), 834–36.

identity. It has a social and also an institutional dimension. Being a disciple of Christ personally is different from being a Christian socially and institutionally. It ceases then to be a merely personal problem and becomes a social and institutional problem and a theological question: Is it possible to be a Hindu-Christian or, for that matter, a Christian-Hindu? How do we define religious identity? Is double or multiple-religious identity possible? If yes, then under what conditions?

These questions may require some explanation. For the purposes of this reflection I distinguish between *identity* and *belonging.* I understand identity as something personal. I am a disciple of Christ. I know many "Hindus" who claim to be disciples of Christ. This is not a sociological but a religious (that is to say, spiritual or faith) claim. But they do not belong to the Christian community as a social and institutional group. To belong to it one has to undergo a rite of passage (baptism) and accept certain obligations. In the passage from Panikkar quoted above, he distinguishes between experience and ideology. I am not raising these questions academically and in the abstract. I am trying to understand people who claim to have a certain experience—partly because I share their experience. The question, then, is whether it is possible for someone to belong to one community but share the religious experience of another community. Such experience may involve beliefs, worldviews, methods of *sadhana*, and so on, while excluding official creeds (doctrinal formulas), rituals, social belonging, and so on.

So, let me say at the outset that I am approaching this question not purely objectively, but as a partisan. More than fifteen years ago I wrote a small book, *Toward Fullness: Searching for an Integral Spirituality.* I wrote in the Preface: "I am obviously searching as an Indian. I can specify this identity further as *Hindu-Christian.*"[5] Theology is faith seeking transformation through understanding, and faith itself involves a commitment. As a believer, one cannot and need not claim to be neutral. Let me also say that I am not identifying "Hinduism" with "Brahminism" as some (Dalit) Christians tend to do today. My argument is that there are, as a matter of fact, people who claim to be Hindu-Christians, and I think that their claim should not be dismissed as absurd if it refers to personal identity and experience and not to creed, community/institution, and ideology. Some people may not make the shift formally but may still live as Christians. Socially

---

[5] Michael Amaladoss, "Preface," *Toward Fullness: Searching for an Integral Spirituality* (Bangalore: NBCLC, 1994), 2. See also idem, *The Dancing Cosmos: A Way to Harmony* (Anand, Gujarat: Gujarat Sahitya Prakash, 2003).

they would be at the margins of both communities, because neither religious community may accept this. Theology can only seek to understand it. For the purposes of this chapter, however, I am not going to analyze myself, but others. I start with some examples and then go on to present my theological arguments. While my examples are taken from different Christian traditions, my theological arguments are influenced by my own Roman Catholic tradition.

Some Examples

All through the history of Christianity in India there have been people who have been on the borders between Hinduism and Christianity. One could call them *liminal* persons. I shall just introduce a few of them here. It is significant that they all tend to be intellectuals who did not simply join a community or an institution, sometimes for nonreligious reasons, but sought to understand and personalize their Christian faith and practice.

Brahmabandhab Upadyay (1861–1907) became first an Anglican and then a Catholic.[6] He became a *sannyasi*, but was forbidden by religious authorities to start an ashram. He was also an ardent nationalist and cofounded, with Rabindranath Tagore, Shantiniketan. He declared that he was socially a Hindu but religiously a Christian. He distinguished between sociocultural and religious identity:

> Our *dharma* has two branches: *samaj dharma* and *sadhan dharma*. . . . We are Hindus. Our Hinduism is preserved by the strength of *samaj dharma*. While the *sadhan dharma* is of the individual its object is *sadhan* and *muktee* (salvation). It is a hidden thing and one to be meditated upon. It has no connection whatever with society. It is a matter known to the *guru* and *shisya* only. A Hindu, so far as *sadhan* goes, can belong to any religion.[7]

Upadhyay's hymns to Jesus Christ and the Trinity contain "Hindu" terminology.[8] In his school he allowed the Hindu children to sing the praises of Saraswati, the Hindu goddess of learning. He himself un-

---

[6] See B. Animananda, *The Blade: Life and Work of Brahmabandhab Upadhyay* (Calcutta: Roy and Son, ca 1947).

[7] Ibid., 200.

[8] For an English translation of the hymns, see Robin H. S. Boyd, *An Introduction to Indian Christian Theology* (Chennai: CLS, 1969), 70, 77–78.

derwent rituals of purification after his voyage to Europe, according to the Hindu social tradition. He also suggested that Krishna could have been God's *avatar* or manifestation for the Hindus, even though Jesus is the only incarnation of God. At this stage he was suspected of having reverted to Hinduism in some way. When he died, both his Hindu and Christian friends had disputes over his body, with the Hindus finally cremating it.

Sadhu Sundar Singh (1889–1929) became a Christian after a personal vision of Jesus Christ. He refused to be associated with any church, even surrendering a preacher's license that he had secured in the Anglican Church. Instead, he travelled widely, preaching the good news of Jesus and probably died a martyr in Tibet. His way of life and manner of teaching had Indian, if not Hindu, overtones.[9] He was guided by the Yoga and the bhakti traditions of Hinduism and had a deep influence on disciples like A. J. Appasamy, who wrote a book on Christianity as a *bhakti marga* (way of devotion).[10] Sundar Singh declared:

> I belong to the Body of Christ, that is, to the true Church, which is no material building, but the whole corporate body of true Christians. . . . We Indians do not want a doctrine not even a religious doctrine. . . . We need the Living Christ. . . . It is quite natural that no form of Church service can ever satisfy deeply spiritual people, because such persons already have direct fellowship with God in meditation, and they are always conscious of His blessed presence in their souls.[11]

Sundar Singh did not belong to any Christian denomination, but he did not belong to Hindu institutions either. He tried to integrate Hindu traditions into his Christian spirituality.

Pandita Ramabai (1858–1922) was an accomplished Sanskrit pandit well versed in the Hindu *shastras*. She became a Christian, translated the Bible into Marathi, and engaged in social work for the liberation of women.[12] She refused allegiance to any established church. Ramabai writes:

> I believe in Christ and His God, and as one of His disciples— though least—am bound to do and believe in his teaching, as I

---

[9] Cf. A. J. Appasamy, *Sundar Singh: A Biography* (London: n.p., 1958).

[10] Cf. A. J. Appasamy, *Christianity as Bhakti Marga* (Chennai: CLS, 1928).

[11] See Boyd, *An Introduction to Indian Christian Theology*, 105–6.

[12] See Shamsundar Manohar Adhav, *Pandita Ramabai* (Chennai: CLS, 1979).

have promised in my Baptism. But at the same time I shall not bind myself to believe in and accept everything that is taught by the Church.[13]

In her lectures in England and in the United States of America she introduced herself as a Hindu. For her, it was more than a national identity, as her friends tried to make out. She says:

My parents were Hindus. I have thoroughly imbibed within me all the good Hindu lessons of morality they taught me. More than half of my life has been spent in the study of the Hindu religion and philosophy, *Smriti* and the *Puranas*, etc. and although there is much that may not be fully acceptable, yet, there are many good things about them.[14]

Panditha Ramabai was neither a Hindu nor a Christian institutionally. Spiritually she was a Christian who followed Christ, but she integrated it with a Hindu way of life.

Pandipeddi Chenchiah (1886–1959) sought to find the "raw fact of Christ" behind the doctrinal statements of the churches.[15] He was deeply influenced by two Hindu masters—Kanchupati Venkata Rao Venkatasami Rao, known popularly as Master CVV, and Aurobindo—in his understanding of the "raw fact of Christ" in a secular and evolutionary perspective.

The fact of Christ is the birth of a new order in creation. It is the emergence of life—not bound by Karma; of man, not tainted by sin nor humbled by death; of man triumphant, glorious, partaking the immortal nature of God; of a new race in creation—sons of God.[16]

Let it be clearly understood that we accept nothing as obligatory save Christ. Church doctrine and dogma, whether from the West or from the past, whether from the Apostles or from modern critics, are to be tested before they are accepted.[17]

---

[13] Ibid., 137.
[14] Ibid., 189.
[15] See Boyd, *An Introduction to Indian Christian Theology,* 144–64.
[16] Adhav, *Pandita Ramabai,* 148.
[17] Ibid., 147.

Chenchiah too declared a certain independence from the institution of the church and felt free to dialogue with and integrate "Hindu" theological perspectives in understanding Christ.

Swami Abhishiktananda (Henri Le Saux) was a French Benedictine monk who was influenced by Ramana Maharishi and sought all his life to have the advaitic or nondual experience according to the Hindu tradition. He claims to have had it. He struggled all his life to reconcile intellectually his Christian experience and this Hindu experience without success. A few months before his death, however, he had a heart attack and seems to have transcended the tensions. According to Abhishiktananda, the Absolute transcends all that is relative, including its relative manifestations:

> People are converted—they receive an initiation [*diksha*], they become Christian, Muslim, Sufi, Vedantin, and so on. All those are superimposed forms. Whereas the essential thing is to strip oneself of all that is superfluously added, to recover one's proper form [*svarupa*] that was lost.[18]

> For the Christian point of view, of course, Christ is the Unique— it is through him that we see all the theophanies. He is the End of them, their Pleroma. . . . Wonderful, but from the standpoint of eternity. . . . The brilliance of the *paramartha* overcasts [overthrows] all scale of values on the level of *vyavahara*! Our Cosmic Christ, the all embracing *Isvara*, the *Purusha* of the Veda/Upanishads. . . . We cannot escape to give him such a full dimension, expansion. . . . Yet, why then call him only Jesus of Nazareth? Why say that it is Jesus of Nazareth whom others unknowingly call Shiva or Krishna? and not rather say that Jesus is the theophany for *us,* the Bible-believers, of that unnameable mystery of the Manifestation, always tending beyond itself, since Brahman transcends all its/his manifestations?[19]

Raimon Panikkar (1918–2010), born to a Spanish Catholic mother and an Indian Hindu father, was brought up a Catholic and came to India only at the age of thirty-five. He spent at least one semester every year in Varanasi and visited the Hindu holy places in the Himalayas.

---

[18] Swami Abhishiktananda, *Ascent to the Depth of the Heart* (Delhi: ISPCK, 1998), 379.

[19] James Stuart, *Swami Abhishiktananda: His Life Told through His Letters* (Delhi: ISPCK,1989), 273.

His book *The Unknown Christ of Hinduism* is well known. His spiritual experience as a Hindu-Christian can be gauged from *Mantramanjari*, a collection of texts from the Hindu scriptures, selected, translated, and commented by him. I began this essay with a quotation from him. Here is one more.

> In the West identity is established through difference. Catholics find their identity in not being Protestant or Hindu or Buddhist. But other cultures have another way of thinking about one's identity. Identity is not based on the degree to which one is different from others. In the Abrahamic traditions (Judaism, Islam, Christianity), people seek God in difference—in superiority or transcendence. Being divine means not being human. For Hindus, however, the divine mystery is in man, in what is so profound and real in him that he cannot be separated from it, and it cannot be discharged into transcendence. This is the domain of immanence, of that spiritual archetype that is called *brahman*. In the Hindu system, people are not afraid of losing their identity. They can be afraid of losing what they have, but not of losing what they are.
>
> I am not such a relativist as to believe that the truth is cut up in slices like a cake. But I am convinced that each of us participates in the truth. Inevitably, my truth is the truth that I perceive from my window. And the value of dialogue between the various religions is precisely to help me perceive that there are other windows, other perspectives. Therefore I need the other in order to know and verify my own perspective of the truth. Truth is a genuine and authentic participation in the dynamism of reality. When Jesus says "I am the truth," he is not asking me to absolutize my doctrinal system but to enter upon the way that leads to life.[20]

This small galaxy of intellectuals who attempted/forged a spiritual encounter between Hinduism and Christianity can serve as a background to my theological reflections on the problems of identity involved in such encounters.

The Problem

From the official Catholic point of view, such an encounter and exchange is itself problematic. A recent Roman document, *Dominus*

---

[20] See Panikkar, "Interview."

Iesus, issued by the Office of the Congregation for the Doctrine of the Faith on August 6, 2000, states that while the church has the fullness of the means of salvation, the other religions are inadequate for the purpose. I shall just quote from the text without any comments:

> With the coming of the Saviour Jesus Christ, God has willed that the Church founded by him be the instrument for the salvation of *all* humanity (cf. Acts 17.30–31). This truth of faith does not lessen the sincere respect which the church has for the religions of the world, but at the same time, it rules out, in a radical way, that mentality of indifferentism "characterized by a religious relativism which leads to the belief that 'one religion is as good as another.'" If it is true that the followers of other religions can receive divine grace, it is also certain that *objectively speaking* they are in a gravely deficient situation in comparison with those who, in the Church, have the fullness of the means of salvation. (no. 22)

The question then is: why should anyone be interested in encountering Hinduism at all? Must a Hindu who has become a Christian abandon Hinduism? The church has the fullness of the revealed truth about God and the assured means to reach God. That is why the people in my list would be tolerated as liminal people, or even condemned as dangerous examples to the faithful.

But before I address this problem I have to clear the ground by addressing another problem that concerns the relationship between Gospel and culture. We saw above how some like Brahmabandhab Upadhyay, distinguished between culture and religion. The possibility of such a distinction, however, has been challenged in recent times. If Christianity is necessarily linked to a particular culture, then we cannot talk about Indian Christians, and certainly not Hindu-Christians. That is why we must discuss the question of gospel-culture relations before we can talk about interreligious encounters.

Gospel and Culture

The church is officially open to the various cultures of the world. It affirms that the gospel transcends all cultures and has to become incarnate in every culture in order to transform it from within. The very term *inculturation,* patterned on the word *incarnation* suggests this. Paul VI said: "The gospel must impregnate the culture and the whole way of life of man. . . . (It is) above all cultures" (EN 20). More recently, however, such openness has been restricted. In *Fides et Ratio* in 1998 John Paul II, for instance, seems to speak in two voices:

> Simply because the mission of preaching the Gospel came first upon Greek philosophy in its journey, this is not taken to mean that other approaches are excluded. . . . When the Church deals for the first time with cultures of great importance, but previously unexamined, it must even so never place them before the Greek and Latin inculturation already acquired. Were this inheritance to be repudiated the providential plan of God would be opposed, who guides his Church down the paths of time and history. (FR 72)

Benedict XVI has said that the Judaic culture in which Jesus communicated the gospel and the Greco-Roman culture in which it took an intellectual shape are normative to all Christians. He told a university audience at Regensburg in 2006:

> I must briefly refer to the third stage of dehellenization, which is now in progress. In the light of our experience with cultural pluralism, it is often said nowadays that the synthesis with Hellenism achieved in the early church was an initial inculturation which ought not to be binding on other cultures. The latter are said to have the right to return to the simple message of the New Testament prior to that inculturation, in order to inculturate it anew in their own particular milieux. This thesis is not simply false, but it is coarse and lacking in precision. The New Testament was written in Greek and bears the imprint of the Greek spirit, which had already come to maturity as the Old Testament developed. True, there are elements in the evolution of the early church which do not have to be integrated into all cultures. Nonetheless, the fundamental decisions made about the relationship between faith and the use of human reason are part of the faith itself; they are developments consonant with the nature of faith itself.[21]

I find this statement and its implications insulting. It pretends that the Greeks have a monopoly on reason and all that others can do is to

---

[21] Benedict XVI, "Faith, Reason, and the University," address at the University of Regensburg (September 12, 2006).

adopt it. We can imagine the complexity of an identity which demands that an African Christian should be "a little Semitic, a little Greek, fully Roman and authentically African," as French-Roman Cardinal Paul Poupard phrased it once.[22] In this way the official church protects its existing creedal, ritual, cultural, and organizational structures. No wonder that converts like Sadhu Sundar Singh and Pandita Ramabai, who became Christians after a serious intellectual and spiritual search, distanced themselves from the official structures of both Hinduism and Christianity. In fact, Ramabai said:

> I have just with great efforts freed myself from the yoke of the Indian priestly tribe, so I am not at present willing to place my-self under another similar yoke by accepting everything which comes from the priests as authorized command of the Most High.[23]

Resistance to ecclesial structures may already be due to the influence of a certain free spirit of searching and experiencing in Hinduism. Such freedom may also be available in the Protestant tradition, though not in the institutional structures of various confessional churches. When, in addition, the ecclesial structures are seen as European and therefore rejected, an Indian identity asserts itself.

Cosmic and Metacosmic Religions

The discussion on gospel-culture encounter supposes that one can make a neat distinction between culture and religion. But culture and religion are closely related. Both deal with the question of meaning. Religion focuses on "ultimate meaning" while supposing the other levels of meaning given by a culture. The different levels of meanings are integrated. When we seek to express the gospel in Indian culture, we may not be able to do away completely with Hindu influences. The question then arises whether such Hindu influences can be integrated if they are not in conflict with Christian meanings.

We can look at this question from two different points of view. When God reveals Godself, God does so in a given social, cultural, and religious context of a people. The influences of this context are

---

[22] I am quoting from my memory of newspaper reports. Cardinal Poupard was at that time the head of the Pontifical Council of Culture. I was living in Rome at that time.

[23] Adhav, *Pandita Ramabai,* 131.

inevitable. While not considering them normative, we have to dialogue with them. On the other hand, we also have to look at the possibility of an unconscious interreligious encounter.

Aloysius Pieris distinguished between cosmic and metacosmic religions.[24] While cosmic religions try to find the meaning of life within the cosmos, which includes the spirit world, the metacosmic religions invoke a "Transcendent Principle." A metacosmic religion takes on board the local cosmic religiosity with its heavens and hells, angels and demons, and agricultural and seasonal rituals and festivals. Some incompatible elements in the cosmic religions may be eliminated and the others reinterpreted to make a new whole. When a metacosmic religion spreads to other areas, it finds new roots in the local cosmic religions. This is inevitable for its survival and growth. This was true of Christianity till the colonial period. After that, rather than spread in the above pattern, it began to be "imported" from Europe and imposed on other cultures. The consequence at the popular level is the phenomenon of double or parallel religiosity, quite prevalent in Asia, Africa, and Latin America. During the celebration of the rites of passage and festivals, alongside the official rituals, there are other local rituals that seem to speak more directly to the people. These rituals are "Christianized" by adding a sign of the cross or a prayer. This is an unacknowledged, perhaps unconscious, sometimes hidden phenomenon of double religious identity.[25]

All the people I have listed above confess to being believers in Jesus Christ, to whom they have surrendered themselves. However, while they no longer "belong" to Hindu institutional structures and despite the differences among them, they all feel rooted in and tried to integrate the Hindu spiritual tradition as understood by them into their Christian experience. Brahmabandhab Upadyay did not fault Hindu students worshiping Krishna and Saraswati, and he himself underwent the rituals of purification—*prayascitta*—after a foreign trip, viewing it as a social ritual. Abhishiktananda and Panikkar undertook pilgrimages to Gangotri and Kailash, sacred to worshipers of Shiva. Abhishiktananda performed the initiation rites of his disciple Marc in the Ganges, inviting Swami Chidananda, a Hindu *sannyasi*, to be a co-initiator, because *sanyasa* is a Hindu religious practice. He was also attached to Arunachala, the mountain on which Shiva is believed

---

[24] Aloysius Pieris, *An Asian Theology of Liberation* (Maryknoll, NY: Orbis Books, 1988).

[25] See Thomas Bamat and Jean-Paul Wiest, eds., *Popular Catholicism in a World Church: Seven Case Studies in Inculturation* (Maryknoll, NY: Orbis Books, 1999).

to manifest himself as a column of fire. Abhishiktananda's own guru, Swami Gnanananda, initiated him into the advaitic tradition. At no time, however, was there any question about his loyalty to Jesus Christ and Christian rituals like the Eucharist.

Interreligious Encounter

Abhishiktananda's *sadhana* or spiritual pursuit was not limited to pilgrimages to Hindu sacred places. His was a search to experience his nondual oneness with the Absolute. Jesus became both the model and the mediation of that encounter with the Absolute. Here is a sample of Abhishiktananda's vision taken from one of his last writings:

> The absoluteness of the ultimate mystery is discovered in the absoluteness of the self itself, of oneself seen in its full truth. The Self is then seen in the self. In the light of pure consciousness, Being shines with its own light. Then the eternity, the aseity, the absoluteness, the sovereignty of God are no longer notions which man tries desperately to understand by way of analogy or negations. They are realized in their own truth in the discovery that oneself *is*, beyond all conditioning. Then God is no longer a HE about whom men dare to speak among themselves, nor even only a THOU whose presence man realizes as facing him. Rather, necessarily starting from oneself, God is discovered and experienced as I, the *'aham asmi'* of the Upanishads, the *'ehieh asher ehieh'* of the Burning Bush. It is not an I which I abstract or conclude from the Thou that I say to him, but an I of which I am aware in the very depth of my own I.[26]

Here we have an encounter between two metacosmic religious traditions. How is this possible theologically?

After the Second Vatican Council in the Catholic Church, there has been a growing appreciation of other religions. While the council itself spoke of "good and holy elements" in other religions and the need for dialogue with them, further reflection has led some to see in other religions the possibility of divine-human encounter. Having no space here to trace this theological development, I shall be satisfied with two quotations. The Joint Statement of the Congregation for the

---

[26] Swami Abhishiktananda, "The Upanishads and Advaitic Experience," in *The Further Shore* (Delhi: ISPCK, 1975), 116.

Evangelization of Peoples and the Pontifical Council on Interreligious Dialogue, *Dialogue and Proclamation*, asserts:

> Concretely it will be in the sincere practice of what is good in their own religious traditions and by following the dictates of their conscience that the members of other religions respond positively to God's invitation and receive salvation in Jesus Christ, even while they do not recognize or acknowledge him as their Savior. (DP 29)

John Paul II acknowledged the presence and action of the Holy Spirit in other cultures and religions.

> The Spirit manifests himself in a special way in the Church and in her members. Nevertheless, his presence and activity are universal, limited neither by space nor time (DEV 53). . . . The Spirit's presence and activity affect not only individuals but also society and history, peoples, cultures and religions. . . . Thus the Spirit, who "blows where he wills" (cf. Jn 3.8), who "was already at work in the world before Christ was glorified" (AG 4), and who "has filled the world . . . holds all things together (and) knows what is said" (Wis 1.7), leads us to broaden our vision in order to ponder his activity in every time and place (DEV 53). . . . The Church's relationship with other religions is dictated by a twofold respect: "Respect for man in his quest for answers to the deepest questions of his life, and respect for the action of the Spirit in man." (RM 28–29)

Today, many theologians believe that every religion can facilitate a salvific divine-human encounter. A seminar on sharing worship took this seriously, stating that if worship rituals in different religions are different symbolic ways to one and the same Absolute, there is no difficulty in participating in them.[27] What, then, is religious identity?

Religious Identity

Why does a person have a religious identity? There are two possible reasons. The first is that a person is born and raised in a religious community and therefore belongs to it. While such a person may

---

[27] Paul Puthanangady, ed., *Sharing Worship* (Bangalore: NBCLC, 1988).

have no problem participating occasionally in the worship of other religions the person's identity is defined by the community he or she belongs to. For example, Ramakrishna Paramahamsa claims to have had the experience of other religions[28] although he was a Hindu and a Shaivite with a special devotion to the goddess Kali. He writes: "I have practised all religions—Hinduism, Islam, Christianity—and I have also followed the paths of the different Hindu sects. . . . I have found that it is the same God toward whom all are directing their steps, though along different paths."[29]

A second reason is that a person has experienced God in a particular religious tradition. The experience is reciprocal: it is not only the person's choice, but he or she has the experience of a special manifestation of God. There is a sense of a "vocation"—a call. This experience constitutes the person's personal religious identity. While he or she is open to the possibility that God may manifest Godself to others through other symbols, his or her relationship with God is something unique. It is not exclusive, but special. Sadhu Sundar Singh and Pandita Ramabai became Christians through special encounters with Jesus Christ; they were not members of a Christian community. Such membership then becomes secondary.

Such a special relationship can also develop with a second religion that one relates to. For example, Swami Abhishiktananda wanted to have an advaitic or nondual experience of the Absolute. He recognized it was "Hindu" and yet transcending Hinduism as a religious tradition. He did not belong to any Hindu community. As a *sannyasi* he was beyond all such communities.

So we contend that while a person may belong to a particular religious community, both sociologically and experientially, he or she can be open to other religious experiences. There is no antagonism toward other religions, and the person may encounter and be enriched by them while still being rooted in one religion. This rootedness could also be in a community different from the one in which one is born, because it is based on a personal religious experience. This was the case of Sadhu Sundar Singh and Pandita Ramabai. In the case of Abhishiktananda and Panikkar, they are rooted in the community they were born in, confirmed also by their personal experience of Jesus, but are open to experience the Absolute through other symbols.

---

[28] See Ramakrishna Paramahamsa, *Cultural Heritage of India* (Calcutta: Belur Math), vol. II, 494, cited in Boyd, *An Introduction to Indian Christian Theology*, 58.

[29] Paramahamsa, *Heritage*, 518, cited in Boyd, *An Introduction to Indian Christian Theology*, 59.

Ramakrishna Paramahamsa and Mahatma Gandhi are corresponding examples from the Hindu tradition. In all these cases there is a realization that the Absolute is one, though experienced through different mediations.[30] One's own religious experience, however, is special and privileged, without being exclusive or inclusive. Panikkar, despite claiming to be 100 percent Christian and 100 percent Hindu, writes about the unknown Christ of Hinduism, not about the unknown Krishna of Christianity.

Identity is always personal, though it is in the context of a community. A person born and raised in a community usually identifies with it. While growing up or because of a particular encounter one may reconfirm one's identity or change it. The change may not be as much against one's former religion as in favor of a new religion. One could also choose an ideology instead of a religion. Even so, one would likely need a community or group of people who think along similar lines.

Multireligious Families

We also have the phenomenon of people born in a multireligious family where the parents belong to different religions. The children, then, grow up, not always as members of a religious community, but in a more neutral situation, open to different influences. I know of a few such multireligious families. In some families one or the other parent is firm that the children are brought up in his or her religious tradition. In countries like the United States the prevailing situation for many is Christian and that affects the children too. In other cases, one or both parents may not be practicing their religion. But what happens if the parents encourage their children to be open and make their own choice of religious identity? I contacted one such family with three young adult children living in Mumbai. The father is a modern Hindu and the mother is an active Catholic. The youngest child, Ashutosh, says: "I do not have a religious identity. I have a spiritual identity. . . . I detest all religions. I believe in a higher power, God, if you like."

The middle child, Nivedita, affirms:

---

[30] This is a theological not a biblical affirmation, although theologians would claim to be rooted in the biblical faith. For elaborate theological explanations of such a perspective on religious pluralism, which is not possible within the short space of this chapter, see S. J. Samartha, *One Christ, Many Religions: Toward a Revised Christology* (Maryknoll, NY: Orbis Books, 1991); Jacques Dupuis, *Toward a Christian Theology of Religious Pluralism* (Maryknoll, NY: Orbis Books, 2002).

I love my double identity because it makes me different. I've been given the power of choice, the ability to think for myself and the gift of being introduced to different faces of God. Why would I say no to any? I believe in a higher power but I also believe that people have to make their own God. Religion is just a social construct that people have made up to please themselves.

The eldest, Gayatri, declares that she likes stories and festivals, nature and sacred places, but not idols and ritual:

I don't have a religious identity at all. I have a spiritual identity. I have a moral identity. I have an ethical identity. I have a code of conduct by which I believe I should live my life, which is not religion because what works for me may not work for someone else. It is not universal. It leaves me more open and understanding and forgiving of others. And yet I chose to get baptized the year I turned twenty-one. . . . I decided to get baptized because being a Catholic is a part of my heritage, a part of my name, and by default, a part of my identity. . . . The feeling of community that belonging to a church gives me is very important. Growing up in the Sri Aurobindo Ashram also gave me a great sense of community. . . . Each one in my Hindu family does their own thing so the sense of community there is missing. . . . Even if you are Christian, being Hindu is part of your Indian heritage.

The way that Ashutosh, Nivedita, and Gayatri are constructing their religious identities is very interesting and instructive. Their religious self-construction is probably not over yet and may be illustrative of what is happening to many young people in the postmodern world, even some born in orthodox families.

In a way Swami Abhishiktananda and Raimon Panikkar are postmodern people too. What is significant is their deep sense of personal identity and freedom. They were also seeking a personal experience of God. They related to a community. But they were liminal people, on its borders, though both were ordained presbyters. Their double identity was indeed a challenge for them and for others who knew them. Swami Abhishiktananda lived in tension much of his life, maybe because Hinduism was new to him. Panikkar does not seem to have had that tension. Some may not have understood them.[31]

---

[31] For a more contemporary example, see S. Painadath, *The Power of Silence: Fifty Meditations to Discover the Divine Space within You* (Delhi: ISPCK, 2009).

A Recent Example

Francis Xavier Clooney is an expert in comparative theology and has written many books comparing Hinduism and Christianity.[32] At the conclusion of a book comparing Christian and Hindu mantras he explores the possibility of a Christian using the Hindu mantras: "There seems to me to be no reason why a Christian cannot still venture to appropriate the piety, theology, and practice of the three Mantras as well as the insights and theology of Desika's *Essence,* for the sake of a deeply Christocentric manner of prayer."[33] He suggests that if the Hindus too engage in a similar practice with Christian mantras then a new interreligious community will emerge. Religious identity would then become very complex.

Conclusion

The problem with Christian identity is that the identity of the individual is subordinated to the identity of the Christian community or the church—especially in the Roman Catholic Church. The church claims to be the body of Christ with a divinely willed hierarchical structure. It determines what Christian identity is: what Christians believe, what rituals they practice, even what their theological reflection should be. So the ordinary Christian feels hemmed in from all directions. But the examples of Abhishiktananda and Panikkar, the tradition of the freedom and primacy of the individual conscience in the face of God fostered by people like St. Ignatius of Loyola, and the postmodern praxis of young people are indicators that new models of religious identity are possible. To liberate them from religious control some will call them mystical. I do not think that mysticism is necessarily involved here. Ultimately, it is for the individual, responding to God's call, to decide what he or she wants to be. This may involve tensions with the community. At the level of the individual, communal identities like Hinduism and Christianity may already be questioned in

---

[32] See Francis X. Clooney, *Hindu God, Christian God: How Reason Helps Break Down the Barriers between Religions* (New York: Oxford University Press, 2001); idem, *Divine Mother, Blessed Mother: Hindu Goddesses and the Virgin Mary* (New York: Oxford University Press, 2005); idem, *Beyond Compare: St. Francis de Sales and Sri Vedanta Desika on Loving Surrender to God* (Washington, DC: Georgetown University Press, 2008).

[33] Francis X. Clooney, *The Truth, the Way, the Life: Christian Commentary on the Three Holy Mantras of the Srivaishnava Hindus* (Leuven: Peeters, 2008), 191.

the postmodern world. The emphasis today may be on the individual rather than the community, though the community remains important. But a community is built up by a consensus of consenting individuals, especially if they are called by God, not by authoritarian structures.

Once again I would like to make it clear that I am not talking about people belonging simultaneously to the social or institutional structures of two religions, but rather about people who seek to integrate in themselves experiential and spiritual traditions they have inherited from different religious groups they have encountered, though they may be rooted in one particular religious tradition. They may be considered marginal by the institution. This may not have been possible when socio-religious structures were strong and the individuals did not have the freedom. But today people seem to be freer to experience and assert their personal identity. I am not making an abstract argument either, but I am trying to understand (and also justify) the religious experience of people whom I have encountered either personally or through their writings. There is a traditional phrase in logic, *contra factum non valet argumentum* (there is no valid argument against a fact). In my experience people with double religious identities, however they may be described, are facts.

I think that the freedom of God, who manifests Godself to whomsoever and in whichever way it pleases God, and the freedom of the individual person to respond to God are sacred. The Spirit is God's gift to everyone. In the Catholic tradition we have tension between the *sensus fidelium*—the consensus of the people of God—and the magisterium or teaching authority of the hierarchy. Today, we may have to add to this the faith experience of the individual. We also have to be clear about the obligation that an individual feels to respond to God in the particular way that God has called him or her, while being open to the reality that God may be calling others through other ways. This means that in building up our identity we must listen not only to our own desires and to the community to which we are related, but also to God, who is calling. God's call may be the most basic of the three elements. Whatever problems communities have dealing with multiple identities on the part of individuals; this trend is here to stay. In any case, realizing and living these new identities are more challenges than causes for conflict.

Chapter 14

From Syncretism to Harmony

All through history groups of people have been in contact with one another through migration, trade, or conquest. Cultures and religions have encountered and influenced each other. The world religions spread across many cultures and cast their roots in them even when they pretend to discourage such a process. As metacosmic religions they integrate local cosmic religions.[1] Aloysius Pieris suggests that when two religions encounter each other their search for integration may take three forms: synthesis, syncretism, or symbiosis. *Synthesis* creates a new religion combining the elements of two other religions. *Syncretism* indiscriminately mixes symbols and other elements from the two religions. *Symbiosis* integrates the two religions in a meaningful way. In practice this means that one religion integrates elements from another religion in a harmonious way without losing its basic identity. We shall keep this framework in mind as we discuss examples of religious practices from India.[3] Our exploration will make clear the criteria by which we identify the process that is operative in a

---

[1] For the distinction between cosmic and metacosmic religions, see Aloysius Pieris, *An Asian Theology of Liberation* (Maryknoll, NY: Orbis Books, 1988), 71–73.

[2] Aloysius Pieris, *Fire and Water* (Maryknoll, NY: Orbis Books, 1996), 66.

[3] For an earlier reflection on syncretism, see Michael Amaladoss, "Syncretism and Kenosis: Hermeneutical Reflections in the Indian Context," in *The Agitated Mind of God*, ed. Dale T. Irwin and Akintunde E. Akinade, 57–72 (Maryknoll, NY: Orbis Books, 1996). See also Robert J. Schreiter, *The New Catholicity: Theology between the Global and the Local* (Maryknoll, NY: Orbis Books, 1997), 62–83; Jerald D. Gort, Hendrick M. Vroom, Rein Fernhout, and Anton Wessels eds., *Dialogue and Syncretism: An Interdisciplinary Approach* (Grand Rapids, MI: Eerdmans, 1989); Peter Schineller, "Inculturation and Syncretism: What Is the Issue?" *International Bulletin of Missionary Research* 16 (1992): 50–53; Robert J. Schreiter, "Defining Syncretism: An Interim Report," *International Bulletin of Missionary Research* 17 (1993): 50–53.

particular case. In keeping with the method of contextual theology I start with some examples—data—and then reflect on them. Let me first evoke three examples. My comments will come at the end.

Popular Religiosity

The first example is that of the practices of popular religiosity.[4] Practices of popular religiosity can be of three kinds. There are practices of popular devotion around Jesus, Mary, and other saints and during the celebration of festivals. These are different from "official" rituals and practices. The people sing their own songs and use their own prayers. They may use Indian musical instruments. They may even dance. They integrate traditional ritual practices. They employ Indian material for decoration. They may dress the statues in an Indian way, clothing Mary in an Indian silk sari, for example. These practices do not pose a problem from our point of view. All they actually do is add an Indian "color," even if it is not "official." A second kind of practice happen at the time of rituals that celebrate the cycles of life (birth, initiation, marriage, death) and of nature (agricultural, like sowing and harvesting, or seasonal, like spring and monsoon). At such times rituals of cosmic religiosity are used. Killing goats and sharing the meat in the sanctuary of a saint comes on the borderline between these two practices.[5]

Let me illustrate the second kind of practice with an example from my own experience. Some years ago my father died. At the time of the funeral I had celebrated mass in front of the house. But before the body was taken to the cemetery a traditional ritual was performed. My sister-in-law (the daughter-in-law of the diseased) was asked to hold a measuring vessel full of paddy (rice). She placed it on the head, the breast and the feet of my father. She did it three times. Then she was led into the home and the paddy was emptied in a corner of the living room. An oil lamp was lit and placed over the paddy. Then the body was taken for burial. The paddy and the lamp remained there for three days, till the end of the period of mourning. It could have been five or seven or more days. People who came late to offer their condolences to the family did so (by weeping, for instance) in front of the paddy with the lamp. The people who performed the ritual may

---

[4] See Thomas Bamat and Jean-Paul Wiest, eds., *Popular Catholicism in World Church: Seven Case Studies in Inculturation* (Maryknoll, NY: Orbis Books, 1999).

[5] See Selva T. Raj and Corinne G. Dempsey, eds., *Popular Christianity in India: Riting between the Lines* (Albany: State University of New York Press, 2002).

not be able to explain the meaning of it. But an anthropologist with some knowledge of symbols may offer the following explanation. The paddy is food and symbolizes life. The paddy touching the body of the dead person and then taken into the home symbolically keeps back the life (spirit) of the person even as the body is taken to the cemetery. It represents the presence of the person in the house for the mourners.

The third kind of practice refers to rituals of healing. One evening I visited the home of a friend. As a priest, I was asked to bless a small child who had been sick for a few days and also to bless the house so as to ward off evil spirits or the "evil eye." In the course of the conversation I found out that when the child got sick, they first went to a medical doctor. As the fever did not abate after a couple of days, as it should have done, they went to the church to light candles and pray before the statue of Mary. Then they went to a Muslim shaman, known in the area as having the power of countering the effects of the "evil eye."[6]

Liturgical Inculturation

My second example has to do with liturgical inculturation. When the Second Vatican Council opened the door to the possible inculturation of the liturgical rites in various cultures, the Indian Church integrated "twelve points," including dress, postures, gestures, materials used, and so on. They were approved by the Congregation for Divine Worship in the Vatican.[7] These twelve points also included waving lamps, incense, and flowers at various moments of the liturgical action. The chants that accompanied the various liturgical actions included the syllable *OM*, which is usually found in the chants of the Hindus in worship and meditation. Around the same time a national theological seminar suggested the use of readings from the scriptures of other religions in the liturgy.[8] This was forbidden by the Vatican even before a formal application was made. Small groups, however, use such texts, not in the official liturgy, but as part of their reflection and prayer in community. All these practices have been decried as being syncretistic by

---

[6] See Michael Amaladoss, "Sickness, Spirits, and Society: The Meanings of Healing," in *Walking Together* (Anand, Gujarat: Gujarat Sahitya Prakash, 1992), 26–38.

[7] See J.A.G. Gerwin van Leeuwen, *Fully Indian and Authentically Christian: A Study of the First Fifteen Years of the NBCLC* (Bangalore: NBCLC, 1990).

[8] See D. S. Amalorpavadass, ed., *Research Seminar on Non-Biblical Scriptures* (Bangalore: NBCLC, 1974).

a small group of people in the church. Many officials in the church either discourage or seek to control such practices even today.

Methods of Prayer/*Sadhana*

My third example has to do with deeper forms of interreligious encounter. Even before the Second Vatican Council there were efforts to encounter Hinduism at a spiritual/mystical level. Jules Monchanin and Henri Le Saux, two priests from France, founded an ashram in Thannirpalli, South India, in 1950.[9] Henri Le Saux—or Swami Abhishiktananda, as he was better known in India—was attracted by the Hindu vision of advaita (nonduality). He sought to experience it. Toward the end of his life he said that he had experienced it. He has narrated his quest, his experiences, and his doubts in his spiritual diary.[10] He had one disciple, called Marc. Marc was jointly initiated in the waters of the Ganges by Swami Abhishiktananda and the Hindu Swami Chidananda of the Sivananda ashram of Rishikesh.[11] When Swami Abhishiktananda died, some of his friends in France wondered whether he had "become" a Hindu, though others stoutly defended his Christian identity.

The ashram movement leads people to explore different Indian methods of prayer. Some take to Yoga and others to devotional practices like the bhajan, which is a repetitive praying chant. A popular example of such integration is Anthony De Mello, who proposed various methods of prayer in a book with the title *Sadhana*.[12] The use of such methods, however, was discouraged by the Congregation for the Doctrine of the Faith.[13] Moreover, the Congregation for the Doctrine of the Faith also warned Catholics about the books of Anthony De Mello.[14]

---

[9] J. Monchanin and Henri Le Saux, *A Benedictine Ashram* (Thannirpalli: Shantivanam, 1951).

[10] Henri Le Saux, *Ascent to the Depth of the Heart: The Spiritual Diary of Swami Abhishiktananda* (Delhi: ISPCK, 1998).

[11] Swami Abhishiktananda explains this in *The Further Shore* (Delhi: ISPCK, 1984).

[12] Anthony De Mello, *Sadhana: A Way to God: Christian Exercises in Eastern Form* (Ligouri, MO: Ligouri/Triumph, 1998).

[13] "Letter on Certain Aspects of Christian Meditation," October 15, 1989, *AAS* 82 (1990): 362–79.

[14] "Notification Concerning the Writings of Fr. Anthony De Mello, SJ," June 24, 1998, *AAS* 90 (1998): 833–34.

These are three types of experiences that I reflect on the following pages.

Religion and Culture

One key that is often used to understand such phenomena is the distinction between religion and culture. In India this distinction is as old as Roberto de Nobili. Until de Nobili's arrival in India, conversions to Christianity were confined to the fisher folk of the coastal areas of South India. When they converted to Christianity, they also became culturally Portuguese in the names they took, the dress they wore, the food they ate, and so on. De Nobili wanted to reach out to the religious elite of Hindu society. He insisted that Indians could remain Indians when they became Christian. He distinguished between socio-cultural customs and religious ones. He said that the Indian Brahmins whom he tried to convert could keep their tuft of hair, the thread over their shoulders, and the ornamental dot on their foreheads. He considered them marks of their social status and not symbols of Hindu belief.[15] De Nobili vigorously criticized and condemned Hinduism as a religion.[16] He was opposed by other missionaries who accused him of introducing Hindu religious symbols into Christianity.

The dispute went up to the Vatican. In spite of various challenges, de Nobili's policy was largely practiced by the Jesuits. The distinction between religion and culture was used to allow practices that were not obviously Hindu. The distinction matured into *Indian* cultural practices and *Hindu* religious ones. Thanks to de Nobili, Christianity in Tamil Nadu, South India, remains one of the most inculturated in the country. At the time of the celebration of life and natural/seasonal cycles, popular religiosity flourishes side by side with official rituals. While the priests are in charge of the official rituals, other ritual specialists (a catechist, for example) or the people then take over. The priests normally ignore or tolerate these. If they are part of popular devotions or festivals they may halfheartedly or enthusiastically encourage it. The reason is the active participation by the people brings crowds to the church. Often the people "Christianize" the rituals by

---

[15] Roberto de Nobili, *Preaching Wisdom to the Wise* (St. Louis: Institute of Jesuit Sources, 2000).

[16] Francix X. Clooney, "Roberto de Nobili's Dialogue on Eternal Life and an Early Jesuit Evaluation of Religion in South India," in *The Jesuits: Cultures, Sciences, and the Arts, 1540–1773,* ed. John W. O'Malley, 402–17 (Toronto: University of Toronto Press, 1999).

the addition of the sign of the cross or a prayer like the Our Father or even the Creed.

The same distinction between religion and culture was used when ritual gestures like the *aarathi* (waving) of flowers, incense, and light were integrated into the liturgy after the Second Vatican Council. It was pointed out that waving of flowers, incense, and light was also used on secular occasions as gestures of honoring someone. They are *Indian* cultural rituals, not *Hindu* religious ones. The fact that Hinduism may use them on the occasion of Hindu worship to honor the Gods and even give them a Hindu religious meaning does not make them Hindu. They remain Indian and so available for use also by Indian Christians. Underlying the religious meaning given to them in a religious context, they have a basic human, social meaning that can be reintegrated in a Christian religious context. This argument leads us to the next step.

Reinterpretation of Symbols

While culture and religion are not the same and can be distinguished in a formal way, they also interact in various ways. Religion is not totally distinct from culture. It is rooted in culture. It is a dimension, perhaps the deepest one of culture. Both are systems of meaning, and they coexist precisely by adapting to each other.[17] Aloysius Pieris distinguishes between cosmic and metacosmic religions. Cosmic religion's search for meaning is immanent to the cosmos. It relates to the various elements in nature like the sun and the moon, the mountains and the rivers, the fire and the wind, though it may see them as animated by spirits. Its view of the world is religio-cultural. The distinction between religion and culture is not too neat. They interact constantly. Metacosmic religion sees the ultimate meaning of the world in an immanent-transcendent being or principle.[18] This is discovered by a special experience, like that of the Buddha, or by revelation, as in Christianity and Islam. It transcends culture. It can relate to many cultures, like the world religions. One culture can relate to more than one metacosmic religion, as in India, for instance. The distinction between religious and cultural elements is easier to see in a metacosmic religion, though even here there is a lot of interaction in practice.

---

[17] See Michael Amaladoss, *Beyond Inculturation: Can the Many Be One?* (Delhi: VIEWS, 1998).

[18] Pieris, *Fire and Water,* 66.

Symbols, like language, are constructs of a culture.[19] Unlike concepts, symbols have a double meaning structure. They can have multiple, even opposite, uses. For example, fire can symbolize the ardor of love: we speak of a warm welcome. Fire can also symbolize the destructive force of anger. Symbols therefore have to be interpreted in the context in which they are used. Religion does not create its own language and symbols. It borrows them from the culture, but gives them a new meaning in the religious context. Given this articulation between culture and religion, symbol and meaning, it is possible that a symbol used with a particular meaning in a given religious context can acquire another meaning in another religious context. Of course, the new meaning must coalesce with the first level meaning of the symbol. Fire, for instance, cannot symbolize coolness. Gestures like washing and imposition of hands and material like food have different meanings in different religious rituals.

Let us now apply these distinctions to the symbol OM. It is understood basically as the tone of primordial sound, the manifestation of waves of energy. It can be seen as the sound form of deep breathing. Yogis speak of the OM welling up from the depths as a person starts to breathe deeply. Both the Buddhists and the Jains use it in their prayer formulas. But they do not give it any special meaning. For the Hindus, OM is the primordial sound symbol of the Absolute. In their cosmology it is the first evolute of the Absolute, before other elements come into being. It is the purest, nondenominational symbol of the Absolute. All the sects of Hinduism, Shivites and Vaishnavites, use it as a symbol of the Absolute. It is not a sectarian symbol. In the Christian tradition we speak of the Word as the first self-manifestation of the Absolute (Father). The Word is the nondenominational symbol of the Absolute. Some Christians familiar with the Indian tradition, therefore, feel that OM can be used as the sound form of the Word and, therefore, the symbol of the Absolute. Some would go further and say that the sound OM contains three elements: A + U + M. It starts with the "A," prolongs itself in the "U," and finds completion in the "M." It is three-elements-in-one. So they see OM as the symbol of the Trinity.[20]

Can Christians use OM as a Christian symbol? Why not? What they are doing is taking an Indian symbol, so far used in the various Indian religious traditions, but giving it a new meaning in the context

[19] Michael Amaladoss, "Symbols and Mystery," *Journal of Dharma* 2 (1977): 382–96.

[20] See Swami Abhishiktananda, *Saccidananda: A Christian Approach to Advaitic Experience,* 2nd ed. (Delhi: ISPCK, 1984).

of their own faith. They are not taking the symbol with the meaning given to it in Jainism-Buddhism or Hinduism. They are reinterpreting it, giving it a new meaning, in the context of their own faith. I think that they have the right and the freedom to do so.

Limits to Freedom

Such freedom however can have limits. Some symbols may be closely associated with the mythological narratives or the history of a particular religion. Most mythological narratives relate to the struggle between the forces of good and evil and the eventual victory of the good. As such, they can be ideally reinterpreted by any religion. But many believers consider history what others may look upon as mythology. It is the foundation of the religious identity of the community. Figures like Rama and Krishna, *avatars* of Vishnu, are objects of faith for the Hindus. I do not think that another religion, like Christianity, can take these figures and reinterpret them in its own context. It will be offensive to the Hindu believers and upsetting to the Christian believers.[21]

Indian Christian artist Jyoti Sahi often depicts the risen Jesus as a dancing figure—dancing out of joy and fulfillment. For a window in the chapel of the National Biblical, Catechetical and Liturgical Centre in Bangalore he designed a simple figure that at first sight looked like a dancing Nataraja, though it lacked all the other symbolic elements that form part of the actual Nataraja image. After some time it was judged by people that, though it could be explained, it might scandalize simple people. So it was removed. This recalls Paul's advice to the Corinthians, not to eat the meat offered to the idols, not because it was sacred to the idols that were not true, but because of the scandal that it might cause to simple believers. But we must point out that a careful explanation can eventually do away with the scandal.

The limitations that go with such mytho-historical symbols, however, are not applicable to symbols that come from nature, like trees, water, light, the sun, the moon, the stars, the sky, and the wind. These do not belong to any one culture or religion. They can be used by all religions. An Indian painter or artist might think more spontaneously of an oil lamp in Indian style than a candle.

---

[21] Consider, however, that Jesus was pictured as Orpheus in the ancient church.

Religious Symbols

We can now take one step further, beyond the distinctions between culture and religion and symbol and meaning. Pieris suggests that a metacosmic religion, as it spreads across many cultures, does not totally replace the local cosmic religion but rather integrates many of its elements. He speaks, therefore, of a process of "in-religionization,"[22] besides inculturation. The elements of cosmic religion are integrated into a new totality in a new religious context. What happens is that the metacosmic religion focuses on the transcendent. It speaks more of the other world than this one. Its official rituals tend to refer to transcendent mysteries. It leaves large areas of life in this world free for traditional rituals. The seven sacraments of the Catholic Church, for instance, mark some moments of the lifecycle of persons in community, not all of them. They ignore totally the agricultural and seasonal cycles. Besides, many of the rituals of cosmic religions also aim at celebrating and stabilizing the social order in addition to religious faith. The rituals around birth, initiation, marriage, and death spell out mutual relationships and responsibilities of different people in the wider family and in the village. This is the reason that the official rituals of the church do not totally satisfy the people. They complete them with many other rituals taken from their own culture and cosmic religion. Since cosmic religion refers to this world, it need not contradict the metacosmic insistence on the other world.

Healing, for example, is an acute need of the people. The sacrament of the anointing of the sick is, in actual practice in many places, limited to the dying. This leaves the field open to other rituals and ritual agents to meet the needs for healing. A prayer or a blessing does not satisfy ritual-hungry people. Rituals that "touch" the body (for example, reiki, pranic healing) can themselves be elements of healing. The horizontal, social dimension is also as important for healing, especially in psychosomatic illnesses, as the vertical, spiritual one. So people adapt traditional rituals for the purpose. In the process they may relate them to a particular saint or to a special sacred place. They may add signs and prayers that Christianize the ritual. The ritual itself is borrowed from cosmic religiosity. There is nothing wrong in this. After all, washing with water, a communal meal, anointing with oil, or imposition of hands were not directly revealed from heaven. They were borrowed from Jewish usage and given new meanings by

---

[22] Pieris, *Fire and Water,* 67.

Christians. Similarly, symbols and rituals from Greco-Roman religious and secular cultures were later integrated into the liturgy. So there is no reason to object to the integration of other cosmic religious symbols and rituals into the Christian popular tradition.

Such integration can be better understood if we look at the structure of rituals. Rituals are community symbolic actions. They have a three-level structure.[23] Let us take the ritual of Christian Initiation. At a ritual level the main symbolic action is washing with water together with the profession of faith. At the social level the main symbolic action is the admission of an individual to the Christian community. At the religious or mysteric level this admission of an individual to the community of Christian believers symbolizes the person's being reborn in the Spirit and becoming a child of God.

The Ritual of Baptism

At the ritual level the actions symbolize purification and commitment in faith. In turn, these ritual actions symbolize the adhesion to the Christian community. This whole symbolic complex indicates the rebirth in the Spirit. The pivotal element in this structure is adhesion to the Christian community and the spiritual meaning given to it. Symbolic actions at the ritual level can change.

The baptisms of desire or of blood (martyrdom) are considered as substitutions for the rite of washing. The ritual of washing itself meant repentance in the baptism of John. It still means purification from sins in Hinduism and can be repeated. Thousands of Hindus throng to the sacred rivers at auspicious occasions. But Christians use it as an initiation rite. So it is a community that specifies the particular meaning of a symbol by integrating it in a particular socio-religious context. Such "symbolization" should not contradict the basic human meaning of a ritual. But this basic human meaning can be further specified and enriched in its own social and religious (faith) context by the community.

We could go a step further. Cosmic religious symbols may be as much cultural as they are religious. So there is no problem in integrating them. What about symbols from other religious traditions? As long as other religions were considered as untrue and devilish, any integration of their symbols and rituals would have been unthinkable. But today we believe that the Spirit of God is present and active, not

---

[23] Michael Amaladoss, *Can Sacraments Change? Variable and Invariable Elements in Sacramental Rites* (Bangalore: Theological Publications in India, 1979).

only in the human hearts of individuals, but also in other cultures and religions (RM 28). If this is so, this Spirit must be manifesting itself in their personal, social, and historical experience, in their scriptures and narratives, prayers, rituals, and symbols.

It is true that every religion is not merely the manifestation of the Spirit of God. It is also the response of humans to the self-manifesting God. So it is bound to be affected by human limits and sinfulness. (This is also true of the church.) Therefore, discernment is indicated, not wholesale rejection. In interreligious encounter, then, even between metacosmic religions, we can be open to mutual influences and even borrowings at the religious level. The official view of other religions today looks on them as preparations, guided by the Spirit, that have to find their fulfillment in Christianity. They have the "seeds of the words" that will find their fullness in the word that is in the church. This paradigm of preparation-fulfillment is challenged by many theologians today.[24] But even remaining within that paradigm the other religions have "good and holy elements" that can be integrated into their ritual and symbolic tradition by Christians.

Being Hindu-Christian

When we compare metacosmic religions, we tend to do so from the outside in the manner of scholars doing comparative religion. Or we look at other religions from the vantage point of the missionaries who come from different lands. We can think of another standpoint from within. For me, an Indian Christian, Hinduism is not an "other" religion, as it is for a foreign missionary. It is the religion of my ancestors. God has spoken to my ancestors through it. It is part of my tradition. I have my roots in it. I could say that I have two roots: Hinduism and Christianity. I will not fully find myself until I can discover and integrate the riches—God's gifts and human creativity—both these traditions have given to me. I am not looking at Hindu scriptures, symbols, and rituals from the outside, as "other," but from within, as "mine."

Obviously, I cannot have my feet in two boats at the same time. I will have to find a personal integration. Being a Christian, my integration of other religious elements will be around my experience of Jesus. I do not have to reject the Christian historical tradition. But I will have to see that the Christian and Hindu traditions interact within me and

---

[24] See, for example, Jacques Dupuis, *Christianity and the Religions: From Confrontation to Dialogue* (Maryknoll, NY: Orbis Books, 2002).

my community in a creative manner. I will then be not only an "Indian Christian" but a "Hindu-Christian," my main identity being Christian. What I say here about Hinduism in my own personal case can be applied by others to Buddhism, Islam, Tribal, Dalit, or other religions, depending on where their roots are. Most missionaries, in spite of the "incarnational" paradigm of mission, do not reach the point where they can look on another religion as their own. Swami Abhishiktananda is a rare example of someone who felt called to the Hindu experience of the advaita and recognized that tradition as his own.

I think that a number of Christians in India today, especially those living in the ashrams, were, and are, following this path. They inspire themselves by reading the Hindu and other religious scriptures. They sing the devotional hymns of the saints of other religions. They use methods of meditation like the Yoga or Viapassana or Zen. Some of them may see them as steps leading to deeper Christian prayer. Others may see them as valuable methods of contemplation in themselves. Some speak of having Hindu or Buddhist gurus.[25] It is also true that we can come across people who are Christian-Hindus, rooted in Hinduism but feeling themselves to be disciples of Christ in many ways.[26] Mahatma Gandhi claimed to be one of those.

Beyond Symbiosis

We seem to have reached the limits of interreligious integration with people who claim to be Hindu-Christian. Is it possible to go beyond this? The experience of Swami Abhishiktananda seems to indicate a further step. When he founded a Christian ashram together with Jules Monchanin, their aim was to witness to Christian mysticism in an Indian context, hoping to attract Hindu seekers to find fulfillment in the Christian experience. In keeping with this goal one of his first books—*Saccidananda*—started with the advaitic (nondual) experience of a South Indian Hindu sage, Ramana Maharishi, and tried to show how it can find fulfillment in the Christian experience of the Trinity.[27] His contact with Ramana Maharishi, however, had a

---

[25] See Dennis Gira and Jacques Scheuer, eds., *Vivre de plusieurs religions: Promesse ou illusion?* (Paris: L'Atelier, 2000).

[26] See M. M.Thomas, *The Acknowledged Christ of the Indian Renaissance* (London: SCM Press, 1969).

[27] See Swami Abhishiktananda, *Saccidananda: A Christian Approach to Advaitic Experience*, 2nd ed. (Delhi: ISPCK, 1984); idem, *Hindu-Christian Meeting Point—Within the Cave of the Heart* (Delhi: ISPCK, 1997).

powerful impact on him. So, leaving his ashram he frequently went to Thiruvannamali, where Ramana Maharishi was, and sought to have the advaitic experience. Ramana was not very communicative. After his death, Swami Abhishiktananda found another advaitic guru in Swami Gnanananda.[28] He was helped by many other Hindu teachers along his way. Finally, he did have the advaitic experience.

To the end of his life Swami Abhishiktananda was faithful to his Christian identity, celebrating the Eucharist and praying the psalms. If we read his diary, what strikes us is his continuing attempt to integrate his Christian and advaitic (Hindu) experience. He did not find it easy. Once he had had the advaitic experience, he did not think that it can find fulfillment in the experience of the Trinity. Sometimes he speaks as if the advaitic experience is beyond all particular religious experiences, including the Christian one. And yet he was not ready to abandon his Christian experience. I am sure he found it still meaningful. Yet he was hesitant to reprint his book *Saccidananda*, though he finally did it with a new introduction. A few months before his death, he had a heart attack. After that, the tension between his two experiences seemed to have disappeared. He did not write much after that to share with us his perspective. But from a few remarks that he made it seems to me that he just accepted the two experiences—Christian and advaitic—as different and no longer sought to subordinate one to the other or see one as being fulfilled by the other. He had two experiences of the Absolute in tension. He did not achieve a symbiosis or integration, much as he would have liked it. How do we understand this experience?

We have been talking about how a particular religion can encounter a new culture or a cosmic religion or another great religion and how it can integrate elements from them into itself without losing its identity. With Abhishiktananda we are facing a situation in which it is not possible to integrate the other religious experience into one's own religious framework. These are two different experiences. They cannot be subordinated, one to the other, in a hierarchical or partial-whole or preparation-fulfillment framework. Their different identities have to be respected. We do not believe in many Absolutes. There is only one Absolute. But different religious groups seek to experience this Absolute in different ways, according to their own historical, cultural, and religious traditions. The different ways are like different languages. One language cannot be subsumed into another. Some may be able

---

[28] Swami Abhishiktananda, *Guru and Disciple: An Encounter with Sri Gnanananda, a Contemporary Spiritual Master* (Delhi: ISPCK, 2000).

to speak both languages, but not at the same time. Each language has a framework that has to be respected.

One of the theories that theologians propose to make sense of the pluralism of religions is *theocentric* pluralism. This is opposed to *Christocentrism*. Swami Abhishiktananda did not propose a theocentric theory of religions. He did not speak about other mediators besides Christ. He would rather say that God, who is Father-Son-Spirit for us, is also beyond all "name and form." This is the apophatic tradition. The advaitic tradition reaches the Absolute, not through another mediator who is in competition with Jesus, but through a different path. Swami Abhishiktananda would have suggested that Jesus himself had such an advaitic experience of the Father. The prayer of Jesus in John 17 seems to indicate this. It also shows that Jesus was keen to share this experience with the disciples. Swami Abhishiktananda would not be equating or comparing his experience with Jesus. At the level of advaitic oneness we are beyond all name and form. At the level of name and form we have the different religious experiences. The advaitic experience is not particularly Hindu. But it is Hinduism that leads him to it. I know that all this sounds very complicated. Perhaps we need not go deeper into this for our purpose here. I would only say that Swami Abhishiktananda was not simply a pluralist. At the same time he was not able to integrate his different experiences in a symbiosis around Christianity, which was his basic identity. I think that his experience would be better indicated by the term *harmony*.

Syncretism or Harmony

It is time now to get back to the examples with which I started. Among the various experiences I recounted I wonder whether I would call any of them syncretistic. There are people who seem to treat the various religious symbols and rituals as objects in a supermarket. They will try one thing or another till they receive satisfaction. There is no commitment to a particular way. There is no attempt at integration. They do not have a clear sense of identity, at least in this particular situation. The phenomenon that is called New Age may fit this description. It may be called syncretistic. These people do not have roots in any religion. They try out various things. They pick and choose. They build up their own practice with elements taken from various sources. I do not see such a relativistic attitude in any of the examples I have given above.

Perhaps the story of the couple who go with their sick child to a doctor, a priest, and a Muslim shaman may need some explanation. There is no problem about their going to the doctor and to the church. But there may a question about going to a shaman. The church does speak about evil spirits. It has official exorcists. But they do not practice very much. That is why people go to shamans, Muslim or Hindu. This happened to me more than twenty years ago. Today, probably, they would go to a Christian charismatic healer who claims to free people from evil spirits. No one would consider this a syncretistic practice. I am not entering here into a discussion about the worldview underlying this phenomenon, particularly the belief in spirits. I only point out that such a practice need not be considered syncretistic within the understanding of people today.

The ritual at the funeral is very significant. It emphasizes the idea that at death the body returns to the earth, but the person does not disappear into thin air. We believe in the communion of saints. The church approves the honoring of the ancestors. People who are dead remain linked to us in various ways. We can relate to them, and they can relate to us. The ritual I described celebrates this. I do not see anything un-Christian about it. It can be easily integrated into a Christian funeral rite.

The rituals of popular religiosity mostly represent phenomena of symbiosis. The people have a "sense of faith." They know to integrate traditional rituals into a new faith framework. There may be occasional exaggerations, but they disappear or are corrected over the years. The only problem is that they are not official, and the elite in the community look down on them. But it is a problem for the elite, not for the people. The people find their rituals quite meaningful. It is the elite who accuse them of syncretism. Such accusations come from a narrow fundamentalist perspective. Fundamentalism can take two forms.

Some people closely identify the cultural elements in which they express their faith with the faith itself. They do not make a distinction between religion and culture. Or they give a privileged and normative place to one particular culture. Many officials in the church give such a privileged place to the Judaic and Greco-Roman cultures.[29] They may even identify them with Christianity. So any effort to integrate other cultural elements into the Christian ritual is seen as syncretistic. Today, a lot of lip service is paid to the need for inculturation. But at the same time every effort is made to preserve the "substantial unity of

---

[29] For the impact of Greece and Rome on early liturgy, see Josef A. Jungmann, *Public Worship: A Survey* (Collegeville, MN: Liturgical Press, 1957); Theodor Klauser, *A Short History of the Western Liturgy* (Oxford: Oxford University Press, 1979).

the Roman Rite" (VL 36). These people are basically not open to other cultural symbols except as external decorations. They see syncretism everywhere. These are cultural fundamentalists. For example, I used to know some people in India who would consider candles Christian and oil lamps Hindu.

Then we have the religious fundamentalists. They think that their religion is the only true one. Anything that comes from another religious tradition is immediately characterized as untrue, evil, and devilish. For them, interpretation is an unknown art. But after the Second Vatican Council we have a more positive view of other religions. Besides, now we see also the possibility of integrating symbols and rituals from other religions, but interpreting them and giving them new meanings and connotations in our faith context. We remain rooted in our identity. But we enrich ourselves from various sources. Sometimes our own complex identity as Hindu-Christian may urge us toward such an integration.[30]

However, there are areas that are still not very clear. Swami Abhishiktananda offers us an example of this. I think that the Congregation for the Doctrine of the Faith was aware of a tension when it sought to discourage people from trying out methods of concentration and contemplation from Asian religious traditions like Yoga and Zen. Some Christians try to use these methods as preparation for prayer insofar as they can quiet the mind and help one to concentrate on one's own religious symbols. But the method itself—Zen is also derived from Yoga—leads one to experiences beyond "name and form." Then it becomes a challenge to "integrate" them in the framework of the name and form *(namarupa)* of Christianity. We have had an apophatic tradition in Christianity. At the apophatic level one can only remain silent. A way of looking at this situation positively is that very few people will reach this level and the Spirit of God will certainly guide them. There are, however, people who propose Yoga and Zen as natural and human— Godless. They seek to give natural explanations of the symbols of various religions. I think that we have to be wary of these people. Human experiences are constructed in some way. Intentions are important. They make our identity. This identity today can be hybrid. But even hybridity has to come to some sort of cohesion in every person and community. Such cohesion, however, need not exclude complexity and tension.[31]

---

[30] See M. M. Thomas, *Risking Christ for Christ's Sake: Toward and Ecumenical Theology of Pluralism* (Geneva: World Council of Churches, 1987).

[31] Michael Amaladoss, "Double Religious Belonging and Liminality," *Vidyajyoti, Journal of Theological Reflection* 66 (2002): 21–34.

Conclusion

In a postmodern world pluralism, with globalization and increasing migration, is a fact of life.[32] We can no longer live in our ghettos, guarding our secluded identities. Hybridity of all kinds is inevitable.[33] That is why some modern theologians see syncretism as a positive process and reject the kind of pejorative connotation that is normally attached to it.[34] Calls to avoid syncretism and claims to guard the unity of the community by safeguarding its identity may be one way of exercising power through control. Pluralism will mean decentralization, and this is seen as a threat by those who are at the center. The unity that they would like to safeguard is the identity as they see and live it. They do not mind people practicing parallel religions or multiple religiosity, provided a facade of unity is kept in official rituals that they dominate and control.

At the beginning of this chapter, quoting Pieris, I mentioned synthesis, besides syncretism and symbiosis. Are there examples of synthesis, in which a third religion emerges out of the interaction of two other religions? The emergence of a new religion is not a common occurrence. I do not know whether some of the Independent Churches in Africa qualify. But in India, Sikhism can be considered a synthetic religion, born out of the encounter between Hinduism and Islam. Like Islam it has no images. Its religious practice is centered around scripture and its ritual recitation. But its scripture contains many devotional poems of Hindu saints. Even today, many Hindus feel a sense of fellowship with Sikhism.

Religions have grown through their interaction with other cultures and religions. Buddhism was born in India as a protest against Vedic Hinduism. But Hinduism progressively absorbed the apophatism and ahimsa of Buddhism so that the latter disappeared from India. Shankara was accused of being a crypto-Buddhist when he championed his theory of the advaita (nonduality). The Mahayana tradition of Buddhism emerged under the impact of the popular religiosity and tantric practices of North India, Tibet, and China. Islam developed the Sufi tradition in interaction with Hinduism. Hinduism itself went through a reform

---

[32] Paul Lakeland, *Post-modernity: Christian Identity in a Fragmented Age* (Minneapolis: Fortress Press, 1997).

[33] Robert J. C. Young, *Colonial Desire: Hybridity in Theory, Culture, and Race* (London: Routledge, 1995).

[34] See Robert J. Schreiter, *The New Catholicity: Theology between the Global and the Local* (Maryknoll, NY: Orbis Books, 1997).

inspired by its contact with Christianity. Christianity did not encounter any challenging metacosmic religion till it came to Asia. It was easy for it to integrate, by subjugating, the cosmic religions of Europe, Latin America, and Africa. But a true encounter with developed religions like Hinduism and Buddhism in Asia may challenge it to change and grow in unforeseen ways. This can be threatening. At least some Christians are not ready for this. So they keep warning people about syncretism.

One of the reasons may be the logical approach Christian thinking inherited from Greek philosophy. Logic is guided by the principle of contradiction. One thing is not another. Reality is looked at through a dichotomous prism: either-or. Identity involves exclusion: I am not the other. Such exclusion means that any coming together of opposites is seen as a denial of identity and unity. I think that this is the fear that is behind easy apprehensions of syncretism. People in the East tend to look at reality, not in terms of "either-or," but "both-and." Their approach is inclusive and integrative. Their sense of identity is rooted, but open. They are ready to hold opposites in tension. They easily move from affirmation to apophatism, but hold on to both. They are less afraid of syncretism.[35]

What is basic to Christian identity is the relationship to God manifested in Jesus. The symbols and rituals in which this relationship finds expression do not really matter.[36] If we really believe that God's plan is to "gather up all things," to "reconcile all things," then encounters with cultures and religions leading to symbiosis and harmony would be normal. Deeper encounters may lead us to explore newer dimensions of experience beyond "name and form."

---

[35] Jung Young Lee, *The Theology of Change: The Christian Concept of God in an Eastern Perspective* (Maryknoll, NY: Orbis Books, 1979), 49–66; David L. Hall and Roger T. Ames, *Anticipating China* (Albany: State University of New York Press, 1995).

[36] Speaking of sacramental rites the Council of Trent spoke of their "substance" as being unchangeable (see J. Neuner and J. Dupuis, *The Christian Faith: Doctrinal Documents of the Catholic Church* [Bangalore: Theological Publications in India, 1990], 1324). The Second Vatican Council specified this "substance" as "divinely instituted" (SC 21). Theologians suggest that only two rituals qualify to be so unchangeable: washing with water in baptism and the community eating and drinking together in the Eucharist. See Michael Amaladoss, *Do Sacraments Change? Variable and Invariable Elements in Sacramental Rites* (Bangalore: Theological Publications in India, 1979).

Chapter 15

Interreligious Dialogue Fifty Years after Vatican II

CHALLENGES AND OPPORTUNITIES

On October 28, 1965, the Second Vatican Council published the *Declaration on the Relation of the Church to Non-Christian Religions (Nostra Aetate)*. Many developments in the field of interreligious dialogue have taken place since then. In the context of the thrust toward new evangelization, it may be helpful to look at the past in order to look at and plan for the future of the church's mission in the world, especially in South Asia. The Synod on New Evangelization said, in its proposition 53:

> The dialogue with all believers is a part of the New Evangelization. . . . Faithful to the teaching of Vatican II, the Church respects the other religions and their adherents and is happy to collaborate with them in the defense and promotion of the inviolable dignity of every person.

There was also concern for religious freedom. In the context of increasing interreligious violence in many parts of the world and, especially, of the widespread persecution of the Christians in many parts of the globe, protecting such religious freedom based on the dignity of the human person and dialogue between religions seems to be an urgent task for the promotion of peace in the world. At the same time, precisely because of the interreligious tensions, interest and involvement in dialogue and collaboration seem to be lessening. This may be a moment to look back at our recent past, with its

211

inspirations as well as tensions, so that we can plan better for our mission in the future.

The Inspiration: The Second Vatican Council

At the council the *Pastoral Constitution on the Church in the Modern World (Gaudium et Spes)* affirmed the availability of salvation as a participation in the paschal mystery of Christ

> to all men of good will in whose hearts grace is active invisibly. For since Christ died for all, and since all men are in fact called to one and the same destiny, which is divine, we must hold that the Holy Spirit offers to all the possibility of being made partners, in a way known to God, in the paschal mystery. (GS 22)

The same pastoral constitution also indicates the possible way in which the grace of salvation is available to humans:

> It is by the gift of the Holy Spirit that man, through faith, comes to contemplate and savor the mystery of God's design. Deep within his conscience man discovers a law which he has not laid upon himself but which he must obey. His voice, even calling him to love and to do what is good and to avoid evil, tells him inwardly at the right moment: do this, shun that. For man has in his heart a law inscribed by God. His dignity lies in observing this law, and by it he will be judged. (GS 15–16; cf. LG 16)

Here we see the Holy Spirit linked to God's voice in conscience. The *Declaration on Religious Liberty (Dignitatis Humanae)* gives conscience a social dimension. Suggesting that humans must not be prevented from acting according to their conscience in religious matters, since the practice of religion consists of those voluntary and free internal acts by which humans direct themselves to God, it goes on to say:

> His own social nature requires that man give external expression to these internal acts of religion, that he communicate with others on religious matters, and profess his religion in community. (DH 3)

A communitarian dimension is also affirmed in *Nostra Aetate:*

All men form but one community. This is so because all stem from the one stock which God created to people the entire earth (cf. Acts 17:26), and also because all share a common destiny, namely God. His providence, evident goodness, and saving designs extend to all men (cf. Wis 8:1; Acts 14:17; Rom 2:6–7; 1 Tim 2:4). (NA 1)

Referring to the "unsolved riddles of human existence," the declaration continues:

The religions which are found in more advanced civilizations endeavor by way of well-defined concepts and exact language to answer these questions. . . . The Catholic Church rejects nothing of what is true and holy in these religions. She has a high regard for the manner of life and conduct, the precepts and doctrines which, although differing in many ways from her own teaching, nevertheless, often reflect a ray of that truth which enlightens all men. . . . The Church, therefore, urges her sons to enter with prudence and charity into discussion and collaboration with members of other religions. (NA 2; see also AG 9, 11, 15, 18; GS 92; OT 16)

The council, in this way, lays the foundation for interreligious dialogue.

The Practice and Teaching of John Paul II

In the spirit of Vatican II, John Paul II invited the leaders of other religions to come together to Assisi to pray for world peace in October 1986. (He did something similar during the conflict in Bosnia and the jubilee year 2000.) Explaining this initiative, he declared, in a discourse to the Roman Curia on December 22, 1986, that all authentic prayer is from the Holy Spirit (no. 11). Developing this further, in 1991, he said in his encyclical *Redemptoris Missio*:

The Spirit manifests himself in a special way in the Church and in her members. Nevertheless, his presence and activity are universal, limited neither by space nor time (DEV 53). . . . The Spirit's presence and activity affect not only individuals but also society and history, peoples, cultures and religions. . . . Thus the

Spirit, who "blows where he wills" (cf. Jn 3:8), who "was already at work in the world before Christ was glorified" (AG 4), and who "has filled the world . . . holds all things together (and) knows what is said (Wis 1:7), leads us to broaden our vision in order to ponder his activity in every time and place (DEV 53). . . . The Church's relationship with other religions is dictated by a twofold respect: "Respect for man in his quest for answers to the deepest questions of his life, and respect for the action of the Spirit in man. (RM 28–29)

John Paul II, however, clarifies that the action of the Spirit in the history of peoples, cultures, and religions "serves as a preparation for the Gospel and can only be understood in reference to Christ, the Word who took flesh by the power of the Spirit 'so that as perfectly human he would save all human beings and sum up all things'" (GS 45; DEV 54). It is the same Spirit that impels the church to proclaim Christ and also guides it to discover its gifts to other peoples, to foster them, and to receive them in dialogue (RM 29). It is in this context that John Paul II goes on to affirm:

Dialogue is based on hope and love, and will bear fruit in the Spirit. Other religions constitute a positive challenge for the Church; they stimulate her both to discover and acknowledge the signs of Christ's presence and of the working of the Spirit, as well as to examine more deeply her own identity and to bear witness to the fullness of Revelation which she has received for the good of all. (RM 56)

Some Theological Tensions

Such openness to other religions and to dialogue with them has given rise to much theological reflection regarding the significance of religions with regard to salvific divine-human encounter and their relationship to the church. Given a wide variety of such reflections, some theologians group them under various paradigms like exclusivism, inclusivism, and pluralism and ecclesiocentrism, Christocentrism, and theocentrism. Such paradigms are not very helpful. They are not faith based, but rather abstract and rational-philosophical classifications. Besides, they are inadequate and mistaken. For example, if we believe that Christ is God, the second Person of the holy Trinity, the opposition between Christocentrism and theocentrism is meaningless. Such a distinction downgrades Christ, humanizing him and making him one mediator among others between God and humans. This is obviously not acceptable to us.

Similarly, pluralism is affirmed by philosophers like John Hick according to the Kantian principle that God or "Absolute Truth" in itself is unknown and unknowable; we have only various claimed personal perceptions, relative to the perceivers and their contexts, without any objective validity. This is pure relativism and is not acceptable. God has manifested Godself to us in history through various prophets and finally through his Son, Jesus, who, we believe, is the fullness of Truth (Heb 1:1–2). Such divine manifestations experienced by humans are not merely humanistic, relative, pluralistic perceptions in the sense of John Hick.

The Church and the Kingdom

Such paradigms, however, bring up the question of how to relate the church to the other religions. John Paul II suggests a solution in his encyclical *Redemptoris Missio*. God has only one plan for the salvation of the universe, which he has manifested in Jesus Christ. St. Paul writes:

> With all wisdom and insight he has made known to us the mystery of his will, according to his good pleasure that he set forth in Christ, as a plan for the fullness of time, to gather up all things in him, things in heaven and things on earth. (Eph 1:8–10)

John Paul II echoes this:

> Salvation consists in believing and accepting the mystery of the Father and of his love, made manifest and freely given in Jesus through the Spirit. In this way the Kingdom of God comes to be fulfilled: the Kingdom prepared for in the Old Testament, brought about by Christ and in Christ, and proclaimed to all peoples by the church, which works and prays for its perfect and definitive realization. (RM 12)

The kingdom of God is proclaimed, inaugurated, and realized by Jesus (Mark 1:14–15). By his preaching and miracles Jesus communicates to us an experience of the loving and forgiving Father (Luke

15), who wants to share God's life with us (John 6) and makes it possible by his own passion, death, and resurrection and the gift of the Spirit. This kingdom is for all people, and all are called to become its members. This call goes out particularly to the poor and the oppressed of the world (Luke 4:18–20). It is an eschatological project, not in the sense that it will happen only at the end of the world, but in the sense that it has started now but will find its final fulfillment at the end of times, so that we live in a period of "already–not yet" (RM 13).

> The Kingdom is the concern of every one: individuals, society, and the world. Working for the Kingdom means acknowledging and promoting God's activity, which is present in human history and transforms it. Building the Kingdom means working for liberation from evil in all its forms. (RM 15)

This kingdom is not merely an earthly reality, though it is being realized in history. The church

> is ordered to the Kingdom of God of which she is the seed, sign and instrument. Yet while remaining distinct from Christ and the Kingdom, the Church is indissolubly united to both. . . . The result is a unique and special relationship which while not excluding the action of Christ and the Spirit outside the Church's visible boundaries, confers upon her a specific and necessary role. (RM 18)

What is this special role? The church is at the service of the kingdom. It serves it by proclaiming and witnessing to the kingdom and by establishing "new particular churches." It also serves the kingdom "by spreading throughout the world the 'Gospel values' which are an expression of the Kingdom" (RM 20). Insofar as the people live "Gospel values" and are open to the working of the Spirit, "the inchoate reality of the Kingdom can also be found beyond the confines of the church among peoples everywhere" (RM 20). It is in this context that we have to say that the church has the fullness of God's self-revelation in Jesus Christ, the incarnate Word, while it may be found in an inchoate way among other peoples. The church also serves the kingdom by her intercession because it is God's gift and work.

Earlier in this encyclical John Paul II explained that, though salvation is meant for and "made concretely available to all," often social and cultural conditions do not allow people to become part of the church, and they are members of other religious traditions.

> For such people salvation in Christ is accessible by virtue of a grace which, while having a mysterious relationship to the Church, does not make them formally part of the Church but enlightens them in a way which is accommodated to their spiritual and material condition. (RM 10)

This is possible because the church is not merely the visible, institutional body, but is also the mystical body of Christ ordained to the kingdom of God.

It is in this context that John Paul II affirms: "The Church contributes to humanity's pilgrimage of conversion to God's plan through her witness and through such activities as dialogue, human promotion, commitment to justice and peace, education and the care of the sick, and aid to the poor and to children" (RM 20).

In his apostolic letter *Ecclesia in Asia* (1999), he warns that salvation by Christ apart from the ordinary means of salvation, namely, the church, "does not thereby cancel the call to faith and baptism which God wills for all people" (31).[1] He then adds: "Interreligious relations are best developed in a context of openness to other believers, a willingness to listen and the desire to respect and understand others in their differences. . . . This should result in collaboration, harmony and mutual enrichment" (31).[2] Pope Francis in *Evangelii Gaudium* (2013) also emphasizes this:

> An attitude of openness in truth and in love must characterize the dialogue with the followers of non-Christian religions, in spite of various obstacles and difficulties, especially forms of fundamentalism on both sides. . . . In this dialogue, ever friendly and sincere, attention must always be paid to the essential bond between dialogue and proclamation, which leads the Church to maintain and intensify her relationship with non-Christians. (EG 250–51)

The Indian Tradition

India is a multireligious country. Hinduism, Buddhism, Jainism, and Sikhism had their origin here. Christianity has been present in India from the time of St. Thomas the Apostle, according to a strong

---

[1] This quotation is from a letter that he wrote to the FABC at its Fifth Assembly in 1991 (*AAS* 83 (1991): 101).

[2] This is a quotation from *Propositio* 41 of the Synod for Asia.

tradition. Islam has also been present from about the eighth century. Interreligious tensions and conflicts were not totally absent. But there was an atmosphere of tolerance. In the third century BCE the Buddhist emperor Ashoka declared in one of his rock-cut edicts:

> King Priyadarsi honours men of all faiths, members of religious orders and laymen alike, with gifts and various marks of esteem. . . . The faiths of others all deserve to be honoured for one reason or another. By honouring them, one exalts one's own faith and at the same time performs a service to the faith of others. By acting otherwise, one injures one's own faith and also does disservice to that of others. For if a man extols his own faith and disparages another because of devotion to his own and because he wants to glorify it, he seriously injures his own faith. Therefore concord alone is commendable, for through concord men may learn and respect the conception of Dharma accepted by others.[3]

In the sixteenth century the Muslim emperor Akbar invited scholars of different religions for a conversation. Two Jesuits from Goa went to take part in them.[4] Akbar himself tried to found a new religion, taking whatever he considered good in the other religions. When the British came, some of the educated Indians responded positively to the message of Jesus in the gospels. They recognized Jesus as an Oriental guru and declared themselves his disciples, though they did not wish to join his church, which was seen by them as a European organization. Mahatma Gandhi was inspired by Jesus's teachings, and by his suffering on the cross, to develop his own policy of nonviolent resistance to injustice. He successfully led India to its independence from British colonialism through a nonviolent struggle.

When the Indian subcontinent was divided into India and Pakistan along religious lines, India chose to be a secular country, not only treating all religions equally, but even offering special rights to the minority religions (and cultures) to practice and propagate their religion.

On the Christian side, already in the early twentieth century, there was openness toward Hinduism as a preparation for the gospel. J. N. Farquahar, a Christian missionary, wrote the book *Christianity the Crown of Hinduism;* and Pierre Johanns, a Belgian Jesuit, published a series of pamphlets, *To Christ through the Vedanta,* trying to show

---

[3] Rock Edict XII, in *The Edicts of Ashoka,* ed. N. A. Nikam and Richard McKeon (Chicago: University of Chicago Press, 1959), 51–52.

[4] John Correia-Afonso, *Letters from the Mughal Court* (Anand, Gujarat: Gujarat Sahitya Prakash, 1980).

that the questions of Hindu Vedantic philosophy were answered by the theology of St. Thomas Aquinas. In 1950, two French priests, Abbe Jules Monchanin and Dom Henri Le Saux, founded a Christian ashram, hoping that the mystical tradition of Christianity, centered on the Trinity, lived in such ashrams would attract Hindus, who also had a mystical tradition. Similar efforts to reach out to Hinduism were also found elsewhere in the country, like Pune, Kolkata, and other places.

These and similar efforts received a boost, so to speak, with the encouragement of the Second Vatican Council to dialogue with other religions. Dialogue groups, in which members of different religions came together for intellectual exchanges, were founded in different parts of the country. The Catholic Bishops' Conference of India had an active secretariat that organized "live ins," in which members of different religions came to live together for a few days, sharing their thoughts and their scriptures and even meditating together on common themes. Christian ashrams were founded in several parts of the country.

Challenges of Interreligious Dialogue Today

But the situation has been changing in recent years. At the political level India still remains a secular country and the rights of the minorities are still upheld by the law courts, but there are many attempts by the state to encroach on them, and tensions on the field seem to be growing. Though there have been Hindu-Muslim tensions, sometimes leading to violence, for over a century, now they have taken new forms inspired by terrorist tendencies. Christians had been targeted by anti-conversion bills in some states. In the last fifteen years there has been anti-Christian violence in some parts of the country. The Hindu majority is becoming restive. There are increasing attempts to assert its identity for social and political gains. One problem is that after incidents of interreligious violence, "peace" is restored through political (police) power, but no serious efforts are made toward reconciliation and peace, respecting truth and justice. Although enquiry commissions are generally appointed, they are largely fruitless without proper follow up.

At the level of the church the ashrams are no longer as alive and active as before, after their pioneers have passed to the Lord. Many dialogue groups have disappeared. Formal meetings of various religious leaders are held occasionally. Dialogues at an intellectual level are rare, and if they continue it is normally in academic or secular settings, like departments of sociology in universities. Given the tense atmosphere in the country in the area of interreligious relations— especially after the recent elections—the program of interreligious dialogue needs to be reinvented and encouraged. We can think of it at four levels: peacemaking, living together, coming together for prayer, and comparative theologizing.

Four Levels of Dialogue

1 *Peacemaking.* The situation in the country today is not one of peaceful living among the religious groups. Even where there no active, ongoing conflict, there are memories of hurts, suspicions, and prejudices. In the age of mass media one tends to identify with the suffering of the other even at a distance. Conflicts between religious groups are triggered not so much for strictly religious reasons, but for economic and political reasons, religious identity being used to weld a group together. It may not be possible for the church and other religious groups to get directly involved in peacemaking. But we can operate at two levels. On the one hand, we can join other nongovernmental organizations in trying to bring out the truth and to obtain justice through the courts of law. On the other hand, we can prepare the people of different religious groups to understand and accept each other, getting rid of their ignorance of and prejudice against others. We can especially focus on the youth in our educational institutions through programs of interreligious and peace education, in which they are introduced to the different religious groups, both in theory and practice, and are also taught the values of reconciliation and forgiveness, dialogue, and peace in the process of building up human communities who live happy and fulfilled lives. The fact that these groups tend to be interreligious is an advantage. Special textbooks and training programs can be devised. This has started to happen in some places.

2   *Living together.* Religious ghettos in which people belonging to the same religion live together in the same geographical area seem to be disappearing in urban areas. But Christian leaders can take the initiative in constituting a group of leaders belonging to all religions (and ethnic groups) to discuss and act upon common civic issues. There can also be participation in one another's social festivals to create a sense of community.

3   *Coming together for prayer.* A third level of dialogue will be to follow the example of John Paul II and to come together to pray for peace and prosperity. This need not be a regular event but is needed

in moments of social crisis. When there has been interreligious violence or some big accidents or natural catastrophes, people can come
together to implore God's protection and help. Even if they do not
pray together, being together before God the Creator in a time of need
can be a unifying experience.

4   *Comparative theologizing.* The fourth level of dialogue consists in
what is known today as comparative theology. In the past, scholars
claimed to study the various religions with scientific objectivity. This
was known as a comparative study of religions. Even a nonbeliever
could do this. Today, religions are studied and compared, taking into
account the point of view of the believers. This is known as comparative theology. This has not been done much in India. We can even go
a step further, by trying to do such a comparative study as a group of
scholars who believe in the different religions engaging in dialogue.

By engaging in such dialogue we are not abandoning our duty to
proclaim the good news of the kingdom of God and to be witnesses
to Jesus in our lives. When we are relating to the religious "other"
in dialogue in the ways evoked above, we do not bracket our faith
convictions but are actually witnessing to our faith and promoting
gospel values. A positive proclamation can occur when there is an
opportunity. We can recall here the advice of Pope Francis: "It is not
by proselytizing that the church grows, but 'by attraction'" (EG 15).

Recognition of the religious "other" does not mean that we subscribe to sweeping statements like "all religions are the same" or "all
religions are true." While we recognize that the religions may play a
role in facilitating a salvific divine-human encounter for their believers,
this does not excuse us from the task of discerning and even judging
them in the light of the revelation we have received from God. At the
same time we need also to be open to a similar judgment on the way
that we live our own faith commitment. Though the church is the
mystical body of Christ, it remains in its visible, institutional manifestation a pilgrim that needs reformation and growth (see LG 14, 48).

While we recognize the other religions as facilitating the salvific
divine-human encounter, we believe that God's salvific plan for the
universe has been manifested fully and in a unique manner in Jesus
Christ (Eph 1:3–10; Col 1:15–20). If we use terms like *inspiration* and
revelation to refer to God's definitive self-manifestation in Jesus Christ,
we do not use the words *in the same sense* to refer to other possible
divine self-manifestations in other religions. Of course, Muslims and
Hindus speak about their scriptures. In the Christian tradition we
speak of private revelations. But all these cannot be equated, from
the point of view of our faith, to the public revelation that God has

granted to us in Jesus Christ. As the International Theological Commission writes in *Christianity and the World Religions* (1997):

> Although one cannot explicitly exclude any divine illumination in the composition of those books (in the religions which have them), it is much more fitting to reserve the qualification of "inspired" to books of the canon (cf. DV 11). (no. 92)

While we have to avoid such comparative statements, we can listen to popes Francis and John Paul II. Pope Francis writes:

> The same Spirit everywhere brings forth various forms of practical wisdom which help people to bear suffering and to live in greater peace and harmony. As Christians, we can also benefit from these treasures built up over many centuries, which can help us better to live our own beliefs. (EG 254)

Similarly, John Paul II challenges us Indians:

> In preaching the Gospel, Christianity first encountered Greek philosophy; but this does not mean at all that other approaches are precluded. Today, as the gospel gradually comes into contact with cultural worlds which once laid beyond Christian influence, there are new tasks of inculturation, which mean that our generation faces problems not unlike those faced by the church in the first centuries. My thoughts turn immediately to the lands of the East, so rich in religious and philosophical traditions of great antiquity. Among these lands, India has a special place. A great spiritual impulse leads Indian thought to seek an experience which would liberate the spirit from the shackles of time and space and would therefore acquire absolute value. The dynamic of this quest for liberation provides the context for great metaphysical systems. (FR 72).

Conclusion

India certainly shares in the global situation that seems to be ruled by individualism and consumerism, profit motivation and corruption in public life, and widely prevalent economic and sociopolitical inequalities. Only religions can offer a sense of values and motivation and inspiration for personal and social transformation. In a multireligious country like India, the religions are called to provide this help to society together. John Paul II, in a talk to other religious leaders in Chennai in February 1986, said:

> By dialogue we let God be present in our midst; for as we open ourselves in dialogue to one another, we also open ourselves to God. . . . As followers of different religions we should join together in promoting and defending common ideals in the spheres of religious liberty, human brotherhood, education, culture, social welfare and civic order.

One element of the religious context that we have to take into account is that, while India is not secularized in the sense that the people have become antireligious or atheist, as in some European countries, religions may remain an otherworldly concern, not playing a transformative role in society. In addition, religions may be becoming indicators of a sociopolitical identity in a conflictual multireligious community. The first task of dialogue in such a situation is to free religions from such a sociopolitical baggage and highlight the values that they stand for. Then we should seek, through dialogue and collaboration, to make them relevant to individual and social life.

What can be the Christian contribution to this common effort? Hindus and others in India have always been attracted by the ethical teachings of Jesus in the Sermon on the Mount. Beyond that, the teachings and actions of Jesus show us God as a parent who loves and forgives. Jesus gives us a new commandment to love one another as he has loved us. He has shown this love in service (washing the feet of the disciples), sharing (the Eucharist), and total self-gift unto death on a cross. His resurrection gives us an assurance that we are destined for life, not death, and that the risen Christ is sharing God's life with us and leading us to all fullness. It is this message of forgiveness of sins and salvation, love, and hope that we are called to share with the people with whom we are in dialogue. But this should not be simply a message that we share, but rather a project of action that we live in community.

Interreligious dialogue is therefore a challenge, but a necessary one, because we are collaborating with God in Jesus who is gathering all things together (Eph 1:8–10), reconciling all of us with one another and with Godself (Col 1:15–20), so that God will be "all in all" (1 Cor 15:28).

Epilogue

Pope Francis and Dialogue

Pope Francis is fast emerging as a model of dialogue both in word and deed. One of his early gestures was his letter to Eugenio Scalfari, a former editor of *La Repubblica*, who had written two articles raising some questions on the pope's encyclical *Lumen Fidei (The Light of Faith)*, prepared by Benedict XVI and completed by Francis).[1] Pope Francis surprised the whole world by writing a public response. This led to a personal dialogue with Scalfari, who reported on it in *La Repubblica*. Scalfari is a self-identified atheist, so the dialogue was significant. In the unrecorded interview Scalfari reports that the pope told him: "I believe in God, not in a Catholic God, there is no Catholic God, there is God."[2] Another gesture, earlier in 2013, was his washing the feet of young people at a juvenile detention center on Holy Thursday. Two of the youth were Muslims and two were women. If we know how such events are carefully planned and orchestrated, this could not have been simply an accident, since the usual practice is to wash the feet of Catholic males. A third event was the common prayer that was organized by the pope to pray for peace in Syria and to oppose any possible military intervention by outside powers. This was more spontaneous than the organized events in Assisi and Rome by John Paul II. Both in Rome and in Syria, Muslims were in the group, praying, besides perhaps members of other churches and religions, even if they may not have prayed together. Before he became pope, in Argentina he had excellent relations with the Jewish community. He published a book of conversations with his friend Rabbi Abraham Skorka: *On Heaven and Earth*.[3] He also had good relations with the Orthodox Church.

---

[1] Francis, "Letter to a Non-believer," September 4, 2013.

[2] "The Pope: How the Church Will Change," dialogue between Francis and Eugenio Scalfari, trans. Kathryn Wallace (October 1, 2013).

[3] Jorge Mario Bergoglio and Abraham Skorka, *On Heaven and Earth* (New York: Random House, 2013).

I would like to explore further this image of Pope Francis as a person of dialogue. I do so in two stages. In a first part I briefly indicate the basic attitudes that seem to be in the background of this character of Pope Francis. In the second I explore the texts, after he became pope, in which he speaks about dialogue. This will give us an idea about how the pope thinks, feels, and speaks about it.

Pope Francis's Basic Attitudes

What are the attitudes that make Pope Francis a dialogical person? I mention just a few so that there is no overlapping with the following section. First of all, Pope Francis has a deep respect for the dignity and freedom of the human person. Everyone knows by now what he said about homosexuals on the plane journey to Rome from Brazil: "Who am I to judge?" He could have said that homosexuality is a disorder and is wrong. But he does not talk in the abstract. He thinks of humans who are living a difficult personal experience. He recognizes their struggle and refuses to judge. Another day, in his homily, he comments on the story in the Gospel of Mark where the disciples are complaining about someone who is baptizing people in his name (Mark 9:38–41). They want to stop him. Jesus tells them to leave him alone and says, "He who is not against us is for us." The pope speaks of the culture of encounter:

> "The Lord has redeemed all of us, all of us, with the Blood of Christ: all of us, not just Catholics. Everyone! 'Father, the atheists?' Even the atheists. Everyone! And this Blood makes us children of God of the first class! We are created children in the likeness of God and the Blood of Christ has redeemed us all! And we all have a duty to do good. And this commandment for everyone to do good, I think, is a beautiful path towards peace. If we, each doing our own part, if we do good to others, if we meet there, doing good, and we go slowly, gently, little by little, we will make that culture of encounter: we need that so much. We must meet one another doing good. 'But I don't believe, Father, I am an atheist!' But do good: we will meet one another there."[4]

---

[4] Vatican Radio, "Pope at Mass: Culture of Encounter Is the Foundation of Peace" (May 22, 2013).

Of course, the church says that those who follow their conscience will be saved, whatever their beliefs. But the pope certainly puts it dramatically and makes it possible for an atheist like Scalfari to dialogue with him. Divorced and remarried individuals may be in an irregular marital situation. But they are human persons in difficult personal situations, and God's mercy will reach out to them too. Such an attitude to persons also indicates a subtle shift from a one-sided emphasis on orthodoxy to orthopraxis.

This leads us to the second attitude that characterizes Francis. How often has he proclaimed God's boundless mercy and the need for us too to convey this loving mercy of God, whatever may be the circumstances and the sin committed? In the past the figure of hell and the image of God as judge have figured prominently in our preaching. The other religions were presented as ways to hell or at least as unable to lead people to God. Francis insists that God's love and mercy reach out to everyone. We have to stress God's forgiveness rather than judgment.

Francis's special devotion to St. Peter Faber points to his third attitude. Peter Faber was one of the first companions of St. Ignatius Loyola and a cofounder with him of the Society of Jesus. While his first companions and roommates in Paris, St. Ignatius and St. Francis Xavier, were well known and admired, Peter Faber was not much known outside the Society of Jesus. He was made a Blessed in 1872 and almost forgotten. Soon after Francis became pope, he expressed a desire to make Peter Faber a saint, which he did on his own seventy-seventh birthday, December 17, 2013. When a Jesuit interviewer, Antonio Spadaro,[5] asked him why he was so impressed by Peter Faber, Francis answered:

> His dialogue with all, even the most remote and even with his opponents; his simple piety, a certain naïveté perhaps, his being available straightaway, his careful interior discernment, the fact that he was a man capable of great and strong decisions but also capable of being so gentle and loving. . . . Ignatius was a mystic, not an ascetic. . . . and Faber was a mystic.

The short list of people for whom Peter Faber prayed every day included his Protestant opponents. He was a person of conversation and

---

[5] For this interview, see Antonio Spadaro, *A Big Heart Open to God: A Conversation with Pope Francis* (New York: Harper Collins, 2013).

dialogue with Catholics and others. I feel that Pope Francis is inspired by this quality as well.

The final attitude that I refer to is his insistence on the joy of the gospel that we have to live and proclaim. We have to resist any attempt at force or compulsion. The fragrance and joy of Truth and Love will spread itself. In *Evangelii Gaudium (The Joy of the Gospel)*, Francis writes:

> Evangelization is first and foremost about preaching the Gospel to *those who do not know Jesus Christ or who have always rejected him*. Many of these are quietly seeking God, led by a yearning to see his face, even in countries of ancient Christian tradition. All of them have a right to receive the Gospel. Christians have the duty to proclaim the Gospel without excluding anyone. Instead of seeming to impose new obligations, they should appear as people who wish to share their joy, who point to a horizon of beauty and who invite others to a delicious banquet. It is not by proselytizing that the Church grows, but "by attraction." (EG 15)

Can we not characterize this as a dialogical way of proclaiming the gospel? Let us now look at some of the texts of the pope, referring to dialogue, in the very first year of his pontificate.

The Context of Evangelizing Dialogue

In *Evangelii Gaudium* Pope Francis speaks about social dialogue as a contribution to peace (Chapter Four, Section IV). Before we focus on this text, however, it may be helpful to look at its context and goal. The centrality of evangelization in dialogue is highlighted when Francis affirms that its goal is "to make the kingdom of God present in our world" (EG 176), and this involves "life in community and engagement with others" (EG 177). The work of Christ and the Spirit in the world has communitarian dimensions that involve being merciful and loving toward everyone. The gospel, therefore, has a social purpose. Francis focuses on two elements of this as more relevant today: the inclusion of the poor in society, and peace and social dialogue (EG 184).

Francis starts Chapter Four, Section II with a general statement: "Our faith in Christ, who became poor, and was always close to the poor and the outcast, is the basis of our concern for the integral development of society's most neglected members" (EG 186). Helping the poor means many things: meeting their basic material needs, reforming the structures that make and keep them poor, and helping the poor to grow and develop as human persons in an integral way. "This means education, access to health care, and above all employment, for it is through free, creative, participatory and mutually supportive labor that human beings express and enhance the dignity of their lives" (EG 192). Development is for all humans because the planet belongs to all. Sometimes we may tend to defend orthodoxy while neglecting orthopraxis. "God's heart has a special place for the poor, so much so that he himself 'became poor'" (2 Cor 8:9) (EG 197). Following God, we too are called to opt for the poor preferentially. It is not merely a sociopolitical option but a theological one, and leads us to dialogue with the poor and to care for them, not only economically and socially, but also pastorally.

> They have much to teach us. Not only do they share in the *sensus fidei,* but in their difficulties they know the suffering Christ. We need to let ourselves be evangelized by them. The new evangelization is an invitation to acknowledge the saving power at work in their lives and to put them at the center of the Church's pilgrim way. We are called to find Christ in them, to lend our voice to their causes, but also to be their friends, to listen to them, to speak for them and to embrace the mysterious wisdom which God wishes to share with us through them. (EG 198)

The economy should focus, not only on production and profit, but also on equitable distribution, which cannot be left to the market forces. It has to be politically managed for the good of all (EG 202–8).

We have to be particularly concerned about the vulnerable people. We can make a long list: the homeless, the addicted, refugees, indigenous peoples, the elderly, migrants, victims of human trafficking, the exploited, mistreated women, unborn children, and finally creation as a whole (EG 209–15).

Francis goes on to stress the importance of building a community of peace, justice, and fraternity and speaks of four principles that can guide development and build a people "where differences are harmonized within a shared pursuit" (EG 221). These four principles are time is greater than space, unity prevails over conflict, realities are more important than ideas, and the whole is greater than the part. Let us try briefly to understand these.

When we are faced with problematic situations our temptation is to seek to set everything in order. But life is evolving, and we have to set up processes that will make things better. "Giving priority to time means being concerned about initiating processes rather than possessing spaces" (EG 223). The fullness is in the future, and we have to keep moving and creating history without anxiety, but with conviction and tenacity. Conflict is inevitable in society. One can simply ignore it, or one can get involved and become its prisoner; but one can also resolve it at a higher plane, building communion in difference. Avoiding syncretism, one achieves synthesis, following Christ who "has made all things one in himself: heaven and earth, God and man, time and eternity, flesh and spirit, person and society" (EG 229). This is peace, which is not a "negotiated settlement," but "reconciled diversity." "Realities simply are, whereas ideas are worked out." So we are called "to reject the various means of masking reality: angelic forms of purity, dictatorships of relativism, empty rhetoric, objectives more ideal than real, brands of historical fundamentalism, ethical system bereft of kindness, intellectual discourse bereft of wisdom" (EG 231). "What calls us to action are realities illuminated by reason" (EG 232). This means that, in evangelization, the word has to become flesh, the gospel has to be inculturated in the lives of the people, thought has to be translated into action. We are living in an era of tension between the global and the local. The global may tend to marginalize the local. The local may try to be imprisoned in itself. What is needed is to be rooted in the local and yet be open to the global. We have to broaden our horizons and see the greater good, but without evasion or uprooting. Community need not suppress individualism but may make it grow further.

> Here our model is not the sphere, which is no greater than its parts, where every point is equidistant from the center, and there are no differences between them. Instead, it is the polyhedron, which reflects the convergence of all its parts, each of which preserves its distinctiveness. Pastoral and political activity alike seek to gather in this polyhedron the best of each. (EG 236)

Francis had a similar suggestion when he spoke to the male general superiors of religious congregations: "The great changes in history were realized when reality was seen not from the center but rather from the periphery. . . . Being at the periphery helps . . . to analyze reality more concretely, to shun centralism and ideological approaches." Speaking to a representative of Jesuit journalists,[6] he

---

[6] See ibid.

insists on creativity and suggests that it has three characteristics: dialogue, discernment, and frontier. Developing the idea of "frontier," he says that we have to be with the people, not in a laboratory. Then he explains: "Ours is not a 'lab faith,' but a 'journey faith,' a historical faith. God has revealed himself as history, not as a compendium of abstract truths." While a laboratory isolates problems out of context and tames them, living on the border makes us audacious and creative.

The gospel is proclaimed to everyone. "The genius of each people receives in its own way the entire Gospel and embodies it in expressions of prayer, fraternity, justice, struggle and celebration" (EG 237). This is the birth and growth of a local church. After explaining these four principles, the pope goes on to speak about social dialogue as a contribution to peace.

Social Dialogue

Three areas of dialogue are covered in Chapter Four, Section IV of *The Joy of the Gospel*: "dialogue with states, dialogue with society—including dialogue with cultures and the sciences—and dialogue with other believers who are not part of the Catholic Church" (EG 238). The subjects of such dialogue are the people as a whole, who have to work together toward a just, responsive, and inclusive society.

The state has to safeguard and promote the common good of society, based on subsidiarity and solidarity and committed to political dialogue and consensus building. The church does not have solutions to every problem but supports programs "which best respond to the dignity of each person and the common good" (EG 241). While the church rejects the claims of positivism, which pretends that empirical sciences are the only source of true knowledge and affirms other areas of knowledge like philosophy and theology, it asserts that the light of faith, like the light of reason, comes from God and that they cannot contradict each other. This is the basis for a dialogue between science and faith that can be "a path to harmony and peace" (EG 242). Such dialogue is opposed to ideological "scientism," which gives to scientific opinion the same weight as to revelation.

Francis looks on other Christians as "pilgrims journeying alongside one another" (EG 244). Such an attitude promotes mutual trust and common witness. The pope suggests, "If we concentrate on the convictions we share, and if we keep in mind the principle of the hierarchy of truths, we will be able to progress decidedly towards common expressions of proclamation, service and witness" (EG 246). What the free and abundant work of the Spirit has sown in the other Christians "is also meant to be gift for us" (EG 246). For example, the Orthodox Churches can teach us the meaning of episcopal collegiality and the experience of synodality. With the Jews we believe in the one God who is active in history and we accept God's revealed word. God continues to work in them and produce treasures of wisdom with which we too can be enriched. We can certainly collaborate in the fields of justice and development, sharing many ethical convictions.

Our relation with the followers of other religions starts with a dialogue of life, being open to the others in truth and love. When we seek social peace and justice, a common ethical commitment "can become a process in which, by mutual listening, both parts can be purified and enriched" (EG 250). In such a dialogue between followers of different religions, both a facile syncretism, which would "be a totalitarian gesture on the part of those who would ignore greater values of which they are not masters," and "a diplomatic openness which says 'yes' to everything in order to avoid problems" (EG 251) must be avoided. Migrations in recent years have made the living together of Christians and Muslims inevitable. This demands a mutual appreciation of the other and a mutual freedom for religious practice. We need to appreciate the Muslims' commitment to God in prayer and their ethical practice, especially caring for the people most in need. We should also "avoid hateful generalizations, for authentic Islam and the proper reading of the Qur'an are opposed to every form of violence" (EG 253). What Pope Francis says regarding other religions is worth quoting in full, since it concerns us in India very much:

Non-Christians, by God's gracious initiative, when they are faithful to their own consciences, can live "justified by the grace of God," and thus be "associated to the paschal mystery of Jesus Christ." But due to the sacramental dimension of sanctifying grace, God's working in them tends to produce signs and rites, sacred expressions which in turn bring others to a communitarian experience of journeying toward God. While these lack the meaning and efficacy of the sacraments instituted by Christ, they can be channels which the Holy Spirit raises up in order to liberate non-Christians from atheistic immanentism or from purely individual religious experiences. The same Spirit everywhere brings forth various forms of practical wisdom which help people to bear suffering and to live in greater peace and harmony. As Christians, we can also benefit from these treasures

built up over many centuries, which can help us better to live
our own beliefs. (EG 254)

The two important points in this text are the stress on the communitarian dimension of the religions and the affirmation that we also can
benefit from their treasures.

The pope concludes this section on dialogue with an important
observation on religious freedom. Religious freedom is a fundamental
right. This includes "the freedom to choose the religion which one
judges to be true and to manifest one's beliefs in public" (EG 255).
Such freedom applies also to people who claim to have no religion.
But in the increasingly secularizing countries of Euro-America the
ideology of religious freedom is leading to unwelcome situations. On
the one hand, it leads to the privatization of religion. People can follow any religion they want privately or in strictly religious places like
churches and mosques, but their belief should have no manifestation
or impact in public life. On the other hand, such privatization leads
to another nefarious consequence. Society claims to be free of any
religion-based ethical principle. It is dominated by a nonreligious,
neutral reason-based and rights-based morality that is imposed on everyone in the public sphere. For instance, recently, the US government
tried to force all hospitals, even Catholic ones, to facilitate abortion
according to US law. The church saw this as an attack on religious
freedom. Religious freedom does not mean the imposition of freedom
from all religion.

However, there may be people who are not religious believers but
who stand by basic moral principles, defending human dignity, community, and freedom. Christians can certainly collaborate with them.
We can recall the remark attributed to the pope when someone drew
his attention to the report that some capitalist ideologues accused him
of being a Marxist for his concern for the poor. The pope said that
he is against Marxist ideology, but he knows Marxists who are good
people and are also concerned for the poor.

Christ and the Spirit

Pope Francis concludes his encyclical with a strong affirmation of
hope. God is at work in the world. On our part we have to be faithful to our commitment to realize the kingdom of God on earth. We
may not always see immediate results. But we believe and hope that

God will make our commitment fruitful in ways and places unknown to us. The source of our hope is twofold. On the one hand, "Christ's resurrection is not an event of the past; it contains a vital power which has permeated this world. Where all seems to be dead, signs of the resurrection suddenly spring up. It is an irresistible force" (EG 276). Correspondingly, "The Holy Spirit works as he wills when he wills and where he wills" (EG 279). "Let us learn to rest in the tenderness of the arms of the Father amid our creative and generous commitment. Let us keep marching forward; let us give him everything, allowing him to make our efforts bear fruit in his good time" (EG 279). The power of the Father, Son, and Spirit is on our side. We believe that the kingdom of God is already present in this world and growing, and that God is with us and alive and "brings good out of evil by his power and his infinite creativity" (EG 278).

Dialogue and Truth

One of the questions that is often raised in the context of dialogue is that of truth. In his encyclical on Faith—*Lumen Fidei*—the pope clarifies that truth is neither merely subjective nor communitarian and oppressive. Truth is born of love and disclosed in the encounter with the Other and the others. It is capable of transforming the individual and of contributing to the common good.

> One who believes may not be presumptuous; on the contrary, truth leads to humility, since believers know that, rather than ourselves possessing truth, it is truth which embraces and possesses us. Far from making us inflexible, the security of faith sets us on a journey; it enables witness and dialogue with all. (LF 34)

We also hear about the dictatorship of relativism. Everyone believes that he or she has the truth. There is therefore no absolute truth. Eugenio Scalfari asked about this in his reaction to *Lumen Fidei*. Since this is a much-discussed problem, often raised in the context of dialogue, since each religion has its own truth claims that are sometimes seen as incompatible, let me quote the pope's answer in his letter to Scalfari.

> I would not speak about "absolute" truths, even for believers, in the sense that absolute is that which is disconnected and bereft of all relationship. Truth, according to Christian faith, is the love

of God for us in Jesus Christ. Therefore, truth is a relationship. As such each one of us receives the truth and expresses it from within, that is to say, according to one's own circumstances, culture and situation in life, etc. This does not mean that truth is variable and subjective, quite the contrary. But it does signify that it comes to us always and only as a way and a life. Did not Jesus himself say: "I am the way, the truth and the life?" In other words, truth being completely one with love, demands humility and an openness to be sought, received and expressed. Therefore, we must have a correct understanding of the terms and, perhaps, in order to overcome being bogged down by conflicting absolute positions, we need to redefine the issues in depth. I believe that this is absolutely necessary in order to initiate that peaceful and constructive dialogue which I proposed at the beginning of my letter.[7]

I do not excuse myself for this long quotation. Dialogue between religions can become a clash between absolute claims to truth. Pope Francis's carefully phrased reflection can nourish our own reflections in such a context. It is also interesting to note that Francis does not speak of the truth as something abstract and rational, but as a relationship that is linked to love, finding expression in a way and a life. He also sets his reflections in the context of dialogue. Need I recall that Christianity itself was known as a Way in its beginnings (Acts 9:2)?

Another issue that concerns dialogue is the manner in which we understand the uniqueness of Christ as the savior. Scalfaro raises this question also. Pope Francis answers it in an interesting manner:

The uniqueness lies, I would say, in the fact that the faith makes us share, through Jesus, in the relationship he has with God who is *Abba*, and from this perspective, in the relationship of love which he has with all men and women, enemies included. In other words, the sonship of Jesus, as presented by the Christian faith, is not revealed so as to emphasize an insurmountable separation between Jesus and everyone else; rather, it is revealed to tell us that in him, we are all called to be children in the one Father and so brothers and sisters to one another. The uniqueness of Jesus has to do with communication, not exclusion.[8]

---

[7] Francis, "Letter to a Non-believer."
[8] Ibid.

Conclusion

What can we Indians learn from the practice of dialogue by Pope Francis? The first thing that strikes me is that he sets interreligious dialogue in the context of social dialogue that seeks to build up the kingdom of God. In India, I think that though we are aware of the fourfold dialogue of life, action, discussion, and experience, we have focused rather narrowly, led by the ashramites, on the dialogue of (spiritual) experience. This focus has helped the development of a theology of religions, which, however, is being misunderstood by people who do not share our experience. There is nothing wrong with this. But at the same time we have neglected the dialogues of life and action. We live together with the followers of other religions in the school, in the marketplace, and in public life.

But religions and dialogue are normally kept out of these areas in the name of secularism, yielding the space to communal and fundamentalist groups. Though Indian secularism is open to all religions and we have not privatized religion, as popular religious practice in community bears witness, we tend to live in religious ghettos. In the meantime, our dialogue of spiritual experience has more or less collapsed and become limited to a very small minority in the church. I think Pope Francis is calling us to what he calls "social dialogue," in which we can make our religious values relevant in projects of collaboration for building up a community of justice, peace, and harmony. This dialogue should be of the people, not of a few theological or spiritual experts. It should also open out to all people, even nonbelievers. We also have to pay more attention to an experiential and active option for the poor. Mutuality in dialogue then becomes important.

What Pope Francis says about the practice of dialogue has theological implications. The pope's views are rather close to our own, since they are not abstract and rational but based on experience. We could learn from his manner of looking at truth and love as intimately related and of getting caught up in the dynamism of life, relationships, and history rather than in abstract speculation. We need to develop a spirituality of hope of a people on the way toward the kingdom of God, built around the presence and action in our lives and in our world of the risen Christ and of the Spirit. Finally, we should be really convinced and happy that our loving and merciful God is not as rigid as some expressions of our religions.

Index

Abhishiktananda, Swami (Henri
  Le Saux), 141, 147–48, 158,
  161–62, 179, 184–85, 187,
  189, 190, 196, 204–6, 208
Absolute, belief in, and global
  vision, 87–88
Absolute Future, 131
Absolute-with-qualities *(Saguna
  Brahman)*, 20
Absolute-without-qualities *(Nirguna
  Brahman)*, 20
Abul Ala Mawdudi, Mawlana
  Sayyid, 73, 93
acceptance, 61–62, 66
*Ad Gentes (Decree on the Church's
  Missionary Activity*; Vatican
  II*)*, xxv, xxvi–xxix, 118
advaita, 9, 89, 196, 206
Agnivesh, Swami, 90
Akbar, 218
al Banna, Hasan, 73
Al Qaeda, 74
Alvars, 10
Amaladoss, Michael, xvii–xxi
Andal, 164
anekantavada, 3, 6
antireligious ideology, 138, 139
antireligious violence, 45
apophatism, 30, 206, 208, 210
a posteriori relativism, 25
Appasamy, A. J., 177
Aquinas, Thomas, 21, 219
Arabization, 94
a-religious ideology, 138, 139
Aristotle, 4, 5

Arya Samaj, 75
Ashoka, 218
ashram movement, 196
Asian Bishops' Conference. *See*
  Federation of Asian Bishops'
  Conferences
Asian Synod, xxxi
Atman, 7, 89–90
Aurobindo, 178
avatars, 10, 20

Bandaranaike, S.W.R.D., 78
baptism, 202–3
Basavanna, 166
Being, realization of, 90–91
belongingness, 158, 175
Benedict XVI, 25, 182
Bhagavad Gita, 8–9, 10, 27, 90,
  166, 168
bhajan, 196
bhakti tradition, 10, 35, 105, 148
Bible, literal truth of, 70
bishops' conferences, xxiii, xxiv. *See
  also* Asian Bishops' Conference; Catholic Bishops'
  Conference of India
bodhisattvas, 92–93
Brahman, 4, 7–8, 10, 89, 171
Brihadaranyaka Upanishad, 12
Buddhadasa, Bhikku, 91, 92
Buddhism, 217, 209. *See also*
  Mahayana Buddhism
  ethic of, 134, 135
  fluidity of, 159
  focused on practice, 140